ARTIFICIAL
Mythologies

ARTIFICIAL
Mythologies

A GUIDE

TO CULTURAL

INVENTION

CRAIG J. SAPER

Foreword by Laura Kipnis

University of Minnesota Press
Minneapolis
London

Published by the University of Minnesota Press
111 Third Avenue South, Suite 290, Minneapolis, MN 55401-2520
Printed in the United States of America on acid-free paper

Library of Congress Cataloging-in-Publication Data

Saper, Craig J.
    Artificial mythologies : a guide to cultural invention / Craig J.
    Saper ; foreword by Laura Kipnis.
        p.   cm.
    Includes bibliographical references and index.
    ISBN 0-8166-2872-6
    ISBN 0-8166-2873-4 (pbk.)
        1. Popular culture in literature.   2. Aesthetics.   I. Title.
    PN56.P547836   1997
    801—dc20   96-8614

The University of Minnesota is an
equal-opportunity educator and employer.

To my parents
whether they like it or not

Now perhaps comes the age of another experience: that of unlearning. [etymologically linked to] Sapientia: no power, a little knowledge, a little wisdom, and as much flavor as possible.

ROLAND BARTHES

Contents

Foreword

Laura Kipnis

Some significant feat of inventiveness, or a serious intellectual athleticism is required to invent a theory of cultural change in the absence of a future tense—and in the absence of subjects, agency, or intentionality. Artificial Mythologies is not only a tactical intervention into current cultural theory but also aspires to define a new discipline. It wants to escalate the riskiness of cultural analysis, to remind us that reading practices can be radical and audacious enterprises. Set amidst the bombed-out ruins of contemporary critical theory, this book means to break in through the back door of current debates about cultural studies in order to trigger the alarm system. Or maybe it's like coming home from a party and finding a debonair cat burglar sitting in your newly redecorated living room, who proceeds to deliver an ironically devastating critique of your self-consciously cutting-edge taste in furniture. At a moment when cultural studies gets to adopt a certain self-congratulatory air as the radical new thing, but one with all the academy-loving safety that its eponymous call for simply more and better "studies" offers it, Craig Saper want us to think, instead, about "cultural invention." Or cultural risks. Or why not cultural overthrow?

The book's title hints that Saper's way of going about all this will be to postmodernize Roland Barthes, that is, to perform one of those mad-scientist mind-body-soul transplants between the early Barthes of *Mythologies* and the later Barthes of *A Lover's Discourse* and *Camera*

Lucida in order to hatch some previously undreamed of hybrid. But (the early) Barthes's target was the confusion of Nature and History, and this now looks a little quaint from Saper's vantage point. We've long ago left Nature—even the appearance of Nature—lying dead by the side of the road and have only Artifice to grapple with and console us. (And one suspects that Saper's deepest affinities actually lie with the Barthes who advised that fully inhabiting the contradictions of your time means making sarcasm the condition of truth.)[1]

This is a book whose lessons, while couched in the idiom of theory, take their energy and impetus from other forms of experimentality. It wants to make positive use of the artificiality of mass media—the very thing most intimately tied to late capitalist hegemony—as a direction for cultural analysis and transformation. Saper offers this redirection variously, as a methodology, a recipe, a machine, and a guide. The book wants to be a manual for taking us to the next thing, which is described, in different moments, as "purposeful change," "cultural invention," and "losing your way." By creating what are designated "artificial myths," a new cultural process is instituted, through which your focus is ever so slightly shifted and refocused. New paths are forged, new vistas are opened, habituated responses are unlearned. What happens then is not entirely clear—after all, it is not as if any cultural theorist gets to invent a direction for change single-handedly—so Saper means only to deliver us to that point just over the ideological horizon from which something new might take hold.

But can you have social change without social actors? Utopian desires without a theory of progress? And when the present landscape is comprised of dead myths, used-up ideologies, and little to counter them but joyless pop culture-hating academics propounding tired negative critiques? Saper's theory of cultural invention is one that resolutely resists positing any psychological subjectivity from which such inventions might emanate. Instead he proposes a deindividuated model of the self, and to exemplify it, he invents a peculiar figure, a new cultural antihero: the artificial mythologist. He (or maybe she, or perhaps some cyborgian switch-hitter) laughs sardonically in the face of the old dead mythologies, watches everyday life as if it were a B movie, or rides it like an amusement park tilt-o-whirl. A trickster, a thief, a courtier, a masochist—to become this figure you must play the fool and ritually reenact those dead cultural myths, posing as their subject in order to destabilize them, before sending them off on their merry way to the boneyard of yesterday's epistemologies.

Well, this certainly raises a lot of questions, and big ones, about the stakes and limits of culturalism these days, given that the relation between "cultural change" and what used to be called social change (in the old mythology) is left somewhat unelaborated here. In other words, there is a story to be told about this book that the book itself does not tell. Perhaps shifting focus would be, as the trickster-mythologist would advise, helpful. So let's try asking this text not to say what it *is* but to say what it is not. Improvising on the notion of a critical cultural practice from Saper's useful provocations, I propose this critical experiment: inserting the foreword writer (a pose, not a subject, obviously) into the interstices of *Artificial Mythologies* to take up residence at those junctures where its aversions meet its big ambivalences, to occupy those spaces it refuses to. Then, once that negative space is enfolded back into the story, it might be possible to ask how this story came to be. What produced its negativities? What is this a response *to*? After all, Saper does seem to be asking us to read between his lines.

By risking getting lost on the path I'm not meant to take, by risking anachronism and studious unseriousness — all the sorts of practices Saper endorses — perhaps I might begin to develop an account of *Artificial Mythologies*'s place in a current cultural-political context. Because whether or not this book is willing to specify its context or account for its own formation (it poses as Harpo Marx at these moments: annoyingly mute), the foreword writer will probably want to wrest exactly these answers out of it, kicking and screaming if necessary. Texts clearly invite such transferential relations with readers, both positive and negative ones. And that the text's very absences, its studied blanknesses are precisely where its reader's desires are most insistently installed would seem, parenthetically, to raise certain paradoxes about Saper's evacuation of psychological subjectivity from his account of cultural processes. (As perhaps does his vast indebtedness to the author of the death of authorship.) So there's one example of a path to get lost on.

But let us try this unmarked path instead. Clearing away the foliage, stepping gingerly over some potholes and around the dinosaur dung, one is confronted head-on with Saper's big bad guy, his hugest aversion.

It seems to be, interestingly, *intentionality*, which is associated with any number of bad smelly things and bad scenes, objectionable on a variety of grounds. And although this book wants to be on the side of invention rather than critique, it is clear that the critique of intentionality is foundational to *Artificial Mythologies*'s invented method.

For Saper, intentionality seems associated with the quest for a sort of mastery that his proposed method would eschew, would in fact run fast in the opposite direction to avoid, choosing (and risking) pathos instead. So his project becomes a tricky one right off: it needs to figure out a way to generate innovation without having exactly any specific intention to do so, or to generate anything in *particular*. Its solution to this dilemma is to put its considerable energies into the task of reinventing what is "already there," and what is most "already there" is, of course, popular culture. Thus, the task of the artificial mythologist becomes one of roaming through the banalities of mass mediated culture and, equipped with a sense of irony and a Barthesian theory of the *punctum*—the off-center detail, that which doesn't fit—producing a series of productive encounters with the unintended. Whether or not what is produced in these encounters is trivial, absurd, or on first glance meaningless, the job of the artificial mythologist is first and foremost not to produce anything *new* but instead to "punctuate" what is already there.

This method has both the virtues and the problems of a certain studied noncommittalness. One thing Saper is explicit about is not wanting to be on the side of any *particular* truth or argument, probably because that sort of intentionality, or specific commitments to specific outcomes, claims the kind of mastery that we're asked to abandon once and for all. The question though, is whether the problem with mastery (a *really* bad smelly thing in this book) is an objection to its form—a metacritical argument about congealed forms of subjectivity, for example—or implies an argument about the content of previous aspirations to mastery. That is, was it the previous generations' specific political *intentions* that were bad, or the phallogocratic zeal for mastery, certitude, and illusory self-knowledgeability with which they vainly attempted to effect those intentions in the world? Is this an argument about political style, and thus a generational argument? Or, if style is substance, and the will-to-mastery too deeply imbricated into previous political projects to rescue their (occasionally good?) intentions, does this argument propose a rupture with the political investments that have been the sustaining ones for much postwar left cultural theory?

What sort of rupture though? From certain perspectives, the distance between the critique of the subject associated with, among other figures, the later Barthes (a good object in this story, the "good enough mother," to borrow from D. W. Winnicott) and the critical theory of Jurassic figures like, say, the Frankfurt School (Saper is not a fan of anything resembling negative dialectics) is smaller than it first appears. The mutual focus on ideology's effect on the subject, the mutual recognition that late capitalism requires certain forms of subjectivity that are held in place through a plethora of ideological discourses, means that for both, any sort of contestation or resistance requires somehow intervening in and reorganizing those processes of subject formation.[2] But from other perspectives, for example, those of post-Marxist and postmodern and postcolonial and feminist and multicultural and queer critics, there are serious questions about the salvageability of previous contestatory projects, whose often overdetermining and overstructuring reliance on (pick one) master narratives, universalism, phallocentrism, or heteronormativity produces a certain fatal narrowness about who gets to be the subject of the story. And about who will run the brave new world meant to spring from the ashes of this old pathetic one. These sorts of suspicions and critical revisions seem to provide the launching pad for Saper's project—if not in name, then in spirit.

None of this is exactly stated here. "Intentionality" seems to be the code word for past mistakes large and small. It's a big burden for one poor word. The result is a certain counter-hermeneutical sense of stumbling around in a darkened context. The book stages a somewhat frustrating refusal to point the way, like an experimental theater piece I once heard about in which the audience are shown to their seats, the curtain goes up at the appointed time, but *nothing* happens. No actors appear. The play doesn't start. Time passes, the audience sits and waits. They start to murmur, shift, look around. Finally someone gets up to leave. It turns out the doors are locked. I can't remember how it turns out, but you can imagine how this experience could prove unsettling. Like other forms of experimentality—Andy Warhol's marathon-length films of sleeping dogs and obdurate skyscrapers come to mind—the refusal to provide an invariably limiting answer, and the sorts of impossible-to-predict spaces that this opens up, *may* initiate the production of new possibilities.

In Saper's version, this is called permission to get lost. So in place of intentionality — that well-lit path that just leads us back to more of the same — he offers the productive accident, the fortuitous error, distraction, detours, and a valorization of various ways to lose one's mastery, like masochism, unsettled subjectivities, foibles, and misdirection. But Saper's problem with intentionality is not only that it quests so hard for mastery; it seems to be, implicitly, that having intentionality dooms you in advance to failure and defeat. Whether the association between intentionality and defeat is an a priori case, or whether it's specifically conjunctural, is not clear given the general reluctance to specify the social. So what precisely has failed, or been failed, and who exactly has been defeated are never named as such. Nevertheless, the sourness of disappointment does tinge the studied optimism of this "guide for cultural invention," providing a gloomy subtext to Saper's adamant aversion to hitching his methodological wagon up to the service of anything in particular. Other, that is, than *cultural* innovation. One might venture to say that there is a certain risk that remains untaken here, a certain *explicitness* that, if one were to venture into this text's negative spaces, must be finally hazarded.

This would be the risk of *naming*. Of course, naming things leaves you open to humiliation and exposure, and while on the one hand, Saper advocates playing the fool, on the other, he seems perhaps a little reluctant to strip down and show us his. You can understand why: naming invariably lacks the elegance and style and alluring diffidence of allusiveness. Or the open-endedness so intrinsic to this project. And literalness makes things a little boring, like the flatfooted genre of the translator's preface, which only becomes sublime and interesting when describing the impediments and difficulties of translatability. An example is the preface to Antonio Gramsci's *Prison Notebooks,* which itemizes circumlocutions like "the philosophy of praxis" or "the founder of the philosophy of praxis" for Marxism and Marx, or the erasure of terms like "class" under the whip of prison censorship. The impediments to translation allow its translators an opportunity to issue sublime, poetically proleptic warnings against their readers' desires to mine unambiguous intentions from veiled and fragmentary objects, all the while cognizant that the reader must do exactly that.[3] While the forms of inhibition governing our veiled and fragmentary textual object are a bit more difficult to specify, it does seem to be the case that *Artificial Mythologies* also deploys its critical energies against something unnameable, which it leaves its reader to decode. ("Ideology" is the favored sobriquet, about as specific as it gets.) Gramsci, at least, knew who was to blame for *his* troubles, even if impeded from committing name to page. But for Saper, knowing who to blame is part of the problem, because if intentionality dooms you in advance to failure and defeat, it also dooms you to possibly mistaking, or misrecognizing, your enemies.

The status and location of power — who, what sort, how it operates — are among the tired old myths Saper means to put into question, right alongside the dead horse of progress. But this can lead to a certain conceptual impasse, because if change is the good object but progress the bad one (too beset by intentionality), this seems to transport us back to some equally hoary Spengleresque notion of cyclical history, the thing that just keeps chugging along on its own, like the Eveready bunny. If the old mythologies are "showing signs of wear," as in his opening paragraph Saper tells us they perpetually are, and further, if "everyone knows this process well," the question of what might account for such transitions is a question not here posed. It just happens.

It's not Saper's project, of course, to describe the social in a way that emphasizes the role of agents versus institutions, social forces and struggles, power and contestation. Here, you're inside representation and looking out. But if somewhat more specified accounts of transition often underpin current cultural theory — transitions to postmodernism, or post-Fordism, or transnationalism, or the widening gaps between social classes domestically, even the "Reagan Revolution" — it's probably because cultural theorists on the left are at some pains to anchor accounts of transitions in social ideologies to material conditions and contexts — even theorists for whom the social is detotalized, or for whom power is dispersed and unlocalizible. If there's no anchor, if ideology simply floats along autonomously, in no particular relation to anything, then why bother about it? Barthes has been criticized from the left for often trivializing the force of the ideological.[4] Saper's work simultaneously presses and resists such questions even more forcefully, given the sort of socially timely and ideologically charged cases he organizes his specific interventions around: television news, multiculturalism, urban decay, and "family values." But given his resistance to naming in the realm of the social, the somewhat formalist description of cyclical processes of demythologization and remythologization risks a fairly apolitical denouement: the old myths must die so that new ones may live. And then, apparently, the cycle starts anew.

I don't believe that this is where Saper means us to end up, but when you take that unmarked path, who knows *what* dead end you'll find yourself in. Because it's precisely around the question of power that the text's contradictions are most keenly felt; inhabiting this interstice is like being in a wind tunnel of whooshing disavowals, given its rather perverse speculations about whether power, as such, even exists. Saper proposes that power these days, even state power, might be merely empty nostalgia, a memory that we—both the Left and the Right—cling to out of fear and desire, specifically our fear that all that may remain is, rather, "an extreme powerlessness." The idea that really there's nobody home—this is what provokes our greatest anxiety. Because where would Left theory be without something to organize itself against?

Bravely, Saper offers this speculation in the context of television reporting on the Gulf War, in the course of detailing a mistake (one of those productive errors the artificial mythologist combs the airwaves for) between two different versions of maps of Baghdad that ABC news broadcast in the midst of the U.S. bombing of Iraq, in which the location of the U.S. embassy shifted around—just as did U.S. policy toward Iraq. Media pundits universally failed to notice this error during their endlessly laudatory coverage of George Bush's cynical little war. And given our own anxieties, the rest of us watch TV in a state of distraction (so the power of media is another nostalgic notion) rather than fully inhabiting its disruptive potential.

Well, this position takes some admirable risks, as any artificial mythologist should. And it is truly an important project to recount power's failures. Power is never monolithic, it has gaps. It can never have the efficacy that our over-Oedipalized investments in it warrant, and this is a point too little stressed in much cultural theory. But at the same time, materiality always trumps theoretical reveries. Dead bodies have a certain claim on our attention—as Saper knows, because he discusses them in an endnote, as the "answers" on a proposed TV game show called "Body Count." (You can only step back and admire his bad taste.) So there's a certain problem of *scale* that this argument leaves its reader to ponder: how do you measure the weight of small productive errors against large-scale death and destruction? Can they even inhabit the same sentence? Because whether or not the smart bombs that destroyed much of Baghdad were smarter than academic theorists—whichever map they happened to be following—putting the death-of-the-author or the crisis-of-the-subject into analogy with the withering away of the state seems, well, premature. It risks glibly trivializing the agentiveness of the state. Evacuating the subject-in-theory does not mean that there is no *object* of state power or other social determinations, although it would be nice. And perhaps this book does point the way toward further evasions and out-maneuvering of such determinations. But still, if agency is a current problem for the Left, it doesn't correspond that agency is a problem for the state. (Of course, by so flatfootedly naming the "moment" that this text inhabits—and is hardly alone in being depressed about—I may be bringing more limiting clarity to this scene than Saper either means to have or would think is advisable.) But I feel the force of his point that I may see it this way precisely because I'm stuck in the muck of old paradigms, and married to a certain political-cultural agenda that it would cause me too much anxiety to divorce.

And, also, the wily subject-poseur, the artificial mythologist—who may be able to evade the tentacles of social determinations because he is never really where you think he is—cuts an appealing figure. Perhaps even a hopeful one. Saper is a fan of *sprezzatura* and reproposes it as the artificial mythologist's credo. *Sprezzatura* is described in Castiglione's early sixteenth-century advice manual, *The Book of the Courtier,* as "nonchalance," the art of saying and doing the right thing at the right time and making it seem effortless—not letting the hard work of being so clever and full of grace show.[5] What an *odd* concept to import to the late twentieth century, especially given the swift kick in the pants Saper means to deliver to the old humanism. Castiglione's manual is meant to guide his readers through the new forms of self-consciousness and sociality that marked the inception and invention of the modern subject.[6] This would be the subject whose expiration date, Saper seems quite adamant, has long since passed.

But has it? What then to make of the fact that Saper's book also occupies the same theoretical moment as the ascendancy (and institutionalization) of what's come to be known as identity politics? Identity politics, if you're thinking like a theorist, can also be read like a metaphilosophical meditation on the status of the subject, one being conducted both in the language of the academy and in the vernacular these days (as is, I will suggest, the Barthesian *punctum* practice Saper describes). The lures and influence of identity discourses have become quite far-flung, although their conclusions lead you down still another path. Identity politics is not only the defiant reinvention of the speaking subject (the joke goes that it was only when women and minorities started to write that the death of the author was announced) but is also defiantly anti-*sprezzatura*. Rather than striving for nonchalance and grace, it wants to insistently display all the hard work and pain and injury of being a subject, to flamboyantly represent a subjecthood striated by the numerous traumas that injustice and inequity—economic, sexual, gendered, or ethnic—pose to identity. The general culture, though, has gotten quickly fed up with the claims of these "victims" on our limited attention and tolerance spans, in popular culture, academic culture, or political culture. Whether it's daytime talk-show trauma queens, or demands for multicultural curricula, or the fight over affirmative action policies, an increasing level of scorn and impatience seems to greet the news that "history is what hurts." Middlebrow intellectuals are busy issuing stern admonitions with titles like *Culture of Complaint,* hoping to convince these overly vocal subjects to just shut up and stop whining.[7] The terrain of the subject appears to be a hotly contested one these days, in both academic *and* popular cultures.

One wonders how the artificial mythologist would navigate these competing claims. With *sprezzatura,* no doubt. But how does *sprezzatura* help in bearing the violences—both physical and psychical—that embodied subjects contend with in contemporary culture? The relation that Saper outlines between *sprezzatura* and the *punctum* practice suggests that what you do with violence is slow it down, replay it, locating the unintentional, the excess, the thing that doesn't fit. Although Saper proposes composite figures like Barthes and Oprah as prototype artificial mythologists, I'd suggest that action-film director John Woo has already staked out this terrain. How about a composite of Woo and Saper?

"Creolization" is a term Saper likes, as opposed to tourism, which changes nothing. Woo is nothing if not an instance of aesthetic creolization: a Hong Kong director whose influences are Martin Scorsese and Sam Peckinpah, who forged experimentality within an industrial practice, and whose directorial style is the cinematic analogue to the Barthesian *punctum* practice that Saper describes. And Woo's obsessions return invariably to scenes of apocalyptic violence. His first American movie, *Hard Target* (1993), was an action picture with class consciousness: rich slime are kidnapping homeless veterans to use as human fodder in a blood sport, hunting them down like hounds after foxes for the amusement of conscienceless aristos. America envisioned as a class war between the landed gentry and the terminally disenfranchised is not so far off, and even prescient given the fact that corporate downsizing is the buzzword of the year after the *New York Times* finally got around to noticing it in a seven-part series of front-page articles, March 3–9, 1996. And the homeless as bloodied trophies of corporate profit-mongering is also not so far off from Saper's proposal of the "Body Count" game show. But from this vantage point, that is, the view from the bottom, there are determinate material conditions acting upon these bodies: exploitation, for example. Vast economic injustices and disparities structure the social and generate social practices. Power is a lived, material reality.

In Woo's sensibility, however, like the artificial mythologist's, it's the moments that stand outside the narrative that fascinate: it's the interesting detail or a passing expression that punctures the moment and opens onto something beyond the frame. Woo has said that when something so moves him, he uses a freeze-frame or slow motion to capture it, to stretch the moment, to capture "a certain beautiful gesture that I want to prolong."[8] It's a new form of paying attention to surfaces that Woo invents for the action picture, just like what Saper envisions for cultural theory. Both take a big risk, and the risk is aestheticization, obviously. The risk is that it becomes nothing *more* than a beautiful moment, or a beautiful theory — that violence, or history, or power are slowed down so much that they dissolve into wallpaper. For the mass media, it's difficult to say whether this is a risk, or the whole purpose. But for the artificial mythologist, this would seem to be the question. Or as Barthes asks, "Is there a mythology of the mythologist?"[9]

Saper's point, though, is that when things seem dead, big risks are the ones you have to take. Hollywood dreams that Hong Kong transplants will revitalize the action genre. And the revitalization of cultural theory with infusions of cultural invention seems like a project worth pursuing, perhaps someday to become an action genre in its own right.

Craig Saper suggested, before reading this foreword but after hearing that its tone might be a little critical, that it be labeled "forewarned" rather than "foreword"—something akin to the Surgeon General's boxed message on cigarette packages. I quite appreciated his sense of humor (and his loyalty to his principles) in the face of an author's worst nightmare. So let me be sure to emphasize that this book will not be harmful to your health. On the contrary, I've learned many things from its useful provocations and must also credit its encouragement of experimentality and antic seriousness for sanctioning the liberties I've taken with it. To whatever degree I've felt impelled to scuffle with the book, *Artificial Mythologies* has accomplished its goal, that is, not just to be *right,* not to tell you what to think, but to set the stage for otherwise unenvisioned possibilities and interventions.

Acknowledgments

This book's specific rethinking of scholarship in terms of action, rather than description, arose from my answers to challenging questions about a paper I presented to the History of Art seminar at the University of Pennsylvania. Christine Poggi also helped me indirectly to refine these ideas during a course we taught together. Jerome Singerman offered careful and poignant commentary on chapter 1. The theories discussed in this book grew out of work with Greg Ulmer and Robert Ray at the University of Florida. Their essays and teachings led to my theory of cultural invention.

Catherine Liu and the Critical Studies faculty at the California Institute of the Arts helped me refine my thinking about theory and humor. Kathleen McHugh gave encouraging moral and scholarly support during my visit to the University of California-Riverside. Margreta DeGrazia, Lynda Hart, Bob Perlman, and Vicki McHaffey have in different ways supported my flamboyant scholarship with collegial support. James English's skepticism about the politics of humor and discussions about institutional politics helped refine my thinking. Réda Bensmaïa offered an encouraging reading and helpful commentary on the manuscript. The editors, designers, and a careful copy editor at the University of Minnesota Press helped move the project along to publication.

The chapter on television grew out of the discussions with my seminar on nonfiction film and television at Indiana University. Two friends and members of that seminar, Tony Rue and Serena Van Buskirk, noticed inconsistencies in the news broadcasts of the Gulf War. Tony Rue shared his complete videotapes of the news coverage and discussed video-art and pedagogy. Barry Mauer approached me at a conference with intimidating and encouraging enthusiasm for a paper, which became the chapter on mapping television.

A much earlier version of the chapter on multiculturalism and identity politics benefited from readings and copious commentary by Carol Flynn, Robert Ray, and Greg Ulmer. I presented an earlier version of some of the same ideas at the conference "After Barthes" at the University of Pennsylvania. The participants' comments, especially Steven Ungar's on rap music and Patricia Lombardo's on cultural studies, helped refine this chapter. Greg Ulmer's work on Nancy Burson's photographs and Jon McKenzie's insights on Burson's work helped focus my thinking.

The chapter on the role of the public intellectual benefited from Gerry O'Sullivan's references to the history of criticisms of curriculum reform. His urgings and Wendy Steiner's work on public intellectuals encouraged me to write the chapter on public intellectuals. Rita Barnard's and Dana Philips's friendship, in spite of their complete distrust and dismissal of my perceived poststructuralist methodologies, led to my thinking about the reception of academics in popular culture. Peter Stallybrass gave a cautionary reading of a much earlier version of the chapter on public intellectuals. Richard Burt and the colloquium at the University of Massachusetts-Amherst on scandal and sexual politics provided important commentary on my discussions of desire and pedagogy.

For the chapter on the aesthetics of social policy, Maryellen Burke insisted we visit an installation by Ilya Kabakov. Jennifer Bloomer read an earlier version of that chapter. Her comments helped me with revisions. Dan Rose and participants in the Ethnohistory Workshop at the University of Pennsylvania also offered helpful suggestions on the representation of social problems. In that workshop, Michèle Richman's role as devil's advocate, in various discussions about theory and culture, helped me strengthen my arguments.

For the chapter on family values, Lucio Privitello and Patricia Gherovici gave me advice on Lacan's work on the Amish. I delivered a section of the family values chapter at the conference on Psycho-analysis and Postcolonialism at George Washington University. Jean-Michel Rabaté inspired me to write on the philosophical implications of the Amish with a haiku he wrote. Without his encouragement and scholarly support in general, this book would never have come to fruition. Lynn Tomlinson, my wife, shared her insights and research sources on the Amish and gave me much appreciated unconditional love and affection.

Writing these acknowledgments has brought back many fond memories. I hope all these readers will have similarly fond memories after reading this book.

1 | Artificial Mythologies and Invention

> But those moments of newness — it's a fallacy on the one hand, on the other it's what you live for.
>
> GREIL MARCUS, *Lipstick Traces*

Mythology and Invention

When the mythologies with which we organize our view of the world show signs of wear, when they become dated, clichéd, or corny, when we notice them as constructions and arbitrary constraints, then we inevitably yearn to change our view of the world and see more clearly. In looking for a new view, we may revitalize old myths out of nostalgia, find new myths more apt for contemporary cultural problems and contradictions, or masquerade with the trappings of myths-gone-by as retro-irony. Everyone knows this process well. Everyone knows how demythologizing and remythologizing continue everyday. Movies and TV programs vary their formulas to make love stories seem new. Codes of objective journalism loosen in order to hype the sensational. Schools include socially relevant curricula, and, in reaction, conservative critics call for a return to older myths as eternal truths.

Commentators carefully and copiously follow this process of shifting myths. Scholars describe tacit cultural constructions, news programs offer ongoing commentary, and commercials appeal to newfangled desires. With all this attention, one might know, in hindsight, *who* introduced a novel idea, an innovation, or even a form of cultural resistance to prevailing mythologies. In many news and popular history accounts, one learns less about *how* these artists, activists, offbeat advertisers, and other innovators made their mark. Mocking reporters regularly describe the antics of trend-setting musicians or actors, the absurd chicanery of avant-garde artists, or the trendiness of wacky college professors. Popular culture tends to greet cultural innovators with rolled eyes and bemused shrugs. This attention to people tends to efface processes. In spite of all the interest in cultural change, the specific process of innovation in media and culture receives little popular or scholarly attention. Most scholars and journalists tell us about the people, movements, or social consequences of cultural change instead of the processes involved in those changes. We know from conservative critics that the political correctness movement tries to change language and history. If that group can purposefully change language and intervene in the myths of our culture, then can we learn those steps to change or intervention? By focusing on the people, consequences, and the appropriateness of changes, popular culture devotes very little, if any, attention to guides for purposeful change. The processes of scientific breakthroughs appear regularly in journals, documentaries, news reports, and advertisements, which regularly explain the machinations of new inventions, from biomedical drugs for heartburn to astrophysical theories of time. When does a report explain the process of a particular cultural innovation or change?

Can individuals affect the course of a myth's development? Does intentional innovation or even resistance to the status quo really exist? Of course it exists. No one denies that change occurs and that individuals play a role in those shifts. Yet, we usually only learn about the changes in hindsight. Looking at the process of change from its emergence, we see that intervention begins with a shift in the way we think about or represent the current situation. In this sense, the first step requires an unlearning of habituated responses, received ideas, and taken-for-granted contexts. The second step requires the popularization of the novel approach and outlook. That second step is a big one. Very few cultural or media critics ever find a large audience. The process of invention depends on the role and status of the public intellectual.

Cultural invention demands an intervention into public debates about culture and politics by those working in the arts and humanities. It depends on a shift away from ivory-tower academics toward the public intellectual. One model of this type of public intellectual comes from America during the late 1960s and early 1970s. Figures like Susan Sontag and Marshall McLuhan held the public's attention and influenced public policy even though their ideas concerned general media and cultural issues. As part of a group of public intellectuals working in the second half of the twentieth century, they differed from earlier figures because they focused on the potential of using contemporary culture as part of an invention process. They formed their thinking from the arts and humanities rather than from scientific research. McLuhan's theories about a "global village" transformed popular conceptions of community to include the importance of being "tuned in" to a current cultural change. Television could function to revitalize culture rather than simply to drain creative potential from the minds of couch potatoes. Sontag's discussions of the camp aesthetic she found in urban gay culture fueled the process of making campy send-ups and retro-irony into national pastimes. Her work not only identified areas of cultural changes and resistances but also suggested how these changes occurred. In this way, these public figures made themselves models of the potential links between the public intellectual and invention.

Another group of influential and well-known intellectuals emerged in France during the 1960s and 1970s. Again, this group of structuralists and poststructuralists influenced public debates with research on media, culture, and philosophy. The changes and controversies they stirred up still swirl around in American popular culture. Among this group, Roland Barthes gained a public reputation that made his books bestsellers and his persona well known on talk shows and in popular magazines. Most literary, media, and cultural critics today discuss Barthes as the author of a method for demythologizing culture or as a participant of the structuralist and poststructuralist milieu of the 1970s. Those moments have now passed, and cultural critics now almost universally consider the era of Barthes to have passed. His work as a scholar who intervened in popular culture as a myth*maker* and inventor of novel critical forms has yet to receive much attention. In an era supposedly "after Barthes," his work returns as a model for a type of cultural and media study as invention. Most scholars think of him as a structuralist or poststructuralist. A less common and usually pejorative appraisal of his work found in casual conversation rather than biographies or critical essays claims he was a journalist, literary critic, and popular figure. In this type of evaluation, his popularity insinuates, in a perverse elitist logic, that he does not match the academic rigor or brilliance of his Parisian peers. To consider his work as a model for public intellectuals interested in cultural invention suggests an alternative to these interpretations of his accomplishments. Neither simply an advocate of a methodology nor merely a dilettante producing novel essays for their popular appeal, he produced models for reading mythologies and, later, for inventing artificial mythologies of one's own.

Although he ultimately rejected his semiotic methods of *exposing* myths, he later produced a series of experimental works, which not only referenced contemporary cultural myths but also invented novel forms and approaches to old problems. While the earlier work described myths' machinations, the later inventive work implicitly described and demonstrated artificial mythologies. Similar to the combination of left populism and popular satire found in his work on mythologies, the later works have a peculiar tone and sense of humor—having the last laugh. That peculiar sensibility, neither ornamental nor superfluous in his work, functions as a crucial strategy for media scholars interested in practical models for cultural and media activism. Marx in *The Eighteenth Brumaire* warns critics not to pose as "the serious buffoon who no longer takes world history for comedy but his comedy for world history."[1] Understanding history as something of a cruel farce allows for a critical distance from contemporary myths that we hold self-evident. Although Marx saw a happy ending to history, he warned against overlooking the joke against those that take the present reality as the rational and universal outcome of history. Seriousness itself may prevent one from laughing at the comedy of history and finding joy in change. Marx's economic theories aside, politics depends on a sense of humor.

In spite of the importance of this critical sense of humor, a supposedly pedagogical imperative separates serious knowledge from laughter in most academic cultural and media studies. As a minor mythology, this lack of a sense of humor in academics has readers and critics expecting "serious" scholarship to dismiss "making fun" in favor of detached accuracy and aloof reasonableness. Of course, scholars, critics, politicians, and other public figures often use jokes to make their essays and lectures palatable. Courses and books on public speaking explain how to pepper an otherwise boring talk with engaging jokes. Using jokes and humor as ornaments gives fun an appropriate place next to serious scholarship. It does not make fun an essential part of serious scholarship. If humor and fun play a role in invention, then teaching students to make fun of, and have fun with, existing cultural and scholarly mythologies may prove advantageous.

On the subject of this kind of inventive carnivalesque play, Peter Stallybrass and Allon White caution that "for long periods carnival may be a stable and cyclical ritual with no noticeable politically transformative effects."[2] When it does "act as a catalyst and site of actual and symbolic struggle,"[3] the carnivalesque implies not only creative disrespect and demystification but also an emergent symbolic system. Barthes's description of cultural invention as an artificial mythmaking suggests how a creative activity can have a critical dimension: making fun makes myths shudder. The artificial mythologist works like an artist attempting to defamiliarize and destabilize cultural studies by watching the cultural scene as if it were a movie or a ride. Others have tested these waters; Barthes gives us a series of exemplary demonstrations.

His later works demonstrate this strategic use of artificial mythology and a playful approach to cultural studies. In that sense, the later works look like examples built on cultural theories first introduced in his earliest works like *Mythologies*.[4] Interpreting his later experiments in terms of his earliest works on myth depends on a speculation that takes the form of a question. It is a question that I imagine many of his biographers must have wondered about in private: What if Roland Barthes had lived longer? What if he had continued to write after the later works, the works that broke emphatically with earlier semiotic concerns, in order to introduce paradoxical arguments and experimental presentations? What if Barthes had returned to earlier concerns with his new attitude and methodologies? One might even argue that he did, in fact, address earlier concerns in the later works with new methods and approaches. In *Camera Lucida,* for example, he returns to ideas introduced in the article on the "third meaning." In *A Lover's Discourse: Fragments,* he examines something like the fashion system he had studied in his earlier work *The Fashion System.* The shift from the work on fashion to the study of love seems subtle at first. For example, he chooses a similar social phenomenon and examines the material traces of this cultural formation. His methodological approach and presentation mark the significant shift away from the earlier work. In the later work on a lover's discourse, his compulsively categorizing semiotician finds himself hopelessly in love and, therefore, unable to find mastery over the object of study. So, what would his earliest work look like if he had had time to return to *Mythologies* after he had finished *Camera Lucida*? Would he have returned to more explicitly "universal" or cultural issues, which some critics have found lacking in the last work? What can we learn about mythology from the *later* works?

Early in his career, Barthes used the image of a car trip through history to describe how mythology works. When a driver looks out of a car's windshield, she sees the landscape as full and present, and, at the same time, she sees the windshield. Myths function as windows framing and mediating our view of the world around us. The slightest change in focus allows the driver to notice the window. A broken window makes the myth too obvious, and we seek new myths, as described earlier. To focus only on the window would cause the car to crash. Barthes suggests a third option besides naïveté or cynical nihilism. Focusing on window and view separately goes against myth's dynamic of both window and scenery taken in together. Barthes explains that when he counters this dynamic, he passes "from the state of reader to that of mythologist" (M, 124). The mythologist takes advantage of the vacillation between noticing the windowpane and seeing the landscape to create what he calls an *artificial mythology*. This counter-myth of "naïveté looked at" neither replaces the window nor transcends it to direct access (M, 136). It simply changes the driver's focus as in a movie that racks or changes focus during a single shot for comic effect or exciting emphasis. In fact, one might argue that artificial mythology plays precisely on a preoccupation of much avant-garde art. Those artworks make life appear as if seen in a movie.[5] Counterintuitively, the moments punctuated by that "like-a-movie" sense destabilize naturalized myths or realities. The artificiality and distance that occur when one sees an event unfolding in, for example, slow motion also create the vacillation between what one sees and how one sees it. Barthes does not tell us much more about this phrase, nor does he allude to it ever again in his other works throughout his career. From this little detail, this little thrown-away gem, or as the Spanish refer to a diamond in a lemon, a *sapates*, springs the possibility of a methodology for the study of cultural and media invention.

That Barthes chose a drive in a car as the model for ideology seems particularly fitting for citizens of the United States because the American Dream depends so much on the mobility of the family car. While the glamour of trains has past and the economic pressures for mass transit no longer seem pressing, the car remains the keystone of contemporary culture. Even E-mail and the Internet have failed to dent the car's hold on the West's imagination. Bicycles, important means of transportation in many economies, especially in Asia, remain a recreational vehicle or, in congested urban areas, a way for speedy messengers to get around the car traffic. These daring bike-messengers are the exception that proves the rule: all of our cultural myths seem to circulate around the car literally. The car is not just as an apt metaphor for mythologies; it is the epitome of American mythologies.

The familiarity of the car makes it not only Barthes's vehicle for the metaphor to describe the interactions of myth, artificial myth, and material history but also an image used in popular culture to describe progress through history. Both metaphors depend on a driver staring out the window at the landscape. Take, for example, the Ford Motor pavilion at the 1964 World's Fair in Flushing Meadow-Corona Park, New York City. The Ford pavilion used cars to carry people through the history of world progress. Cars functioned there as both the epitome and vehicle of progress. The pavilion played host to many of the 51.5 million visitors to the fair with a theme of "peace through understanding." That slogan could double as the emblem of myth: healing contradictions in the name of understanding in order to keep the peace. The World's Fair's grounds, built on an old garbage dump and swamp, literally covered over the stench with myths of progress. As passengers entered the pavilion, Ford Mustangs, Thunderbirds, and other models shuttled each family through the history of the world from the dinosaurs to the future.[6] Even a child could drive the car because each car was connected to a moving track. Just as the Mustang driver seemed to steer through world history, individuals, in contemporary society, seemed not to notice the predetermined track pulling their myth-cars along. What a perfect image of the machinations of ideology and mythology!

The nuances of this ride have important implications for understanding how it also serves to explain artificial mythology as well. The 1964 World's Fair displayed a tone and design quite different from the 1939–40 fair at the same location. The earlier fair had a futuristic monumentality, while this fair had signs of a pop-art aesthetic everywhere: a giant tire, giant pop-art prints on the side of one building, the moving sidewalk, which took visitors on a visit with a computerized pope, and so on. The Ford pavilion was no different. Even as it presented the most obvious example of a mythological view of history, and even as the promoters sought to create a mechanized verisimilitude to prehistoric times and the future, the obviousness of its staging, the use of actual Mustangs for the drive-through, and Disney-built creatures throughout the ride had a pop-art flair. The pop-Disney connection had many links including Claes Oldenburg building his "Ice Bag" in a Disney workshop.

The artificial myth works the way a pop artist paints. It changes the viewer's focus so that myths look larger than life, out of proportion to the naturalized world around. Out of context, enlarged, and, therefore, making the familiar strange, the pop artwork makes both the banal object and the monumental look silly. For example, the giant clothespin by Oldenburg at the center of Philadelphia across from city hall suggests both a tool for drying clothes and the grandness of modernist public art. On the one hand, its shape resembles Brancusi's modernist sculpture of a couple kissing. In that sense, the clothespin allusion pokes fun at modernist monumentality. On the other hand, the clothespin simply changes the focus of the public slightly, punctuating or stressing the irony (the banal object, a clothespin, as huge monumental public art) or the comedy of a possible mistake (someone put a giant clothespin in front of city hall). One could imagine a visitor saying, "Now that is some clothespin." Of course, the recognition of putting the city's dirty laundry out for public scrutiny may only occur for a fleeting moment for a passerby. Anyone can miss the joke, just as anyone can mistake the World's Fair as realism rather than Disneyfied. Pop's parody sometimes fails to reach the very audience it aims to provoke.

Laughter as Methodology

Similar to the pop artists, Barthes begins with the banal and specific rather than the grand scheme. By playing the fool, he defamiliarizes critical viewpoints. While in his earlier work on myths, Barthes uses a semiotic strategy and strikes the pose of a scientist unearthing hidden contradictions, in later works like *A Lover's Discourse: Fragments,* he appears to take a particularly unfashionable pose, working through debased myths instead of rejecting them outright. At first this strategy resembles the adventures of Bouvard and Pécuchet, who travel through fields of learning like tourists on vacation, stumbling on disappointments and letdowns as they bungle each new endeavor. That image of their "ineffectual inclinations, their inability to feel satisfied, the panic succession of their apprenticeships" forms the basis for a counter-myth, a "bouvard-and-pécuchet-ity," an artificial mythology of naïveté looked at (*M*, 135). Quite different from the earlier works that reflect a competent mind always finding the hidden message by using traditional norms of scholarship and sophisticated scientific methods of analysis, Barthes's later works show an ill-fated struggle to know and understand. Instead of applying semiotics to the problems at hand, he finds only a loss of his semiotic mastery. He confronts a block to any positivistic knowledge; over and over again he meets an impasse to any metalanguage, any definitive summary of a field. Faced with these problems, he does not retreat to solipsism. He invents an artificial myth by enacting with bouvard-and-pécuchet-ity various roles and activities: a romantic lover's obsessive list making, an eager tourist's superficial journal, an autobiographer's fragmented digressions, and a photo collector's utterly personal favorites. Each of these enactments plays through a particular cultural myth about love, travel, family, and death. Instead of simply debunking a myth about love, for example, he poses as a lover waiting in vain for the beloved to return. These situations often put the narrator in comic predicaments (e.g., getting hopelessly lost trying to use a confusing map and an impossible address to orient himself).

It is as if the narrators of these later experimental works were visiting a big city called Semiotics, Political Decoding, or Demythologizing only to find themselves lost among these markers of a hip modernity that sees through myths and cultural clichés. The readers laugh not only *at* these feckless wanderers through knowledge and methodologies but also *with* these outsiders at modernity's metalanguages, including the methods used to demythologize. In his wanderings through systems of knowledge like a character in a novel or movie, Barthes invents artificial myths out of the failures, weaknesses, and disorientations built into our cognitive maps of the world, those methods of understanding like semiotics. Although the participant, the character, does not enjoy the experience of having cognitive maps fail, the reader, or observer, of these experiments delights in watching a semiotician's foibles and slapstick as he tries in vain to decode the world of love, travel, subjectivity, and so on. These figures of love and learning, travel and otherness, family album, and death and memories appear not only in the clichés of middle-class everyday life but also in the most sophisticated academic conversations and debates about teaching and desire, multiculturalism and tourism, family values and media, and death and memorialization. These themes preoccupied Barthes in his later works because he saw important intersections ripe for innovation in these areas. Likewise this book examines these themes again in light of contemporary cultural conflicts.

The novelty that grows out of these farcical encounters leaves the narrators to reinvent themselves without the benefit of either the guiding hand of mythologies or the clear-sightedness of semiotics or other metalinguistic methods. The "controlled accidents" go beyond our hero's mishaps to a method of "yielding to the path of the initial dispatch."[7] These accidents and mistakes have, at first, no positive value or meaning. They merely represent an impasse and an opening for a detour. Barthes detours. He finds the impasses and detours right there where "everyone" goes. As a traveler, for example, unsure of his own frame for understanding what he tours, he does not mock myths from a transcendent semiotic or scientific position; he poses as a tourist. He occupies the smudged, effaced, and clichéd in order to find a language for that which resists current naturalized ways of understanding literature, media, and culture. Taking the detour on the cognitive maps called naturalized myths produces the outlines of change: new paths, vistas, and constraints. In short, artificial mythologies are recipes for cultural invention.

A commonplace notion of invention suggests that an idea spreads out from a central event and place. From the initial "eureka" of the creative genius, the idea slowly seeps its way through the streets and around the globe. It is this romantic myth that Barthes criticizes. He argues that innovation depends less on inspiration than on a system that allows for combinations to occur. In rejecting the myth that inventions are "born out of the blue," this book examines how particular conceptions of media and sociocultural problems and issues stymie innovation. How scholars, experts, and the public at large conceptualize various social problems and cultural issues can squelch the production of possibilities for solutions simply by not considering particular paths or detours. The potential detours depend on a sense of humor and an openness to the *apparently* absurd solution.

In this book, the strong interpretation of Barthes and his work detours the mythologies surrounding this literary critic. It makes a critic considered quintessentially French seem more like an American folk hero. It makes a critic well known for having two very distinct projects during his career merge his earlier work with the later work to create an alternative to both of those structuralist and poststructuralist stages in his career. It makes a serious critic advocate laughter as methodology. It makes his work, recently thought of in terms of the author's life and experiences as a gay man, for example, seem to have less to do with an author's life than with the reader's uses of his work. To those readers *not* familiar with Barthes, the critic's name might add an air of legitimation, and the specific citations certainly help clarify and strengthen my arguments. Yet, claiming that this most eminent and influential scholar and critic wanted to make laughing no laughing matter may strike some more familiar with literary theory as putting Barthes in short trousers. That reading would give me a bit too much credit. It would miss Barthes's own speculative imagination, his own willingness to use laughter as an analytic strategy. If we dismiss his laugh, we miss the chance to understand his strategy to dissolve any metalanguage the moment it constitutes itself. That is, he engages in a *bathmology,* a statement with a series of interpretations ranging from the naive to the ironic.[8] His laugh teaches the reader to listen not only to what the writer says but also to the texture, tone, and *bathos* of his humor.

In a figurative comedy of errors, the participant in artificial mythology loses the way among the well-known and well-worn places or topics in the memory city-theater called naturalized understanding. The map may refer to a critic's life and contributions or to a cultural situation. When that "mishap of disorientation" occurs, the poor narrator has "a sense of anxiety and even terror that . . . reveals how closely it is linked to our sense of balance and well-being. The very word 'lost' in our language means much more than a simple geographical uncertainty; it carries overtones of utter disaster."[9] In working through the overtones of "getting lost," Kevin Lynch lists the elements of disorientation in the image of the city: direction ambiguity, characterless path, lack of differentiation, elastic intersection, weak or absent boundary, point of confusion, and many others. These are the same problems the narrators of Barthes's texts encounter. When Lynch's warning against disorientation is taken as a model of ideology in general, the trials and travails of the narrators look like an effort to get lost in ideology's myths or an effort to take a *dérive*.[10] Instead of following the course set out by ideology, a map that makes life easier or livable in many respects, the narrators lose the way, creating an artificial mythology.

Counter to classical rhetoric, where *inventio* recalls stored information by successfully navigating along habituated routes from topic to topic, artificial mythologies stumble and fall on purpose in order to invent new potential conceptions. In a discussion of memory and writing, Plato rejects the performances of epic poetry because knowledge in that aural cultural practice depended on an *artificial* memory system, which made use of visual images, temporal "becoming" rather than transcendent "being," and a mixture of fact and fiction and audience participation. These artificialities can also disrupt the reality of naturalized mythologies. As Jacques Derrida explains, even though Plato agrees that writing is "good for memory," writing is for Plato "external to memory, productive not of science but of belief, not of truth but of appearances."[11] Plato objected to the passive recitation of poetry because it created a monument of memory rather than living memory. In their efforts to visit or recite these monuments rather than think for themselves, the audience lost any hope of thinking as individual creative subjects. Plato coined an appropriate phrase for the epic audience, who he claimed had a lost sense and could not reason for themselves; he called them sight-seers. Rather than calling on a creative inspiration that precedes writing and other *artificial* systems, one can make use of an inventive practice that *uses* rather than dismisses the artificial. Noticing the mediation, artificiality, and constraints on the view out the car window, that metaphor of mythology, does *not* enable the driver to transcend sight-seeing. Rather the driver uses the artificiality of the view as a starting point for speculating on particularities, anomalies, and details that do not fit with an abstract view or myth. In an essay on Schumann's "lieder cycles," Barthes eloquently expresses the connection between appreciating that which resists abstraction and an aimless wandering through cognitive maps of our understanding:

Even the lieder cycles do not narrate a love story, but only a journey: each moment of this journey is in a sense turned back on itself, blind, closed to any general meaning, to any notion of fate, to any spiritual transcendence . . . a pure wandering, a becoming without finality: at one stroke, and to infinity, to begin everything all over again.[12]

What if Barthes began over again and rewrote his mythological investigations after the later works?

The commentaries on Barthes's career almost universally suggest that, at least by the time of *S/Z*'s publication in 1970, Barthes had transformed his (naive) view of semiosis or meaning production. In the earlier works like *Mythologies*, ideology supposedly congealed from false consciousness. The dominant class promoted ideology through the spread of specific fictions or mythologies. In *S/Z*, on the other hand, cultural forces still inform literary texts, for example, but in the later work the imposition does not arrive as a monolithic force. In the earlier works, each mythology repeated in various incarnations essentially the same ideology. The deeper meanings of mythologies always repeat the same limited set of messages. In the later work, suggestive words, phrases, and images have multiple or infinite meanings. The earlier work sought to uncover the singular meaning from a multitude of situations; the later work sought polysemy from even the apparently most trivial details. Even in regard to his attitude and prose style, most critics agree that his later work abandoned didactic explanations and traditional structural analyses in favor of reflective essayistic texts that seemed to disparage structuralism. Barthes's own remarks about his earlier works suggest that he rejected the unsophisticated methods and concerns of the earlier work. Like his commentators, he wrote that his earlier analyses constrain the polysemy and merely attempt to lift a veil exposing dominant cultural institutions' operations.

In challenging any effort to bring the early work together with the later work, commentators recount his many methodological changes. The early works do not address a major preoccupation of the later works: the relation of knower to known. To make a link between the early and later works risks missing the major change in his career from semiotic analysis to works that dropped the conventional distinction between theory and practice. As poetic involvement replaced detached objectivity, his later texts rejected the political and scientific metalanguage of the earlier projects. His adoption of *new* concerns during the last decade of his career surprises scholars little now. The shifts in his thinking have become the indexes of his character and find ample motivation in his efforts to avoid codification. To Barthes's dismay, it seemed as soon as he published one project, it would inevitably find its way into the reifying hands of academics, who would turn his playful and elusive texts into systems of thoughts and methodologies. He feared his works would become popular and recuperated by the institutions he sought to criticize.

Following the code of Barthes, we can conceive of him in his later life as constantly trying to stay one step ahead of the literary and theoretical avant-garde by changing his epistemology. More importantly, the epistemological changes represented a complete and irreversible break with the past rather than a gradual evolution toward a mixture of methods. Barthes himself charted the many changes in his epistemological (or, finally, "bodily") position. After spelling out four "genres" or "phases" in his work (social mythology followed by semiology followed by textuality followed by morality), he adds his numbered explanatory remarks:

> (5) each phase is reactive: the author reacts either to the discourse which surrounds him, or to his own discourse, if one and the other begin to have too much consistency, too much stability; (6) as one nail drives out another, so they say, a perversion drives out a neurosis: political and moral obsession is followed by a minor scientific delirium, which in its turn sets off a perverse pleasure.[13]

He understood his early projects, which he groups within "social mythology," as a "political and moral obsession." The "perverse pleasures" of the fourth phase, it appears, have no place in the serious and obsessive work of uncovering and dismantling bourgeois ideology—the work in (or of) *Mythologies*.

If his hedonism does not mesh with his earlier concerns, neither does the epistemological body and soul searching seem to facilitate his project of objectively exposing the process of "naturalization." Whereas the primary tool of *Mythologies* seems to be a universal science, his later texts employ a different tool: his body. While his later texts often attempted to generate new (or fantastic) reading strategies of stories and cultures, especially in the "textuality" phase (*S/Z, Sade, Fourier, Loyola,* and *Empire of Signs*), or produce poetic spectacles from his encounters with the everyday, especially in his last three projects (*Roland*

Barthes, A Lover's Discourse, and *Camera Lucida*), his earlier tasks apparently merely described the operation of connotations and "second order signification." *Mythologies,* according to this code, is a descriptive project. The project here interprets the earlier work through the lens of the later work.

The concern for extreme particularities marks much of Barthes's work. In a discussion of travel guides, he complains that these guides give travelers only an abstract reading of a place and exclude the possibility of appreciating the nonmonumental and the temporal. He explains that "generally speaking, the *Blue Guide* testifies to the futility of all analytic descriptions which reject both explanations and phenomenology: it answers in fact none of the questions which a modern traveler can ask himself while crossing a countryside which is real and which exists in time" (*M,* 75–76). Barthes seeks that which resists an abstract or transcendent view of reality (i.e., he resists both myths and metalanguages). These views always presume to exist outside the vicissitudes of time, the lives of people, and the contingencies of place. Rather than leave a vacuum in their place for some romantic notions to fill, he proposes methods and procedures to approach the artificial, ornamental, or anomalous. As he shifts away from the enlightenment project of *Mythologies,* especially in the last ten years of his life, the tourist guide no longer functions merely as an illusory veil or displacement of reality. In the later experimental works he makes a decisive break with efforts to appreciate abstract or underlying aesthetic forms, linguistic structures, or demythologized knowledge. While his early works contain flashes of the importance of the particular, he does not yet incorporate those moments of insight into a larger project. In the later works, he no longer attempts a complete elucidation of a terrain. Instead he provokes the reader to approach the absolutely particular in readings, viewings, travels, and so on. In American academic scholarship, the challenge comes less from the eternal values usually found in museums, histories of art, and canons of literature than from the *pseudo* science of supposedly neutral and objective descriptions of culture. As Barthes notes, the myth of travel embodied in the *Blue Guide* had already begun to give way to statistics and rankings of the banal: "Notice how already, in the *Michelin Guide,* the number of bathrooms and forks indicating good restaurants is vying with that of 'artistic curiosities' " (*M,* 76). Who can doubt the veracity of a guide that gives addresses, telephone numbers, and prices of motels along the road, and who would think to question the validity of such truths? In his early work, like *Mythologies,* Barthes demonstrates how these everyday facts hid many underlying assumptions. In his later work, he notices how our attention to only *banal* facts discounts and ignores the particularities these facts presumed to offer. By focusing attention on either the monumental or the statistical social geography, the (culture or media studies) guide user either misses the trees for the forest or the forest for the trees. Traveling is neither the tour of the monumental nor merely "certain boring and useless things: customs, mail, the hotel, the barber, the doctor, prices" (*ES,* 13).

What is traveling? Intersections. The rendezvous becomes that momentary intense intersection, like a train station, an empty value, which sets in motion a perpetual combination of lines. In this book, the intersection of the interests of cultural studies scholars *and* widespread popular concerns forms the basis for each of the investigations. Of course, these two contexts never coincide exactly, and parts of the discussion seem destined to work at cross purposes to each other. Instead of merely ignoring these odd conclusions created from the overlap of the popular and academic paradigms for researching the most pressing problems confronting contemporary culture, this book finds ways to appreciate the intersection of these two discourses. Barthes's work in the 1950s joined the most sophisticated academic research to the most common popular practices; this book returns to this conjunction.

The Punctum as Practice

> Not only does spontaneity require practice, but it can take time to arrive at immediacy, and when you do, it's not something to dismiss.
>
> HENRY LOUIS GATES JR., on rap-meets-poetry

Although most critics have interpreted the *punctum* as a peripheral detail opposed to the studium, the aesthetic or social meanings in a photograph, *Camera Lucida*'s readings of photographs depend on the use of a punctum practice. The intense intersection, what Barthes calls the *punctum,* appears as something not quite in harmony, a problem or an impasse, always pointing to other routes and destinations.[14] Like Proust's madeleines, they provoke something like, but not identical to, involuntary memories.[15] The train station epitomizes this crossing of lines and promise of potential by always alluding to other destinations. This place of other places functions as a relay of desire: always pointing to something outside itself. Like a passenger jumping at the arrival of "his" train, Barthes gets hooked not because of an interesting detail in a photograph, for example, but because of where that detail promises to take him. He plays these particularities like Huysmans's Des Esseintes plays the smell organ in *Against Nature*. In that sense, *the punctum's importance for media and cultural studies has gone unnoticed*. It is not an ontological entity. It is a possibility, a sense of timing, a pragmatic practice. The significant accomplishment in inventing the punctum has less to do with a neophenomenology, as some critics have claimed, than with a term to describe an activity in relation to knowledge. He does not oppose the punctum to the studium, everything one learns in school. Rather Barthes describes an interaction between analytic knowledge and pragmatic practice. He demonstrates how media action can commingle productively with more traditional scholarship. The relationship resembles the play between *sprezzatura,* the ability to speak as if on the spur of the moment and to have a sense of timing and humor, and *mediocrita,* the practice and knowledge that the speaker draws on when speaking.

In his reading in *Camera Lucida* of a photograph of a hydrocephalic girl and a microcephalic boy (popularly known as a pinhead) in an institution in New Jersey (taken in 1924 by Lewis W. Hine), Barthes claims he "hardly sees the monstrous heads and pathetic profiles (which belong to the studium)" (51). Instead he sees the "off-center detail, the little boy's huge Danton collar, the girl's finger bandage" (51). Despite his claims to the contrary, he does not dismiss all knowledge, he does not discard the studium. Here he mobilizes cultural knowledge differently. He does not focus on what aesthetics teaches is the center and central meaning of the photograph. Acting something like Zippy the Pinhead, he sees only the Danton collar and claims to hardly notice the children's heads. To recognize a "Danton collar" makes use of a cultural knowledge of costume and history. It uses the studium the way a courtier uses *mediocrita*: in order to serve a sense of *sprezzatura* or the punctum practice.

Modern universities teach students to speak on the spur of the moment in order to serve the studium, to express clearly and quickly the "correct" answer. *Camera Lucida* sides with the courtier's practice over the modern student's drills. While court behavior depended on quick wit and clever comebacks and medieval universities required mobile imaginations, the *modern* university arises completely out of the studium:

> A University (Latin *universitas*) in the relevant medieval sense is a legal term, meaning a guild or a corporation, a group of men engaged in a common activity of any sort and having a collective status, that is legally recognized to be self-governing and to exercise control over its own membership. In the strict sense of the term, there was no university in Paris until the masters and scholars in the city had formed their own corporation and had been formally recognized to have legal standing. This happened no earlier than between 1208 and 1215. A *studium,* on the other hand, is a place of study, a city where there are several schools, that is, masters offering instruction. . . . The medieval concept of the *universitas* was not tied to a specific place in the way the *studium* was; nor was the university intrinsically defined by function, again in contrast to the *studium.*[16]

Understood in terms of this interpretation of a studium, the punctum functions as *an institutional practice rather than merely a textual effect like a detail.* The punctum practice differs from the studium or school practice:

> The school context may be the wrong context for developing widely applied thinking skills. . . . For learning about learning to be achieved, there must be a decontextualization of the message, a discrimination of the message from its particular instances of use. Learning depends upon freeing the message from the constraints of the situation at hand.[17]

It is not that schools teach irrelevant information but that information is always contextualized to solve school or academic problems. The practice associated with the punctum allows information to move away from the school context of problem solving. The "impossible context" of nonsense functions like the punctum practice by a progressive decontextualization of information that leads to learning.[18]

According to researchers in both psychology and cultural histories, an openness to apparently unrelated or trivial factors functions as an asset to invention. Moreover, how we frame our problems allows or restricts that openness. As Robert Sternberg and Lynn Okagaki write, school tends to contextualize or frame knowledge so it only seems "relevant for doing the kinds of problems that are found in school."[19] They go on to suggest that outside of school "problems and problem solving are not neat and clean. . . . Non-academic problems are messy, ill-defined, and sometimes unanswerable. With non-academic problems, even identifying that there is a problem is crucial."[20] The problem-setting logic postpones conclusion and shows the process of construction. In the logic of a retroactive fantasy, the reader's path creates the writer's path. By interweaving codes and references, the logic produces what Bertolt Brecht called an alienation effect, "distance made explicable" (ES, 54)—the same effect produced in an artificial myth. This procedure merely "designates": "What is designated is the very inanity of any classification of the object" (ES, 83). Barthes does not merely record his ego's subjective wanderings; instead, he gets the last laugh on those critics who would confine Barthes to the ranks of trifling dilettantes by demonstrating with careful precision how to write about *cultural invention without a psychological subjectivity centering creativity.* He thinks around what he cannot think, writes beyond or off the subject, and makes much of little. Barthes offers a method to think beyond ourselves, beyond or other than our habituated experience of reality. Susan Horton explains that the "sense of something not-quite-right, something not-quite-in-harmony, or something missing in our picture of the world...triggers the process of invention and results in our 'getting an idea.' "[21]

In attempting to elucidate the sense of timing in this punctum practice, Barthes describes how the practice involves knowing how to trigger memories and reveries. Just as Proust's involuntary memories begin with a childhood scene of waiting in his bedroom for his mother to kiss him good night, Barthes's memories also begin with an absent mother figure. Analogous to this connection of the mother's figure with involuntary memory, the most potent punctum, for Barthes, is his *not* including a photograph of his mother in his book *Camera Lucida.* The noninclusion creates suspense and sets the reader wondering first what that picture looks like and then, more importantly, speculating on what pictures the book's *readers* would *not* include in their own collections of poignant photographs. It makes the abstract notion of a psychoanalytic "structuring absence" into a concrete demonstration. No longer does psychoanalysis function as a descriptive analytic project. It works through practice. Rather than a photograph allowing the past to live on in our presence, certain photographs function, for Barthes, as textual time machines.[22] For example, a photograph of a man condemned to die puts us into a past time or an anachronism of culture; as Barthes writes, "He is dead and he is going to die..." (*CL,* 95). The analogy between the death mask and the photographic image still holds, but his ecstatic logic allows photography to "reverse the course of the thing" (*CL,* 119). This "temporal hallucination" indicates an emergent symbolic system. As Barthes writes,

> I want to change systems: no longer unmask, no longer to interpret....
> Let us imagine that the science of our *lapsi* were to discover, one day,
> its own *lapsus,* and that this *lapsus* should turn out to be: a new,
> unheard-of form of consciousness?[23]

The punctum, as a *lapsus* in our understanding, forces a vacillation and a detour. The reader or spectator stumbles. Interpretation becomes "an action of thought without thought, an aim without a target" (*CL,* 111). That is, the punctum practice produces potential routes of invention rather than a description or target to analyze. The punctum uses that which does not fit. Not yet a fit idea for selecting, it remains recessive.

One can use peripheral details as part of a decentered reading strategy. That strategy would not focus on the intended meaning of a film but on details that are poignant to the reader. Rather than using details as examples to prove a point about a film's form or meaning, this method uses peripheral details as an alternative way to understand films. The use of peripheral details calls into question what it means to read, and it shifts the ground of a student's wandering attention from media illiteracy to a political activity. Rather than the reader's attention following the story or appreciating the filmmaking, the reader's decentered attention floats in what Roger Cardinal describes as "mischievous curiosity."[24] Passive spectators will find this strategy practically impossible, but active spectators will succeed if they add something to the film that, as Barthes explains, is nonetheless already there. In arguing that we must add something to the film that is already there, Barthes suggests that saying "any old thing" will result in the same unproductiveness as saying the "same old thing." The punctum requires the spectator to find something as of yet unsaid, something different, supplemental, or leftover. By actively scanning the literal and figurative periphery of a text's message, concentration becomes crucial at the very moment when our minds or eyes or ears wander: attention to distraction becomes a foundation of artificial invention.

Cardinal explains how to recognize details that function as punctums. He places Barthes's work on "third meaning" and the punctum in relation to other similar work like the surrealist's "paranoid criticism." That criticism emphasizes "irrational knowledge fed by tangential features of the film shaped in the light of oneiric associations—a kind of errant dream-criticism."[25] As in Cardinal's decentered reading, the punctum practice simply adds a caption, a comical comment, or anything that focuses the eyes differently on what is already there.

There are obviously intended significant details. For example, in Alfred Hitchcock's *Notorious,* the heroine, a government agent who marries a suspected Nazi to uncover his scheme, picks up the key to the wine cellar where her husband has secretly stored uranium. When he goes to kiss her hands, she hugs him, drops the key behind him, and kicks it under a table. In the next scene, we look down in an establishing shot over a large formal party; in a single shot, the camera cranes down until the screen fills with the heroine's hand; we see the key back in her possession. This is an example of a central and centered detail. In the last scene of Orson Welles's *Citizen Kane,* the camera cranes over a warehouse of Kane's belongings. In the penultimate shot of the film, we see workmen throw a sled into the furnace; the word on the sled, "Rosebud," was Kane's last word, and the missing clue for the newsman's unsolved investigation of Kane's life. In both of these examples, we cannot help but notice these details. Indeed, they are arguably two of the most famous scenes in the history of the cinema.

In producing films, directors use details to build or conclude a narrative. The understated detail appears as a reinforcement of themes or narratives, or as part of less conventional narratives. The final scene in Michelangelo Antonioni's *The Passenger* and the opening scene of Francis Ford Coppola's *The Conversation,* a film strongly influenced by Antonioni's *Blow-up,* use understated details to build or conclude the narrative. The last scene of *The Passenger* begins when the hero lies down to take a nap; the camera records only what one can see when looking out the window at the dusty dirt plaza. Assassins, who have pursued the hero throughout the film, arrive, and (as an understated detail) we see the assassin in the room only briefly in a reflection in one of the windows. Later, the hero's wife arrives, and when asked if she knows the victim, she says, "No, I never knew him." The hero's newfound girlfriend says, "Yes, I knew him." The actresses deliver these lines nonchalantly, leaving only the viewer to understand the significance. No close-ups punctuate the dialogue. This scene, which leaves the viewer to piece together these understated details, concludes both the narrative and thematic lines of this film about switching identities. *The Conversation* begins with a crane shot of a city park in San Francisco. The camera follows a mime and then follows various other characters around the park. As we piece together the relationships between the various characters, we learn that a surveillance team has an elaborate system to record a couple strolling around the park. The enigma, why the surveillance tracks such a normal couple, involves the spectator and the investigator in a nightmarish look at the implications of voyeurism. Many of the initial scene's details become quickly recuperated into the narrative and thematic structure.

Contrary to the intentionally placed significant detail, peripheral details can appear even in the most tightly controlled films. To stress his point, Barthes chooses Sergei Eisenstein's *Ivan the Terrible,* Part I, a film famous for the director's careful control over every element of the film's form and mise-en-scène. We need not look for peripheral details in unseen or peripheral films; we need not search through rare archives to find the marginalized. One can find the peripheral detail in the most controlled sites. Barthes does not find the peripheral in an authentic nonartificial experience away from the crowd as in a modernist or romantic dream. Like a tourist who stands in front of the monument and cannot help but notice some insignificant and unimportant detail, we need not leave the tourist attraction or the movie theater to find it. We need not mock the tourists and praise the discoverer. For those dreams of conquering new territory, of finding the authentic where no one has looked before, carry with them the baggage of colonialism, imperialism, and even sexism. The peripheral detail, the tourist's attraction, is neither heroic nor uniquely authentic.

The decision to focus on an apparently carefully controlled film, *Ivan the Terrible,* and the recognition that peripheral details appear even in the most trite, crass, and insipid films suggest how one can use this method in analyzing other films. Instead of being used to interpret films, the punctum functions here as a practice using recessive ideas or peripheral details. In a discussion of an often cited educational film, which Western relief workers attempted to use to teach a group of indigenous people the importance of boiling water, Barthes suggests how punctums also provoke a particular practice:

> According to an old experiment, when a film was shown for the first time to natives of the African bush, they paid no attention to the scene represented (the central square of their village) but only to the hen crossing this square in one corner of the screen. One might say: it was the hen that gazed at them. (*RF*, 239)

Pecked by the punctum, Barthes investigates a "kind of subtle beyond—as if the image launched desire beyond what it permits us to see..." (*CL*, 59). As he explains, the punctum's gaze "is located *beyond* appearance: it implies at least that this 'beyond' exists, that what is 'perceived' (gazed at) is truer than what is simply shown" (*RF*, 240). As Jacques Lacan explains, "In our relation to things as constituted by the path of vision and ordered in the figures of representation, something shifts, passes, is transmitted from stage to stage, in order to be—invariably, to some degree—elided: this is what is called the gaze."[26] Resistant to one's consciousness, the gaze alludes to a staining or a *resist* as in the dying of fabric: a stain in an image. This *not* seeing something, of something missing or lost, functions as neither part of a personality nor as an element in a discursive structure, except as a loss or blockage in that structure. Jane Gallop explains this "blind field" as something outside the frame in her discussion of photographs where "things continue to happen outside the frame."[27] She discusses how in those cases even certainty escapes the frame. Barthes's word choice in his discussion about the lack of intention involved in punctums betrays his doubt: "the detail that interests me is not, or *at least not rigorously,* intentional, and *probably* it must not be...it does not *necessarily* attest to the photographer's art" (*CL*, 79–80; emphasis added by Gallop). Barthes "cannot be certain the detail that pricks him is not intended."[28] But, faced with this and other uncertainties about the "unsayable," he admits he has "no other resource than this *irony*: to speak of the 'nothing to say' " (*CL*, 93). Each frame of reference, which can appear as a photograph, a narrative, a video, a metaphor, or an essay's argument, contains links to something outside the frame. The punctum practice links frames and makes intersections.

In *Camera Lucida,* Barthes discusses a photograph of a man condemned to die, Lewis Payne. Lewis Thornton Powell, who called himself Payne, was a son of a Baptist minister in Florida. After escaping from prison, he wandered adrift in the North penniless and half mad until he joined John Wilkes Booth and planned to abduct the president. After Lincoln's assassination, Payne was captured and convicted of conspiracy to commit murder. Barthes mobilizes this information, this studium, using a punctum practice. He explains that the photograph of Payne has a punctum that spreads out to fill the whole frame, not merely one detail. The punctum that fills the whole picture also functions as a link, but not because a detail does not fit into this frame of reference. It functions by a number of frames of reference overlapping or crossing. It functions as a hybrid cross among frames of reference. The mix of the Payne of history, the pain of absence, and the pane of representation indicates how Barthes organizes his album of photographs using a particular practice. These mixing ideas form the basis of the organization around a hypnotic *spell*. Payne is dead, and he suffers the pain of waiting to die, and the pane between Payne and us is a pane between the past and the future. Of course, the fact that these puns only appear in English, not in the original French, does not discount their importance. The practice depends on readers and reading, not merely on what appeared in an original version. It depends on the potential or recessive idea. Artificial Myth functions as a collection of recessive ideas, detours among established topics of the studium. The recessive ideas intersect even though they do not yet fit.

Described as not merely a "semioclasm, the deliberately irreverent destruction of signs as we know them,"[29] this practice changes our relation to maps of knowledge. As Barthes explains, the map changes from an abstract and visual grid based on print culture to a gestural practice based on an alternative sensibility. This practice has *less* to do with definitive meanings than with potential combinations and with changing the setting or frames for understanding. Barthes explains, "you cannot speak on such a text, you can only speak in it, in its fashion, enter into a desperate plagiarism."[30] The practice finds the intersections among different symbolic systems instead of working toward progress in any single system or epistemological frame. In the attempt to account for more than one symbolic system, or to explore the potential of an interference in our home languages, the driving and traveling metaphors again become significant. Every anomaly announces, by definition, that a singular language system or way of understanding cannot account for every incommensurable difference. These signs are not easily assimilated; they remain *recessive*, only apparent in between systems or in the crossing of differences. The textual model reads/writes the unassimilated (strangers, tourists, anomalies, etc.) as the basis for invention's peculiar economy of attention. The practice connects fragments according to the magnetism of gossip or graffiti; it writes through street talk as the popular mixes with the personal and specialized discourses. It builds on the fascinations or manias usually discarded by conventional reading practices. It allows for the intensity, patience, and personalized analogies necessary for generating associations. Like what Gilles Deleuze and Félix Guattari call a *minor literature,* this "deterritorialized language, appropriate for strange and minor uses," disrupts the usual connection between individual and a social background.[31] The minor logic of invention changes the relationship between individuals and their organization of knowledge. It encourages and preserves the relay/translations of recessive ideas. As an institutional practice it "associates intellectual activity with delight. This swerve of affect from alienated thought to carnivalesque thinking occurs by exploiting the indirections of metaphors, images, and key words employed in theoretical explanations."[32] This institutional practice makes "passages" between dominant languages of selected knowledge and the writing of artificial mythologies.

Barthes explicitly refers to the punctum as "what Lacan calls the *Tuché*," the occasion or encounter. And Lacan mentions the *Tuché* in describing how the gaze functions. Joan Copjec, in a discussion of Lacan's theory of the gaze of the Other, has teased out the salient features of a theory that focuses on discontinuity, particularities, and blind spots. In that sense, her work is useful for a discussion of Barthes's work. In an attack on apparatus theory she writes:

> It is not the long arm of the law that determines the shape and reach of every subject, but rather something that escapes the law and its determination, something we can't manage to put our finger on . . . an indeterminate something which is perceived as extradiscursive.[33]

These are precisely the terms Barthes uses to describe the punctum in *Camera Lucida.* Copjec goes on to explain that this "indeterminate something" functions as a kind of limit or impasse in a subject's efforts to make sense (of the picture, sound, world, etc.). She explains that the "different positions are structured so as to circumscribe and thus define an absence at the fantasy's center. This absence or 'kernel of nonsense' holds the fantasy and the subject in place, limits the subject.... It provides the link between the subject and social discourse."[34] The link that Copjec identifies between the "kernel of nonsense" and social discourse helps to highlight how the use of a punctum practice can inform an innovative cultural practice. This kernel of nonsense provokes laughter as a methodology that seeks to change the discursive context in which literature, films, and other cultural performances are read and (mis)understood. It responds to recent theoretical imperatives to appreciate films, and culture in general, in terms of, or as, a context of reception. Always received in a discursive context, film does not exist as something autonomous, outside of arguments, discussions, viewing patterns, and so on. One might see a film in a first-run theater or in a classroom. One watches films in contexts, and those films, in turn, create contexts. Reading and watching become crucial to changing film's role from a passive tool of hegemonic control to part of a generative process. The shift in understanding contexts as part of a hermeneutic explanation to using contexts as part of generative practices requires an appreciation of how the authentic no longer should be the teleological center orienting research. As an alternative to describing how cultural myths exert hegemonic control, one can use artificial mythologies by making use of existing social structures and adding markers, pointers, and magnification.

Artificial Myth: Connecting Studium to Punctum in Cultural Change

Marshall McLuhan's moral judgments and his supposed insistence on technological determinism have caused his works to fall into disfavor with the academic community. In fact, his most important works, *The Gutenberg Galaxy* and *The Medium Is the Massage,* were both out of print from the early 1970s until the early 1990s. In spite of the problems with his work, he offers helpful readings of how to understand changes in conceptual maps. In that sense, his work can suggest clues to translating myths into artificial myths. In the *Gutenberg Galaxy,* he argues that Shakespeare's *King Lear* dramatizes the painful consequences of the emergence of a visually based individual consciousness.[35] In the previous social order, centralized authority relegated each member to a peculiar role in the hierarchy. Power shifted from one's predetermined role in society to a job-centered definition of self. And, according to this new ideology of the self, individuals make their own fate by becoming skilled in specified and demarcated domains of knowledge. When Lear proposes the division of his land with authority decentralized, he disrupts the stability of the hierarchical roles. In that sense, the play functions as a model of the process by which people "translated themselves from a world of roles to a world of jobs."[36] To conceptualize his plan, Lear uses a map, "a novelty in the sixteenth century" and a "key to the new vision of peripheries of power and wealth." The map highlights "a principal theme of *King Lear,* namely the isolation of the visual sense as a kind of blindness."[37] Once the territory is conceived of in terms of a map, the journey inevitably involves analytico-referential reason. One cannot *see* an alternative. Although subjects now had free choice and individual consciousness, they sacrificed the ability to make connections across rationally unrelated domains of knowledge. The isolation of one sense, vision, creates a specialist bias. Subjects do their jobs according to their expertise in demarcated domains of knowledge rather than playing their roles across boundaries of specialized domains. While the maps in *Lear* function as naturalized myths, *the Fool creates artificial myths as commentary on the unfolding events.* The maps create rational domains of knowledge, which only a fool can disparage.

Homer's *Odyssey* chronicles a similar shift in cognitive maps. Ulysses' "voyage to the self" uses a travel narrative to explore the breakdown of a passage to an alternative consciousness.[38] That passage functions as an analogy for the connection between what some biologists refer to as the left and right brains. The passage created a *bicameral* mind with both sides interacting regularly. The right brain, the place of "the Gods," produced voices and visions that the left brain would obey without free choice or conscious decisions. The left brain would speak and think without the sense of an internal cognition. Achilles in the *Iliad* represents an example of the bicameral mind. His destiny was determined by "the Gods." Julian Jaynes, another often disparaged generalist in the humanities, argues that consciousness arose with the "breakdown of the bicameral mind." Although he tends to rely on biological determinism, he connects the dissolution of the bicameral mind to subjective consciousness's relation to language. Jaynes explains that physiologically we have the neurological structures for speech and language use in both the left and right areas of the brain.

Yet, in the modern world, we almost always find speech functions localized in the left area. Most other important functions are bilaterally represented in both hemispheres. Indeed, many neurological researchers have demonstrated that *biologically* we do *not* have left and right brain differentiation.[39] What Jaynes explains is that the dissociation is *metaphoric* not biological. The metaphoric use of language generates consciousness. Metaphoric language sets up an inside and outside (including the inside self and outside world) without any remainder. The way conscious subjects use language creates the impression that the voices and visions of the right brain have no *say,* no sway over our thoughts and actions. Without consciousness, the voices and visions of the right brain (i.e., "the Gods") would direct each subject in peculiar directions. Ulysses in his disagreements and battles with "the Gods" not only marks the emergence of consciousness but also indicates a new power relation. Jaynes notes that a series of erupting volcanoes forced apart communities. In efforts to organize these scattered people, consciousness arose in relation to state power. Reason became the glue that held subjects together in a common goal. As Deleuze and Guattari note, Ulysses is the first man of the modern State.[40] The right brain, place of "the Gods," now appears under the rubrics of the unconscious, savage mind, child, and even "feminine style."

In theorizing this connection between two types of thinking, Jacques Derrida characterizes his approach to art with the term "passe-partout," which is not only the mat board joining/separating frame and painting but also a term of passage. As David Carroll explains, it "provides passage everywhere."[41] This passage "between the outside and the inside, between the external and internal edge-line, the framer and framed, [and] the figure and the ground" produces a critical discourse that travels among fact, fiction, theory, art, and other discourses without terminating.[42] As Carroll concludes, "the term that perhaps best characterizes Derrida's approach to art . . . the term that is fundamental to his borderline aesthetics . . . is a term that appears frequently in his essays: passage."[43] To locate the punctum passage, one need only tour the conventional map or order of things:

> There are pass-words beneath order words. Words that pass, words
> that are components of passage, whereas order-words mark stoppages
> or organized, stratified compositions. A single thing or word
> undoubtedly has this twofold nature: it is necessary to extract one

from the other—to transform the compositions of order into components of passage.[44]

Artificial mythologies mediate the conventional or studium with the contingencies of the punctum. The use of artificial mythologies does not merely dispense with the current conception of a situation or problem. It places it in a different context the way a cartoon places speech in a balloon. It allows the left brain of the studium to connect to the fissures, lines of break, and anomalies of the right brain's punctum practice. It combines scholarly elements like pieces of a puzzle according to the *magnetism* of graffiti or rumor. The new combinations always suggest an otherness, difference, or as yet unrealized possibilities. This use of language strategy travels among cultural codes to create a "passage" to another way of knowing.

Connecting the studium's copiousness, *mediocrita,* or rationality to the punctum's reveries, *sprezzatura,* or free associations associates intellectual activity with delight. Understanding cultural invention in terms of a language game, the rules and properties of a category of discourse, allows this connectivity to function as a generalizable model called artificial mythology. In finding the frame for this method, Barthes occupies, like a squatter, other language games: "When no language is available to you, you must determine to steal a language— as men used to steal a loaf of bread" (*RB,* 167). Jean-François Lyotard has equated these games with "the minimum relation required for society to exist . . . the question of the social bond, insofar as it is a question, is itself a language game, the game of inquiry."[45] Lyotard's statement allows us to see that Barthes's language game describes a particular social bond, not the reified ancient city of language but the shifts in attention around cultural mythologies. It is as if one wandered around Wittgenstein's city of language:

> Our language can be seen as an ancient city: a maze of little streets and squares, of old and new houses, and of houses with additions from various periods; and this surrounded by a multitude of new boroughs with straight regular streets and uniform houses.[46]

The logic involved in artificial mythologies depends on forgotten connections, on impropriety, and on truth as an experiment. Just as the logic of jokes and dreams suggests to Freud a writing practice (i.e., the talking cure or a hypnosis based on animal magnetism), Barthes's logic demands a writing practice that has the "grammar of tempura" like Certeau's "rhetoric of walking." Certeau explains how the "long poem of walking manipulates spatial organizations."[47] Like Barthes's wanderings through Tokyo or the topics of love, the rhetoric of walking rejects the transcendent view from the skyscraper. This abstract knowledge represses "all the physical, mental and political pollutions" that would obstruct the rational view of the city. It flattens out "all the data in a plane projection." The "ruses and combinations of powers that have no readable identity proliferate ... they are impossible to administer." Just as the cities Barthes wanders through resist maps, metaphors, and rational grids, the clear abstract map of the "concept-city" decays (*Life*, 94–95). As Certeau explains:

> In analyzing what escapes this decay of the concept of totality, he focuses on the microbe-like, singular and plural practices. His description of walking rejects a formal mapping of a particular route. Surveys of routes miss what was: the act itself of passing by. The operation of walking, wandering, or "window shopping," that is, the activity of passers-by, is transformed into points that draw a totalizing and irreversible line on the map. (*Life*, 97)

Indeed, walking connects "a sequence of phatic *topoi*" and "affirms, suspects, tries out, transgresses, respects," and so on, the trajectories it "speaks" (*Life*, 99). This wandering rhetoric uses the mythologies of everyday life in a particular way:

> For the technological system of a coherent and totalizing space that is "linked" and simultaneous, the figures of pedestrian rhetoric substitute trajectories that have a mythical structure, ... a story gerry-built out of elements taken from common sayings, an allusive and fragmentary story. (*Life*, 102)

The coherent grammar of Western discourse does not help the inventive practice just as "the technological system of a coherent and totalizing space" tells us little about Certeau's walking; instead, each of the sights, sounds, smells, and experiences on the walk must actually build the method. We cannot get much of an idea of how the invention process works from merely drawing out its trajectory on a map. Choosing objects, dividing them up, and combining them into poignant groupings help create the logic for invention. This logic depends on the improprieties among public and private spaces, self and other, and on the impropriety of a foreignness in home (languages). No longer in a foreign city, the theorist feels like a tourist at home.[48]

Punctum as Sprezzatura

In suggesting a connection between Barthes's work and invention, Eric Charles White describes *inventio* with the Greek word *kaironomia*; its etymology suggests the moment in archery when the arrow will have the power and angle to hit and penetrate the target.[49] Like the *sprezzatura* described here, this conception of invention stresses that originality produced in the contingencies of a particular occasion depends on rehearsed spontaneity and a special discursive practice. Barthes calls this practice the "middle voice." What he hints at is a different tone of voice neither simply a naive sincerity nor an ironic smirk but a speculative inventive tone difficult to place and fix on the spectrum running from naïveté to irony.

Speculative invention from the middle voice undermines the notion of the self as noncontingent, essential, discrete, or autonomous. The tone of voice, always dependent on what Lacan calls "the voice of the Other," floats among a number of possibilities. The middle voice disrupts the Imaginary certainty of an autonomous ego. It transforms subject and object in an endless dynamic of repetition and difference, never coming to rest in a symmetrical certainty; and like the will-to-invent, it keeps desire in play by fixing neither object nor subject. Instead, it mediates differences according to the logic of invention. Knowing the right moment and the lines of fissure allows us to wait while generating possibilities without immediate concern for truth, sincerity, or authenticity. It allows for artificial brainstorming. As Cicero explains, the logic of *inventio* concerns the orator's ability to "hit upon what to say."[50] Barthes's method allows *language to strike.* It allows language to hit us with something to say. As it forestalls the use of habituated categories, it allows for alternative frames or taxonomies. In *The Fashion System,* he writes that "the taxonomical imagination, which is that of the semiologist, is both psychoanalyzable and subject to historical criticism."[51] In many of his later works, Barthes uses an alternative taxonomic descriptive system. He alters it by *dramatizing* it, making it work in a particular performance or setting rather than in an abstract generalization. In *S/Z,* Barthes dramatizes the taxonomy Sarrasine wants to establish.[52] The categorizing of everyone in the binary opposition of male or female is an attempt to set up a relationship between Zambinella and himself. To his fatal surprise, Sarrasine finds his taxonomy, disrupted by the *castrato* Zambinella, who exists simultaneously outside the difference between the sexes and as a representation of the taxonomy's illusory symmetry. Zambinella functions as the middle voice in *S/Z*'s allegorized version of the Balzac story "Sarrasine."

By following how a text addresses a reader, Barthes writes what calls him to read, what holds his attention, and beckons him to read on. This tracking of the address depends on the appreciation of extreme particularities, "the singular image which has miraculously come to correspond to the speciality of my desire" (*LD*, 34). Suggestiveness replaces the notion of a correct context of reception. This drifting of meaning has a profound impact on the tone of research. Gregory Ulmer describes this shift in terms of Barthes's study of Bernard Réquichot. Réquichot's scribbles, scrawls, and unintelligible script represented to the artist an impasse in communication leading to despair and suicide. "But what was a process of despair for Réquichot is bliss for Barthes. What began as a critic's concern for connotation... developed... into a perverse pleasure."[53] For instance, the examples from "Japan" in *Empire of Signs* function like fetishes, charged not with symbolic meaning but perverse pleasure. Barthes's "work proceeds by conceptual infatuations, successive enthusiasms, perishable manias. Discourse advances by little fates, by amorous fits" (*RB*, 110). It allows us "to venture in directions towards which certain words vaguely point, words which, for some as-yet-unaccountable reason, captivate us and provide what Barthes calls a 'flush of pleasure.'"[54] In explaining how we can use Barthes's strategies as a research method, Robert Ray argues that "a particular phrase or vocabulary can reanimate a whole domain. Such 'constitutive' words do not simply explain in colorful imagery something already known... rather they 'suggest strategies for future research.'"[55] He goes on to explain that the crucial factor in using these suggestive figures depends on their open-ended meaning. He writes:

> Such "constitutive" words or phrases are precisely not yet ideas, but rather maps for which the territory must be, not found, but invented; incomplete allegories, clues (Sherlock Holmes's dog that does nothing in the nighttime), hermeneutic enigmas, what Walter Benjamin called "the rumor about true things." Barthes himself offers several names for these research-generating terms: "*mots-valeurs*," "fashion words," "manna-words," "color-words."[56]

The amorous fit, in its heightened ability to attend to "fashion words," leads to a method through which to appreciate and use implications rather than reject them as trivial.

Artificial Myth as Method

In a report to the French Minister of Research and Industry on culture, technology, and creativity, researchers concluded that "the myth that inventions are born out of the blue must be definitively rejected . . . and a large-scale system for the spread of both technical and artistic culture will have to be devised and implemented."[57] Algirdas Julien Greimas's "semiotic square" understood in the context of Barthes's work on artificial mythology illustrates how a system for the spread of innovative culture works. The semiotic model offers an abstract metalanguage with which to understand the creation of artificial myths.

Although the narrators of the later works would wreak havoc with precisely this type of cognitive map, charts and maps still have value even if their fragility makes them prone to parody and pastiche. The value of this particular mapping has less to do with locating artificial myths in a cultural landscape than with understanding the dynamics of creating artificial myths from the interaction of cultural categories. The accompanying semiotic square explains the circulation of meanings or perspectives that move among four cultural contexts of reception: mythologies, demythologies, new mythologies, and artificial myths. Instead of finding some essential quality in any particular object, the graph illustrates how meaning depends on changes in contexts and appreciations of a particular object. This reception model of cultural objects looks somewhat different than older forms of history of art that also study the meaning of cultural objects. An older school of art historians traditionally finds essential aesthetic meaning in particular objects called "authentic masterpieces," and cultural historians find creative genius behind "authentic inventions." In contradistinction to these ways of understanding art and culture, this semiotic square illustrates how meaning arises from *shifts in reception*. Changing the reception of an object can create an invention from the commonplace, the residual, or rubbish. This book uses the square as a blueprint or *a machine for cultural inventions,* not merely as a map of cultural change.

How does this cultural invention machine work? An object can come under the scrutiny of cultural historians, and it can come to rep-

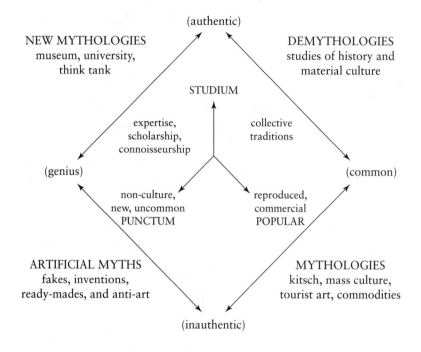

(authentic)

NEW MYTHOLOGIES
museum, university,
think tank

DEMYTHOLOGIES
studies of history and
material culture

STUDIUM

expertise,
scholarship,
connoisseurship

collective
traditions

(genius)

(common)

non-culture,
new, uncommon
PUNCTUM

reproduced,
commercial
POPULAR

ARTIFICIAL MYTHS
fakes, inventions,
ready-mades, and anti-art

MYTHOLOGIES
kitsch, mass culture,
tourist art, commodities

(inauthentic)

resent an element of material culture. Its meaning will have less to do with shared myths than with the effort to unmask its mythic power. In that realm, it will have a negative meaning because it will stand for the trickery involved in mass culture. In both these shifts of context, the object becomes a marker for something more authentic than mass culture. Its meanings also become part of the studium. The same object can also move toward another realm of inauthenticity. As James Clifford writes, in reference to his somewhat different use of a similar semiotic square, "various forms of 'anti-art' and art parading its un-originality or 'inauthenticity' are collected and valued (Warhol's soup can, Sherrie Levine's photo of a photo by Walker Evans, Duchamp's urinal, bottle rack, or shovel)."[58] The residual or emergent meanings appear in "zones of contest and transgression... as movements or ambiguities among fixed poles."[59] That is, the emergent meaning, like the punctum practice, moves among the fixed poles of the studium.

With these few notes in mind, the shift from the descriptive machine for making authenticity to a generative machine for making artificial mythologies begins by changing the reception of objects from "kitsch," for example, or "commodities" to artificial myths, which consist of "ready-mades," "pop art," and "inventions." The reservoir of recessive ideas circulating in collections of junk, the tarnished idea, shifts to an artificial myth when received as emergent. So, to produce artificial myths requires a machine for changing reception and for digging around through the in-between zones, in traffic, and in the ambiguous and contested. Already this map's usefulness wears thin in providing answers about the process of the interstitial areas. At least it begins to illustrate how an artificial mythology can function as something besides a description of existing cultural artifacts. It can function as a machine or method for producing cultural invention. It involves the simultaneous *loss of a contextualized meaning,* and the *inclusion of the discarded and inappropriate,* a sieve-order:

> Things extra and other (details and excesses coming from elsewhere) insert themselves into the accepted framework, the imposed order. The surface of this order is everywhere punched and torn open by ellipses, drifts, and leaks of meaning: it is a sieve-order. (*Life,* 107)

The improper, disordered, and irrational function as elements of invention. Certeau describes the effects and forms associated with this impropriety:

> [B]outs of surprise (in the same way there are bouts of fever), the sudden jubilatory, semi-ecstatic forms of "astonishment" or "wonder" . . . have been, from Aristotle to Wittgenstein, the inaugurators of philosophical activity. Something that exceeds the thinkable and opens the possibility of "thinking otherwise" bursts in through comical, incongruous, or paradoxical half-openings of discourse.[60]

He goes on to explain that these philosophers find "events of a thought yet to come" (*Heterologies,* 194). In regard to Barthes's work, Gregory Ulmer explains, "this 'impropriety' is necessary in any case because Barthes addresses a level of reality that exists at the limit of knowledge excluded from the extant codes of both opinion and science."[61] Even scientific breakthroughs, as Paul Feyerabend argues, depend on making moves forbidden by methodological rules and appear initially as artificial myths: "Theories become clear only after incoherent parts of them have been used for a long time. Such unreasonable, nonsensical, unmethodological foreplay thus turns out to be an unavoidable precondition of clarity and empirical success."[62]

The impropriety of cultural invention makes use of variations, substitutions, and multivalence without deciding on how these choices support a particular truth or argument. In that sense, this logic allows for brainstorming without unnecessary criticism. It builds on the fascinations or manias usually discarded by conventional reading practices and allows for the intensity, patience, and personalized analogies necessary for generating associations. It understands variations of expectation as indicators of emergent ideas, metaphors, or even a new paradigm of understanding. It does not merely offer a negative criticism of a dominant ideology of reading, writing, or thinking. Instead, out of the failures of empirical reading strategies, it makes a minor language. The details that resist taking a meaning within current symbolic systems (i.e., dominant ideologies of reading) suggest an unheard-of symbolic system. These *extreme particularities* appear as temporal problems or anomalies in reading. At those moments something happens. "This something—which is etymologically an adventure—is of an infinitesimal order: it is...an anachronism of culture...an illogicality of itinerary" (*ES*, 79). These "changes in reading" indicate a disruption of the symbolic system, that logic of binary oppositions that holds our conceptions in place. The notion of anomaly shifts as well:

> It has been noted that the origin of the word *anomal* ("anomalous"), an adjective that has fallen into disuse in French, is very different from that of *anormal* ("abnormal"): *a-normal,* a Latin adjective lacking a noun in French, refers to that which is outside rules or goes against the rules, whereas *an-omalie,* a Greek noun that has lost its adjective, designates the unequal, the coarse, the rough,...a phenomenon of bordering...the borderline—the anomalous....Sorcerers have always held the anomalous position...at the borderline of the village, or *between* villages.[63]

What exceeds the institutional explanations builds the language of invention from the otherness of the commonplace. The social milieu does not serve as a mere background, but rather it allows one to, in Deleuze's and Guattari's terminology, "pickup ideas." Invention as a minor method allows one "to become a nomad, an immigrant, and a Gypsy in relation" to one's own language.[64] Barthes focuses on the "delicate communication" of someone drawing directions and explaining how to follow the visual cues to a particular address. In reading these diagrammatic directions, Barthes recovers the writing practice by retaining "the gesture of my interlocutor reversing his pencil to rub out, with the eraser at its other end, the excessive curve of an avenue, the intersection of a viaduct" (*ES*, 34). The fabrication of the address fascinates him more than the address itself. By following the gestural marks in each reading and by rereading that address, he creates an occasion to recover the process of constructing a narrative: "When an artist struggles with material...sounds, words...it is...that struggle and that struggle alone that is in the last instance being told."[65]

Instead of a single abstract metalanguage, like a printed map, this logic requires us to engage with, experience, and write the text the way a lost visitor might wander through a foreign city: slowly with surprises and hesitations. The cognitive map does not appear continuous, unified, logical, or complete. The wanderings no longer uncover denotative meanings or certain destinations. The text becomes a situation rather than a substance. It has less to do with definitive meanings than with potential combinations and with changing the setting or frames for understanding. Invention, neither centered on speech nor limited by reason, writes its own rules as it explores an unheard-of symbolic system. In *Empire of Signs,* for example, Barthes selects materials according to lines of force and rifts in symbolic systems; he combines materials according to a type of *magnetism.* We can follow one series from the arrangement of the dinner tray and the description of things floating in soup to the arrangement of food at the floating market to the chopping of vegetables to the uses of chopsticks to the preparation of sukiyaki. All of these topics deal with the problem of division, scale, and arrangement. The way each topic moves around this motif, however, is quite different. Barthes describes food arrangement in terms of painting, then in terms of cultural materialism, and then in terms of anthropology. If we drew a line on a map, it would go from eating experience to eating experience, but it would miss the suspicions, affirmations, and transgressions; it would look at the food without tasting and touching; it would walk without listening to the street talk.

The Laughing Majority: Artificial Myth Today

> It may be noted by the way that there is no better start for thinking than laughter.
>
> WALTER BENJAMIN, "The Author as Producer"

What is an artificial myth, today? On the one hand the answer is simple. Barthes defines myth as a type of speech; artificial myth is a type of writing.[66] While the speech of myth has a veneer of natural-ness, the artificial myth depends on the written-ness, the obvious me-diation. If talking about things creates myths, then reading allows for artificial myths. One who listens to a myth believes it. One who reads through a myth begins to appreciate artificial myths. The abili-ties to read against the grain, to create humorous often ironic dis-tance between the reader and the message, and to disrupt the power of listening all create the circumstances for an artificial myth. *Artifi-cial Myth is a type of writing.* Of course, it is not *any* type of writing: language needs special conditions in order to become artificial myth. It is not an object, concept, or idea. It is a mode of signification. Can everything become an artificial myth? Yes, for the universe is infinitely fertile in ambiguous and ambivalent suggestions. That suggestiveness is only a beginning, not an end itself. Already an unheard majority be-gins to make its presence known by laughing. To take up that laugh-ter as a method for cultural invention through artificial mythology is the goal of cultural and multicultural studies that privilege pragmatics over abstractions. The chapters in this book apply the method of ar-tificial mythology to problems and cognitive maps in cultural and me-dia studies including the reception and conceptualization of photog-raphy, cinema, television, urban architecture, and public relations.

2 | Mapping Television

Maps

In this chapter I examine a peculiar mistake in a network news broadcast on the first night of the Gulf War. Although every major newspaper and television commentary discussed in detail the particularities of that program's coverage, and in spite of the many scholarly criticisms of the television coverage, not one of the popular or scholarly descriptions to date has discussed the obvious and unfortunate error. Noting the detail in the maps of the broadcast stresses a detail already in the broadcast. The stress changes the broadcast's suggestiveness forever. In this chapter I use a punctum practice, the punctuating of details, to create an artificial mythology about television's power to influence and persuade. In that sense, I examine this oversight in terms of the reception of television and the mapping of dissent in the United States. The punctuation of the oversight allows for that *fleeting flash of hilarity* missing from naturalized myths. I go on to discuss the implications of this slip-of-the-maps for media studies, and how the change in the terrain alludes to psychoanalytic as well as more directly political concerns about cause, displacement, and mourning.

Although the Gulf War seems like ancient history in the television's mobile memories, O. J. Simpson's drive down the highway inspired someone to mark the event with a similar slipup. In a Howard Stern-inspired call to the live news coverage of the standoff, a man in stereotypical Black dialect identified himself as a neighbor who could see O. J. "all slumped down" in the Ford Bronco and went on to comment that "he be looking mighty sad." He ended the call by saying "Ba, Ba, Booey." The newscasters quickly notified the listeners that it was a practical joke. The staged event, somewhat different from the mistakes discussed in this chapter, received some media attention. Once the mistake is noticed, the news programmers will attempt to contain the embarrassment even as new mistakes emerge. What embarrassment will go unreported to the melancholic delight of those watching history unfold supposedly without much participation? This book responds to this other, laughing majority by suggesting strategies, methods, and demonstrations.

Contradictory Maps

The situation of the ABC evening news broadcast on January 16, 1991, presents a number of problems for a tactical intervention. For one thing, everyone has commented endlessly about the events of that evening and especially the media coverage. More importantly, the specific event that makes that evening remarkable today was not noticed by any of the commentators. As Walter Goodman wrote in the *New York Times,*

> The first tentative word that something was happening came a few minutes after the start of the "World News Tonight" on ABC, when Gary Shepard, on the telephone from Baghdad, told of seeing an "incredible panorama of flashes" from his room at the Rashid Hotel on what he called "a very black and clear night." A minute or two later, he reported, "Obviously an air raid is under way right now."[1]

His description also made an implicit connection (which John Fiske has pointed out explicitly) that the news is a melodramatic genre: "Threats, rumors, power failures, sirens, lights; the evening had all the elements of a good old thriller." It was "the most exciting television evening ever."[2] Howard Kurtz, in the *Washington Post,* added that it was like old-time radio broadcasts reminiscent of Edward R. Murrow's radio reports from London. Of course, Kurtz's article made the standard kudos to CNN for its media coup via special telephone lines.[3] Tom Shales, also in the *Washington Post,* went further and reported on CNN's "blindingly brilliant moment." He also noted that "the timing was eerily convenient for the war to break out during the evening news."[4] An example of the antiwar coverage, the *Village*

Voice's issue of February 5 reported on the protests around the country including the Washington, D.C., march, which drew between 150 and 200 thousand people. The *Voice* pointed out that even though this huge antiwar sentiment was unheard of at the *start* of a war, there was little coverage of any of the protests by the mainstream media. Indeed, the group Fairness and Accuracy in Reporting organized a protest against the major networks' coverage. The group pointed out that leading up to the war, only one percent of all the war-related coverage dealt with dissent, and even that coverage was patronizing and simplistic. The *Voice* editorial argued that we have the "Pentagon's puppet show—the mainstream media—to thank for Bush's popular support."[5] With all this careful attention to details, by both the Left and the Right, no one commented on a small but certainly important displacement during the first report of war on ABC.

While Shepard spoke about "something happening," ABC showed a number of maps of Baghdad. Using the "very colorful" map, Peter Jennings told viewers that he would locate Shepard on the map for them. One map of Baghdad was shown, and then another, almost identical map appeared; the (almost unnoticeable) difference is crucial: at least one significant building had changed in that switch of the maps. The location of the U.S. embassy moved from the west bank of the Tigris River to the middle of an isthmus across the river. On the second map, the "Presidential Compound" appeared in the same location as the U.S. embassy had appeared in the first map. Other key "targets" like the "Ministry of Defense" and "Iraqi radio and TV" remained in the same locations. The shift was particularly noticeable because the bend in the river and the isthmus are easily recognized on both maps, and the U.S. embassy appears near the center of both maps. Jennings never mentioned the displacement of the building, nor which map was supposedly "correct." The displacement happened without comment. Goodman pointed out that "the network's use of maps was helpful throughout," and he even singled out ABC's use of maps; he wrote that Mr. Jennings was "especially clear with the assistance of particularly colorful maps in explaining what was going on and where."[6] An analysis of the maps' coloring will have to be saved for another time. The accuracy of the maps was apparently not an important issue for Goodman, or maybe he just was not paying close enough attention. Admittedly, to point out a trivial mistake in a map's accuracy seems presumptuous in the light of the fact that people were dying. Yet, the argument here concerns why this displacement was unremarkable, unnoticed; why was no one paying close enough attention? Other errors are usually dutifully discussed and commented on by newspapers and media analysts. This displacement went unnoticed? It seems impossible to imagine that on that night especially no one noticed a mistake in the accuracy of a map. The discourse surrounding the war was about accurate maps and smart bombs that could read them. What is the significance of the mistake?

Who noticed the mistake? What neither the Left nor the Right can bear to admit is the possibility of an empty news media, merely a shell of power, the possibility that no one is paying attention to what is supposed to shape, manipulate, or guide, depending on the critic's point of view, a national consensus. The Left regularly releases "fact" reports about who owns the media, about how many white male heads appear on news programs, or about the distortions and omissions in the news media. Admittedly, there was no agreement on the Left about the justification of the invasion. Mitchell Cohen of *Dissent* argued that the Left should not equate America's frustration with Saddam Hussein with "the US invasions of Panama and Grenada [because] it undermines its own credibility in opposing future Panamas and Grenadas."[7] The Right responded with complaints about "liberal bias." There are exceptions to this as well; some on the right opposed intervention and were upset with the "cheerleading" media. Even though there were never two monolithic opposing groups, "everyone" watches the news, and precisely because there is heated disagreement, many scrutinize every detail especially for fairness and accuracy. So, why with so many eyes focused on the evening news, did no one notice (or at least not point out) the displacement? What anxiety was too great that neither the Left nor the Right noticed—nor even perceived? Is that not the very definition of repression—not even noticing the displacement? This symptom does not point to a trick, to a conspiracy, or even to the bunglings of the ABC news team. It points to something that does not fit into political discourse. It points to the fringe or border of that discourse; it marks a limit to that discourse. It exists in the discourse and marks its failure, its hole, its impasse. This trivial minor point was apparently so trivial that with all the trivial mistakes that the media do point out to us and "cover," it was merely passed over. No one even mentioned it. Commentators mentioned other "gaffs" (e.g., an announcer talking about a map before it appeared on the screen), and they bemoaned the fact that we never saw enough ("not one dead body"). Those kinds of displacements fit into the prevailing political discourse.

Mapping Attention

The ideological maps of television used by many critics contain a contradiction. These maps position television as both a mindless distraction *and* as a thought-control machine. On the one hand, critics hold the "boob tube" as the great distracter responsible for lower verbal scores on the SATs and for an epidemic of unthinking "couch-potato" children. On the other hand, television as an extremely powerful manipulator apparently condenses and distorts reality for particular ideological ends. The apparent contradiction might disappear if the critics compared the television to hypnosis. The machine would then function to influence the unconscious desires and impulses without any conscious awareness. The viewer would fall into a lulled state of intense attention just as the hypnotized subject appears to doze off after being distracted by the swing of the watch. Just as some people respond more to hypnotic suggestions, some viewers would respond more to the hidden or subliminal messages piped into our homes. Although this conspiracy theory has a certain cachet among the suspicious, most critics note that television does *not* encourage an intense concentration as does hypnosis. For example, "channel surfing," talking during programming, leaving the set on while doing chores or leaving the room, and laughing *at* the programs, advertisements, and news suggest that the experience of watching television does *not* induce an intense concentration that allows for the reception of hidden messages. The critics usually argue that television's messages use easily recognized clichés from a shared culture to reinforce and encourage particular existing ideologies. Both left-wing and right-wing critics tend to understand the news, for example, as putting a particular "spin" on the facts. A news program will not hypnotize the audience. And it will not engage in a conspiracy against the viewer's opinions. Rather the news frames stories and puts a spin on those stories to make them more interesting and provocative, and to support (unintentionally) particular ideologies shared by producers and viewers. When viewers sense a discrepancy between a news program's spin and their own "take" on a story, then the ideology begins to show through, whether liberal or conservative. Focusing on the way television frames an issue is extremely useful. The question here, however, has to do with the relationship between distraction and influence.

Does television distract even from its own messages? Does it put the spectator in such a trance that nothing of substance, not even its own meanings, messages, or ideologies come through in complete form? The sociopolitical analyses common in "cultural studies" and the content analyses used in the social sciences and media studies have charted and explained how media constructs, insinuates, and distorts information. Critics and scholars have also demonstrated and explained how television distracts the public from other media, primarily print sources, by acclimating viewers to quick, simple, and easily understood images and associations. Some critics have charged that the common use of images and associations on television, even on news programming, replaces rational logic with associational logic and superficial visual thinking. Again, in these widely accepted interpretations of television's effects and affects, the contradiction between television as something that distracts completely and causes us to miss the point and television as a manipulator that depends on the spectators getting the point of the messages seems unresolved. One might argue that the associations and distractions lead to particular ideological messages. One might contend that the loss of attention spans caused by television leads the spectator to get only one message and miss the nuances. This essay does not challenge these arguments. In fact, the example discussed here encourages similar interpretations. The example analyzed pushes to the fore the problems and possibility of television as a mobile target, rather than a monolithic power. The case offers strong evidence for television encouraging both a mobile attention as well as a lack of attention. It challenges scholars to consider the significance of anomalies, mistakes, inaccuracies, distortions, practical jokes, and so on, which few comment on in the press or in scholarship. Neither the mainstream press nor the dissenters discuss these inconsistencies. Neither the *New York Times* nor critics of that newspaper, like Noam Chomsky, note these anomalies let alone comment on the significance of these mistakes. If the mistake is trivial, then it deserves to fall by the wayside. What if the mistake has great importance and occurs during a serious news event watched and discussed by every news commentator in the world? What are the implications for studying television when something important seems to have gone unnoticed? Does this example of distraction challenge in any way arguments about television's ability to manipulate public opinions, emotions, and even violent actions?

The debate about whether media distracts or leads to heightened attention and immersion finds its roots in essays written about popular culture by members and associates of the Frankfurt School. The best-known argument about the terms *distraction* and *concentration* comes from Walter Benjamin's writings on cinema. Because of his influence over a wide spectrum of critics as different as Jacques Derrida and Terry Eagleton, these critics often contest the meaning and interpretation of Benjamin's essays. The journal *New German Critique* has dedicated many pages to the nuances of his work and its significance for cultural, media, and literary studies. Instead of entering into this debate directly, I make a more modest claim here concerning the usefulness of my interpretation of Benjamin's discussions of terms like *concentration* and *distraction*. Although these terms have more complicated meanings than our quotidian notions, the use of them here does overlap with media and cultural theorists' use of these terms in discussing television.

Benjamin begins thinking about the impact of cinema on spectators by initially positing distraction and concentration as polar opposites. *Distraction* often appeared, before television, as a key term in describing the impact of the popular arts. Not only do writers refer to the distracted mass absorbing the art or performance, but commentators often refer to these arts as distractions. *Distraction* is both a synonym for attractions and a description of its effect on spectators. On the other side of the spectrum, *concentration* is a term often applied to the necessary abilities needed to appreciate avant-garde art. A commentator might discuss how the spectator enters into the avant-garde modernist experiment in an intense state of concentration. The opposition is both historical and based on common sense. Historically artists described their work to the public in terms similar to those used by newspaper critics. Those promoting a distraction would not want to confuse the potential audience into thinking they would actually experience some artwork requiring great concentration and immersion. Likewise, the high-modernist avant-garde artist would not want the public to think of the artwork as a mere distraction, a frivolous pleasure appropriate for a night out on the town. They wanted the audience to approach the work with an intensity and concentration not found in popular distractions. The writers in the Frankfurt School, especially Theodor Adorno, wrote a number of essays arguing that revolutionary thought was only born out of the intense experience found in high-modernist art. Even though the art seemed pitched toward a bourgeois audience rather than a mass popular audience, the artwork's requirement of an intense concentration negated the use of art as a mere *commodity* or dalliance. The serious purpose of art, to unlock the utopian spirit, was only found in works demanding concentration.

Before continuing with the specifics of this argument found especially in Adorno's work, it is important to place Benjamin's argument about distraction and concentration in this intellectual context. Counter to the belief in high modernism's ability to encourage utopian desires, Benjamin writes that popular cinema has this ability to release a utopian yearning in the public at large. Popular movies have the potential to collapse the apparent opposition between distraction and concentration. These movies accomplish the simultaneous distraction of the spectator's attention and, paradoxically, the demand for concentration. They pull off this stunt by constantly interrupting and overlapping the spectator's associations. Just as it presents one set of images, dialogue, and (live or recorded) sounds, the cinema replaces them with another set of images. This constant shifting puts the public in the position of the critic. *The public thrills at the effects,* and like the critics, they then notice the construction of art. Even in the movies that Benjamin must have seen while he discussed and wrote about the cinema, movies made by Charlie Chaplin, for example, the effects of editing and framing are delightfully startling and noticeable.

The important point that Benjamin adds to his argument is that this position of the public as critic requires no attention when watching a movie. He writes that "the public is an examiner, but an absent-minded one."[8] Concentration joins with distraction to make the knowledge of structure pleasurable. In his argument, Benjamin builds on Bertolt Brecht's well-known theory of the "alienation-effect." This alienation or distanciation, according to Brecht, creates the situation for the spectators to concentrate on the construction of the object. By disengaging from the art object, the spectator liberates herself or himself from the dictates of a naturalized narrative. In that state of disengagement, the viewer can look beyond the narrative to the underlying structures of the object. The spectator can then reject the assumption that the causal structure of the narrative is an inevitable or natural sequence of events. From that sort of realization it takes only a small step to begin noticing that the historical narrative sequence of events also does not have a necessarily natural or inevitable causal structure. Once the working class, according to Brecht, recognize that the present situation and its connection to a historical progression can take another route, changing their fate for ever, the step toward revolutionary change is close at hand. The disengagement also produces the same pleasure usually associated with popular distractions. The audience is distracted from the narrative by musical interludes, placards or intertitles, and other interruptions. They then concentrate on allegorical and structural questions. As is Benjamin, Brecht is concerned with changing the audience's relationship toward work. He wants the work usually associated with concentrated effort to have a joyous distracted element that will engender a sense of an interactive community versus a sense of narrative or historical inevitability.

If one reads the phrase the "work of art" from Benjamin's famous essay on "The Work of Art in the Age of Mechanical Reproduction" as indicating the effort or work involved in learning from art, then Benjamin suggests that the process of learning (i.e., of making connections across domains and noticing a structured view of history) combines with pleasure or distraction to suggest, at least symbolically, a world in which labor is joyous and work is play. In that sense, mechanical reproduction destroys the *work* of art. This thesis is usually taken to apply only to the aura of the work of art: reproducing an artwork challenges the work's meaning as a unique object with a lineage of ownership and increasing value. The original is one among many. Because that thesis has such profound and far-reaching implications for a political analysis of media, the other reading of the phrase "work of art" does not play a part in commentary on Benjamin's work, and that neglect also discounts the importance of the cinema's ability to produce a distracted concentration. In his concern about the audience's response, Benjamin shifts his argument from the workings of the film medium, and its status as art, to audience interpretations of reality. This becomes the basis for much future cultural criticism that primarily examines an audience's reactions to reality or simulations. In fact, the very notion of cultural studies grows out of this concern with audience reactions to cultural simulations rather than a preexisting formal element in a particular medium like film or television. The explosion of interest in cultural studies parallels the emergence of television as a major factor in modern culture and the corresponding questions about audiences that television's format seems to provoke.

TV as Target

Media theorists have long struggled with questions concerning spectators' attention and the significance of fleeting images. Their theories often use one of four methodologies: the social-scientific content analyses originally used to study the effectiveness of U.S. propaganda films in the 1940s and 1950s, sociopolitical psychoanalytic studies imported from film studies of the 1970s and 1980s, the sociological cultural studies arising from British Marxist literary studies of the 1970s and 1980s, and moral sociological criticism popular throughout the twentieth century. In the area of cultural theory, film studies, partly because it became an academic discipline long before "cultural studies," has provided the most influential models of research. Today television has displaced movies as the major source of popular distraction. Noël Burch, an influential film theorist, turned his analytic skills toward American television to implicitly *test the function of distraction and concentration in watching television*. Burch argues that television trivializes everything through its ability to distance us from any particular message. In that sense, it distracts completely. Burch notices that television's format has the cumulative effect of inducing "disengagement" from the messages. Whatever the audience sees, no matter if it is a news program or a commercial, does not "really count." Burch inserts these observations into the history of the theoretical debate about distraction and concentration. In line with Brecht and Benjamin, the filmmaker Jean-Luc Godard built distanciation into his films. These effects would create a critical distance for the spectators to examine the construction of the film, and, by extension, the constructedness of social and political situations. Burch comments that the powerful distancing effects "ought to make Godard green with envy."[9] Instead, television has co-opted distanciation for its own trivializing ends. Burch suggests that the viewer absentmindedly watches the interruptions and breaks in the narrative progression. Although Benjamin and Brecht believed this absentmindedness accompanied the concentration on structure and could possibly make the audience into critics or examiners, television appears to merely produce alienation without end. While some alienation may produce ironic and potentially motivating readings, the endless trumping of one image with another opposite association makes for cynical detachment rather than sophisticated engagement, according to Burch. In watching television, distinguishing the significant from the ornamental or the real event from the illusory spectacle becomes difficult or impossible.

Many cultural critics have focused on this difficulty or impossibility in choosing the actual from the simulated in the society of the spectacle, the phrase Guy Debord uses to describe what others call the media age. Some critics, following Debord, bemoan the loss of authenticity in the light of television's endless stagings. Some critics almost celebrate this simulated situation. For Burch and others, television's ability to distance viewers from any particular message, trivializing all the messages, quiets sociopolitical concerns rather than heightens them. The television has produced a distancing effect that keeps one enclosed, paradoxically, within the televisual world. Jean Baudrillard describes this distancing effect found in television as similar to "the distancing effect within a dream, which tells one that one is dreaming, but only on behalf of the censor, in order that we continue dreaming."[10] In some sense, this reading of distanciation in television has many similarities to Benjamin's theory of the movies' political potential. Just as the dream predetermines the individual's reaction, the mass audience response predetermines the individual reactions, the laughter, for example, which the mass audience will produce in each individual.[11] When the audience laughs, it carries almost everyone along as in a wave of bodily enervation. Benjamin's comments on the cinema as similar to psychoanalysis also form the basis for film theory's concern with understanding how cinema manipulates viewers, using distraction to mask an underlying concentration and immersion of viewers. He argues that in the cinema the audience no longer has the "natural" distance from reality usually associated with a classical painter's view. Instead of taking a position similar to this classical painter's, the audience takes the position of the camera. In that sense, the audience takes the position of the dream machine rather than merely of the dreamer. Just as psychoanalysis introduced participants to unconscious impulses, the cinema introduces audiences to unconscious optics or optics outside the control of any one individual. For Benjamin, taking the position of a dream machine, with all of its slow-motion, freeze-frame, or crosscutting effects, allows the audience to see reality as something unfamiliar and to see differently than from a conscious position.

The audience's participation also depends on the quantity of spectators. The television obviously increases the amount of viewers and should, therefore, function as a more intense extension of the cinema. Benjamin explains that the quantity of spectators changes the quality of the experience. In a translation of Marx into a cultural rather than economic realm, he argues that quantity transmutes into quality. Increasing the quantity of spectators changes the mode of participation. In television, with the addition of many possible programs, which can be mixed with the "simple movement of the hand, hardly more than a sign," and videotape recorders, which intervene with "interruptions and isolations...extensions and accelerations,"[12] television increases the most important effect of film identified by Benjamin: "At any moment the reader is ready to turn into a writer...even if only in some minor respect."[13] Applying these fragments from Benjamin's work on cinema to television offers a counterargument to Burch's pessimistic portrayal of television. The television does distract endlessly, but the mechanism increases the amount of audience members and increases the possibilities of reception. The increase of viewers changes the quality of the television programming from a mere distraction to something that can potentially combine the distraction from any single message or narrative with the often corrosive and ironic concentration involved in making and mixing unintended messages. While Benjamin and Brecht saw the revolutionary potential as a product of production techniques and a shared common audience response, a use of their terms *concentration* and *distraction* for understanding television will inevitably stress the importance of their work on audience reactions rather than their interest in production techniques. Once one recognizes audience reaction as integral to television, the audience's use of VCRs and remote controls as home mixing machines blurs the apparent opposition between production and consumption. The mass audience creates the possibility for unauthorized readings. Overlapping and constantly interrupted associations have the potential to interrupt the spectator's interpretation. Whereas interruptions break the play's or movie's narrative progression, the interruptions in television now intervene in the spectator's mobile interpretations. On the one hand, a nondeliberate parody clings to everything. On the other hand, the interruptions constantly force the spectators to shift their unmasking rituals.

For better or worse, the television watcher becomes a critic. This viewer as critic does not resemble a traditional art critic. In the article "The Work of Art in the Age of Mechanical Reproduction" (1936), Benjamin defined "aura" as the unique existence of art objects in a fabric of the tradition of aesthetics.[14] The art critic focuses on a work's aura, while the television viewer-as-critic for the most part discounts any aura and views television as a transient message. John Berger, in *Ways of Seeing*, explains how the aura of art distances spectators from images. In his discussion he uses the vocabulary of a hypothetical art critic in order to mock the aura:

> Terms like "harmonious fusion," "unforgettable contrast," reaching "a peak of breadth and strength" transfer the emotion provoked by the image from the plane of lived experience, to that of disinterested "art appreciation."[15]

This art critic's distanciation makes the object a sacred testament of the eternal values of civilization: Beauty, Truth, Genius, Good Taste, and so on. Spectators appreciate art for its (cult)ural value until mechanical reproduction creates the conditions for spectators to notice the importance of distribution in forming an art object's value. The object's ability to conjure a cultural heritage rests on its uniqueness or its authenticity. Under this schema, the artist creator is like Christ: both had to touch the object for it to have special powers. Mechanical reproduction wrests the work of art from this semireligious realm of ritual by disrupting the concept of authenticity. To ask for the original of a television program makes no sense. For the broadcast and taping, it has no original.

In "The Work of Art" article, Benjamin celebrates the disintegration of this art historical aura. Later, after Theodor Adorno's criticisms of his argument, Benjamin reformulates his position. Adorno objects to Benjamin's assumption that the loss of the ritual use-value of art creates the condition for both political action and critical thought. He suggests that only class struggle will force a transition out of capitalism. Even if films could create a forum for politics or engender class consciousness, their present domination by capitalists prevents any progressive use. Film audiences passively receive the sounds and images that manipulate them into conforming to the dominant social order. These spectators consume the commodity of "cinema," but rather than noticing any liquidation of the traditional value of cultural heritage, spectators let their desires function as grist for the socialization mill.[16] The homogeneity of the film industry assures a homogeneous product: consumers without community.

In response to Adorno, Benjamin admits that the aura does contain the locus of community. Without a shared structure of meanings in a collective memory, neither communication nor community can exist. He agrees with Adorno that capitalism and mechanical reproduction destroy the communal and ritual basis of collective memory. Benjamin argues that certain works combine both the experience of the loss of aura (i.e., the present as ruin or crisis and art as an exchangeable commodity) and, by an artwork's incompleteness, a space or gap for the spectator to find another aura of unauthorized connections. This disturbing aura allows the audience to have memories of the future. This other aura fractures the economy of identification (i.e., disrupts our appreciation of a work's beauty, unity, creative use of conventions, etc.) and creates a screen for the projection of other possibilities. Television never claims to have an aura in the art historical tradition. Its very lack of originality and flaunting of triviality causes dismay in critics like Burch. Television never presumes to have a place in a transcendent pedigree. Instead, its aura has everything to do with immediacy, reality, spontaneity. Its aura puts each image in a shroud of actuality.

News as Target

Bill Nichols has described how even television news programs structure their portrayal of reality.[17] Even most amateur scholars of television would assume that the news packages real events. In fact, the news programs now routinely discuss how journalists and broadcasters put a specific spin on the news. Liberal and conservative commentators regularly complain that the messages of the "media" have an unfriendly slant. Nichols's work goes beyond these complaints to examine the specific rhetoric employed by the news broadcasters. Television news, using an "artistic" exposition, relies on the speaker's (the anchor's) effect on the audience. The supposed referent for the news is no longer a pro-filmic event (i.e., the event before it appears on the news) but, rather, an anchorperson. The anchor uses credibility, emotional appeals, and demonstrations of real or apparent truth to influence the audience. She or he relies on shared assumptions to demonstrate not merely reality but also truth. The specific rhetoric dresses the common assumptions in the garb of natural reality. In this sense, the "message" of the news has less to do with any literal meaning than with the "attitude" elicited (*Image,* 178). The news programs differ from Hollywood realism, for example, which uses an expository rhetoric. That traditional expository cinema invokes and promises to gratify the "desire to know." It often uses an inartistic exposition, making the sign and referent appear to merge into a realism. The invisible style of the cinema explicitly excludes any transcendent anchor. The film may contain a voice-over, but this is usually the voice of one of the characters in the story.

The news would look strange if the victim of a flood or a terrorist caught planning a bombing narrated the news with a voice-over. The rhetorical organization of the news, like the Hollywood film, effaces its construction through specific strategies of organizing the visual and sound track. The traditional ethnographic film effaces its construction through natural reality; it presents events unfolding. While narrative films and the news repress the context of production, the ethnographic film hides its production of meaning. That is, the news and the movies both leave the viewer with a strong explicit sense of what the images mean. The ethnographic film leaves the viewer with the impression that there is no particular meaning. The film still has a meaning; it pretends not to have any particular meaning or position except to claim that "this situation is the way that it is." Written ethnographies often use science to avoid admitting they are producing meaning; again it looks as if they are merely discovering the facts. Nichols advocates that ethnographers switch to a poetic model when they make films (*Image,* 252). The difficulty will be to examine the uniquely historical event (or text) and not hide the fact of the film's function as a re-presentation. The new model he advocates creates a "balance" between association and explanation, historical specificity and cultural generality, referentiality and reflexive structures that indicated the film-as-constructed. The meaning of the film will arise, then, from the interplay between the two sides of the opposition: representation and structure. This struggle between representation of an event and showing how a film is constructed resembles Barthes's conception of an artificial mythology. In both models, the spectator can choose to understand the film neither as direct access to reality nor as a solipsistic retreat into a formalist experiment, for example. Although Nichols does not suggest an alternative to the news programming he examines, his comments on ethnographic film offer a way to identify aspects of an artificial mythology for news broadcasts.

Nichols discusses the use of voice-over in John Huston's *The Battle of San Pietro* (1944) as an example of an alternative to traditional documentary (*Image*, 185–95). Because Huston plays with the anchor position, the film's play between voice-over and visual images suggests how to conceive of the news as something besides an anchoring of images. In the film, Huston shoots the visuals of the battle to give the feeling of being there on the ground. Just as the foot soldiers run around in fear and confusion during the middle of the battle, the filmed version of the actual battle makes little visual sense: we see men advancing through the woods, and we do not know where they are in relation to the enemy or to their fellow soldiers. We see a man throw a hand-grenade and then a reverse shot shows an explosion, but we cannot tell where these events take place in relation to the battle. We do not know if the soldiers are making progress or losing ground. Nichols points out that the syntagmatic construction of this film depends on the verbal and visual tracks (not just Christian Metz's "grande syntagmatique," which charted every possible combination of the visual track alone).[18] The play between the voice-over and the visual makes this film particularly interesting for our purposes. To fill in the lack from the visuals, the voice-over usually serves to anchor and place the images for us. Here the voice-over enters and describes in relatively upbeat terms the point of the battle, while the visuals create an increasing confusion. The images show soldiers dying and confusing maps, while the voice-over almost cheerfully ignores these images. In Huston's film, the indexical markers of reality (i.e., men dying) become symbols for pointless sacrifice and unjust suffering: the voice-over does battle with the visuals.

Usually, if neither action visuals nor voice-over can position, explain, or anchor the film, then charts and maps are used to orient the viewers. The maps used in the film just complicate matters, making the dying men appear as pawns in a futile game played by strategists. *The Battle of San Pietro* names a literal and structural allegory. The title of the film refers to a village in Italy named after Saint Peter. In the book of Peter in the Bible, he talks of the spiritual significance of suffering. He argues that the fires of persecution purify the victim. Even a supposedly subversive reading (i.e., the soldiers suffer unjustly) is explicitly addressed by Saint Peter when he discusses the victory of unjust suffering. The Pentagon delayed the release of the film until World War II was almost over. The confusing maps, which hint at the pointlessness of the battle, and the voice-over that fails to anchor the images contribute to making this a powerful indictment of the sense-lessness of war.

The particular use of the voice-over suggests how a news broad-cast might also show signs of fissure. The points in a news broadcast where the visuals contradict the anchor already open on to an artifi-cial mythology where the anchor's power begins slipping away. The signs of wear in television's aura happen when the distractions over-whelm the concentration on the event as actual and the meaning as anchored. Burch notices how television's distractions look much like the early cinema. Television returns us to a particular cinematic ex-perience, the nickelodeon:

> It is strange to see the many ways in which United States network television constitutes a return to the days of the nickelodeon: a continuous showing cut up into brief segments of from one to ten minutes, with an audience that drifts in and out, the incredible mixture of genres, the confusions between reality and fiction . . . program format . . . a series of six to ten minute shorts with songs or lantern slides between each. (Burch, 31)

Burch condemns the "nickelodeon" effect in his dismissal of televi-sion as distraction. Counter to Burch's dismissal, one might instead read the effect as suggesting a tension or contradiction in the myth of television's reality. In this interpretation, the effect suggests an open-ing for an artificial mythology.

Map from Cinema to Television Studies: Aberrant Attention

Introductions to film studies use, in some form, two descriptive theo-ries. Formalism explains how films are put together and how the construction of a film creates meaning. Semiotic analysis looks at how films create meaning through a system of reference to cultural codes (rather than strictly formal codes). These theories have an enor-mous influence in film studies because they allow students both to learn conventions of reading and to gain a critical distance from the media texts they read. The discounting of the formalist New Criticism's approach to literature has not caused film studies to abandon these dominant reading strategies. It has clung to those strategies because media studies has added a historical and political dimension to the type of formal analysis typical in New Criticism. The debate about the privileged or competent reader was effaced in media studies by the political imperative to combat the cinematic apparatus's hegemonic control over spectators. To understand how a film exerted control over viewers, film theory used formalism, psychoanalysis, and semiotics. After carefully reexamining the theories that film studies imported, theorists from Mary Ann Doane to Colin Mac-Cabe realized that the cinema's control was neither certain nor complete. Indeed, much of the psychoanalytic film theory since the mid-1980s has criticized the mistaken notion that films can control or even create subjects.

Although many critics have described how studies of the "cinematic apparatus" never adequately accounted for aberrant readings, psychoanalytic concepts do have distinct and peculiar power in explaining how one thing (e.g., a supposedly transcendent view) displaces another (e.g., a social context, the labor of construction, the camera, etc.).[19] This particular brand of contemporary film theory uses psychoanalysis and Marxism to help explain both the seduction of images and the elusiveness of the underlying causes or "apparatus." Theorists wanted to know how Hollywood films hid the sociopolitical context of production. Specifically, they wanted to understand how the filmmaker's (and by extension the culture's) view of the world became confused with, or displaced by, the spectator's view; that is, they asked, how does "their view" (the culture's view) become "your view" without provoking any protests? In this mode of research, the film's world *appears* to open up in front of you as if seen through a window. The cinema, in that sense, represents a perfect example of how a culture naturalizes ideology: it makes social constructions into natural facts. In this scenario, the movies say, "the world just is." In a related way, psychoanalysis explains that a sense of self displaces the recognition of the social construction of identity: one's perceptions seem natural rather than constructed. When one identifies one's view with the self, the self or ego constantly masks the cultural construction and framing of that view. The discontinuities that remind us of our tenuous situation (e.g., neurotic symptoms, slips of the tongue, forgetting, images in a dream, and other psychopathologies of everyday life) represent the anxiety-provoking eruption of the social context (either "the family drama" or the voice of the "Other"). Taken out of the context of cinema studies' fascination with a relatively monolithic apparatus controlling and directing attention, the theory becomes useful for a study of attention in terms of hiding, displacing, and identification. Do these psychoanalytic theories have any relevance for studying television's ability to encourage a lack of attention? In spite of its productive influence over the past twenty years, "apparatus theory" has fallen into disfavor especially among those scholars interested in television. They complain that film theories do not account for the mobile attention common when watching television. And they argue that television needs a set of methodologies specific to its social, technical, and current aesthetic configuration.

In answer to these complaints against merely importing film theories to explain television, a number of alternative research strategies have specifically attempted to appropriately account for the infinite diversity of television's audiences. For example, the deconstructive analyses of John Fiske, which became popular in the middle and late 1980s, suggested many alternative readings of programming that seemed to have singular and obvious messages. These studies focus on audiences that do not pay attention to the dominant or intended readings of television programs, and valorize aberrant ways that individuals and groups use popular culture. Instead of describing how monolithic media fool or manipulate the masses, this increasingly common research practice uncovers subversive *readings* of popular culture by various dispossessed, oppressed, or marginalized groups. This research, associated with British cultural studies, uses ethnographic-style practices to discover that everyone gets a different message from television programs. These studies illustrate that instead of blindly following along with Big Brother, small groups and individuals have become more heterogeneous in their interpretations; in this sense, a spectator might interpret, or be influenced by, both the oppressive and politically progressive content of a single program or event.[20]

One of the major problems facing television studies concerns its relationship to culture and cultural change. While many commentators bemoan the problems created by television and the inadequacies of TV news programs as a singular news source, the emergent academic discourse of media studies has provided mostly descriptive readings rather than speculative suggestions or experimental models for alternatives. The growth of public-access television and electronic multimedia sources has led to an explosion of potential alternatives. Academic research has only slowly awakened to these changes. Hamid Naficy's work on public-access television argues that large subcultures interact with very specific public-access programming.[21] Narrow casts now have more impact on particular groups than more traditional broadcasts. Still, even Naficy's work does not go beyond a descriptive project to suggest models and demonstrations.

Building an artificial mythology takes neither a naive nor a cynical, nihilistic view of understanding television news. Instead this type of analysis changes the scholar's and viewer's focus. The particular conceptions of television, television's news, and television's relationship to sociopolitical power can sometimes stymie innovation. How television studies, media experts, and "viewers like you" (to borrow PBS's slogan) conceptualize the function, workings, problems, and issues surrounding watching television inevitably will close down other conceptualizations. Sometimes the *apparently* absurd solution will open paths to unthought-of possibilities and potentialities. Just as Barthes focuses on details that do not fit into wider conceptions, this project examines a detail that few noticed. What are the implications of this significant detail? Television scholars can use their knowledge differently, as a provocation rather than merely as a description. Timing has a major role in understanding this alternative to traditional media studies. It takes the given, the obvious, and begins to find the weaknesses and inaccuracies in the map — both literally and figuratively.

Unfortunately, this "cultural" research basis for explaining the way "people" read messages has led to a predictable formulaic approach to analysis. Judith Williamson criticizes this approach as "left-wing academics . . . picking out strands of 'subversion' in every piece of pop culture from Street Style to Soap Opera."[22] Or, put more strongly by Meaghan Morris, the critics now *produce* the banality they used to find in television and cinema. Morris's article "The Banality of Cultural Studies" offers an elegant and persuasive criticism of these current theoretical practices. After reading through current journals, like *Cultural Practice,* and the latest books on pop culture, she imagines "that somewhere in some English publisher's vault there is a master disk from which thousands of versions of the same article about pleasure, resistance, and the politics of consumption are being run off under different names with minor variations."²³ This hilarious fantasy, an ironic cross between the Reagan administration's image of "televisions-as-toasters-with-pictures" and Bouvard and Pécuchet in the electronic age, goes far beyond a mere criticism of banality. It suggests a strategy for intervening in the discourses surrounding the production of knowledge. One might call this use of a kind of desperate or ironic humor to talk about the production of knowledge a theory joke. Indeed, an *interventionist* graffiti or fleeting joke on, and of, the often bleak moment, event, or situation is precisely what Morris goes on to discuss later in the same article.

Artificial Attention

The "flash of hilarity" in the situationist tactics displaces, among other things, the quiz-show logic of factual citations commonly found in criticisms of contemporary culture. It is never sufficient criticism to merely state the facts. Nevertheless, it does not take much vulgar reduction to recognize the listing-of-facts method in important variants of cultural studies. Some scholars muster the facts together to prove how the media "manufacture consent," how big business owns the media, or how the mainstream media actually fail to report the facts.²⁴ Other scholars use statistical evidence from psychological experiments to make statements about reception. And another trend in scholarship about contemporary culture is the list method; one article listed each and every company who supplied arms to Saddam Hussein.²⁵ All of these studies are enormously useful and viable; they do tend, however, to lead to an antitheoretical and anti-intellectual bias that may foster a quiz-show mentality among readers regardless of the authors' intentions. William Boddy explains that in quiz shows in the 1950s, "knowledge represented the accumulation of discrete facts, atomized and offered unproblematically within *a priori* categories and levels of difficulties, presided over by the authority of college professors, bank presidents, and armed guards; the model of knowledge precluded reflection, explanation, or the activity of thought."²⁶ As a benign form of fact collection, this quiz-show logic insists on an anti-intellectual and antitheoretical basis for thought. In one 1957 article on the popularity of the (later infamous) quiz-show contestant Van Doren (who, it was later revealed, was fed the answers or told to guess incorrectly), the connection between fact accumulation and the anti-intellectual bias is made clear:

With all respect for Mr. Van Doren, who is a highly intelligent and cultivated man, his performances have nothing to do with learning or with thought. Americans have always venerated the fact, and the quiz show has merely underlined this aspect of our culture.[27]

The mere accumulation of factual evidence not only seems to legislate against theoretical reflection but also has had little effect in swaying public opinion. The public knows that "we" killed somewhere between one hundred and two hundred thousand people so far in Iraq; yet, precisely because of the connotations surrounding those facts (rather than the facts themselves), many people feel "proud" that America has *helped* the people of Iraq.

Todd Gitlin, in his discussion of the reasons for the excessive violence in the media, *inadvertently* suggests why the mere showing of the fact of killing or the facts about the fallacious reasons motivating a war may not actually dampen public opinion. In his discussion of the increasing violence in movies and in pop culture in general, Gitlin argues that the producers of this excessive violence usually depict absurd caricatures of macho men killing like machines.[28] The production of this "schlock by mostly male writers occurs out of a need to deny dependency and femininity in themselves" (246). These writers "deny their own castration" with knives and chain saws (247). Movies become "machines for the sadomasochistic imagination" (248). If we take the small step in applying these claims to political strategies, we can quite easily see problems in most rational fact-accumulation criticisms of the war machine. While the Left insists on criticizing the unfairly cruel exploits of the war machine, the ultra-Right and many others lap up what they (secretly) want to express themselves: this is senseless unnecessary killing, but we want to hurt and even risk being hurt ourselves. Significantly, Gitlin adds that many spectators "shrug off" the violence "or camp it up, recognizing that movie violence is a sort of exclamation point" (248). One might argue that his interpretation of how spectators interpret films makes him sound like the banal broken-record version of cultural studies that Morris criticizes. The language Gitlin uses to argue that (cynical) subversive readings do occur suggests a tactical approach rather than a merely descriptive approach. Violence becomes a kind of "punctuation." Gitlin does not stress that the camp reading changes the punctuation of the film; the reading does not actually add anything to the film, but it punctuates the violence so that it becomes parodic or, at least, comic book-like.

It functions by insinuation. Interventionist tactics do not state the facts; they displace them with insinuations for a *fleeting flash of hilarity*. In discussing a similar tactic, Homi Bhabha proposes a "melancholia in revolt."²⁹ In that proposition, he makes the connection between tactics and a psychoanalytic politics. In explaining his tactical suggestions, Bhabha uses Frantz Fanon's argument about the colonized peoples' efforts to create a symbolic space and Derrida's notion of the encrypted piece of discourse that cannot be incorporated or mourned fully. Melancholia is a reaction to "the loss of a loved person, or to the loss of some abstraction ... such as one's country, liberty, an ideal and so on" (101). With this definition in mind, Bhabha explains:

> What is particularly important for understanding historical and cultural "loss" in this context is the inversion of meaning that constitutes melancholic address and its identification with its object. The melancholic discourse, Freud says, is a plaint in the old fashioned sense. Its insistent self-exposure and the repetition of loss must not be taken at face value for its apparent victimage and passivity. Its narrative metonymy, the repetition of the piecemeal, the bit by bit, its insistent self-exposure, comes also from a *mental constellation of revolt*. (102)

There is in the melancholic's flaunting of the wounds of loss a revolt like the flash of hilarity found in situationist tactics. More importantly, the importance of psychoanalysis now shifts from a diviner of pathologies toward an arts of timing. Using psychoanalysis in this pragmatic fashion rather than as a tool for some transcendent knowledge about contemporary culture makes a descriptive theory into a pragmatics of tactical intervention.

With assumptions about how spectators are fooled by the news or, conversely, how they read messages in contradictory ways, surprisingly few scholars have studied the power of a *lack of attention*. What if the news could not overcome that impasse or obstacle? This impotent news media, neither evil nor giving us "just the facts," neither manipulating us blindly nor doing the best they can under the circumstances, would have an entirely different valence in cultural studies if it actually *inhibited attention*. Our collective desire (Left and Right) demands a powerful, potent news media and a government that is actually *in power*. It would be difficult to imagine an oppositional politics confronted with a government and a news media not completely in power. It would be difficult to admit that the symptomatic displacement that appeared on that "most memorable" night—the embassy displacement—went unnoticed or unnoted. No mention of the mistake was made in either the mainstream or alternative press or in any scholarly discussion or any talk show or call-in radio, and so on. Only much later would we learn that (as rumors had predicted) our embassy in Baghdad had shifted its position, giving Iraq mixed signals about invading Kuwait. The embassy had moved on the political map, and ABC had *unintentionally* noted this vacillation in their two contradictory maps. Simply stressing this coincidence has implications for how scholars interpret other events and images on TV. The activity of coding, stressing, and noting what might otherwise fall out of history is already the most important activity media scholars perform.

It would be difficult to admit that try as we may, neither "they" nor "we" know where we stand, where we are on the map, in the big picture; there is instead an extreme powerlessness. And, the anxiety over this powerlessness—shared by news media and spectators alike—explains why the symptom appeared as a displacement and, then, disappeared from memory. As Freud comments "all symptom formations [are] brought about solely in order to avoid anxiety."[30] In regard to repression, Freud explains that "danger situations to which the ego is sensitive cause the latter to give the anxiety signal for inhibition."[31] What provokes so much anxiety to cause us not to notice or to inhibit noticing? What if this displacement did not fit (a *lack* of fit) into the prevailing political discourse? Even the most radical revolutionary wants to know that the evil daddy patriarchy of advanced capitalism is still manning the fort; even the most dyed-in-the-wool, red-blooded, gung ho American male wants to believe that leaders (even if they are Oliver North and Manuel Noriega) have power and potency. In this logic, the United States is super-power-full. In the Gulf War, "we" supposedly won because of a particular kind of power. Everything supposedly depended on knowing precisely where to drop the bombs; that is, *everything depended on having accurate maps,* which were then keyed into "smart" bombs. The smartness of the bombs resides not in their ability to kill or destroy but in following an electronic map in order to hit the target accurately. What if the maps are inaccurate? Yet, no one *said* anything about ABC's inaccurate map. Confronting our dumbness changes everything.

The problem for cultural studies, as Shoshana Felman explains in terms of literary studies, is, "How can I interpret *out of* the dynamic ignorance I analytically encounter, both in others and in myself? How can I turn ignorance into an instrument of teaching?"[32] *Is there a way of writing or theorizing that accounts for the play between anxiety and ignorance?* If, as one theorist notes, "the first goal of the critical model of power-as-hegemony is the project of demystification by theoretical activity,"[33] then what if a lack of knowledge, a misfit in the political discourse, appears somewhere between mystification and knowledge? It is not a matter of seeing more clearly, of getting a more accurate map. What I am proposing is to let the event disrupt the way we go about doing research. This pragmatic theory of displacement attempts to understand psychoanalysis in the context of Situationism. The method offers a tactics of surprise. This combination is especially useful for cultural studies of attention because it focuses on the relationship between intervention and the unnoticed displaced detail. The unnoticed movement of the American embassy is a perfect example of where this intervention occurs; one does not create anything new, one merely *punctuates the situation.* As a form of punctuation, Jacques Lacan's "short sessions" made questions of time and timing crucial for the analytic experience. And those interventions came during sessions where the analyst added very little to the conversation. Lacan merely punctuated the discourse. What Lacan called "Logical Time" does not correspond to chronological time; it is time in a series of effects (one's sense of self played out as an effect) inscribed as meaning. In this sense, psychoanalysis functions as theory of a surprise that has an effect — it insinuates. It uses an art of timing to intervene in the series of effects; it breaks the chain with a surprise. What "constitutes these suspended motions as signifying is . . . their interruption . . . the subject's doubt — revealing itself. . . ."[34]

By changing the punctuation of a situation, one also changes how it functions as an effect. The effect no longer looks or sounds the same (the second time it is played). Even the cause of the situation changes. While the classical notion of cause in psychoanalytic theory depends on the notion of a hidden deep structure, recent work in Lacanian psychoanalysis has offered a very different definition of cause. Jacques-Alain Miller explains that cause "involves a breaking up of the chain" of discourse and meaning, not as a determining law. Instead of a deep structural motivation, cause "always implies the notion of a missing link...discontinuity." The cause interrupts the regularity and functions by surprise![35] And Miller explains that the analytic situation makes use of the surprise as a part of an interventionist interpretation. Cause breaks the chain of discourse in a way similar to the "flash of hilarity" discussed by Morris and the "melancholic revolt" discussed by Bhabha. The "most recurrent interpretations are not so effective as what comes from surprise."[36] This surprising punctuation sets up a situation of transference, not a transference of the "family drama" as in classical notions of psychoanalysis, but a transference of one's relation to lack. It puts the spectator in a situation similar to mourning—an opening of the wounds. Barthes has eloquently summarized the punctuation point and mourning in his discussion of the punctum. The punctum, in the context of mourning and transference, refers to the detail that does not fit in with the ego's knowledge (i.e., the studium). The unassimilable piece broken off from one's sense of the how the world fits together (i.e., all the social, political, aesthetic, or other learned discourses) returns to haunt the spectator. It bruises, wounds, and bothers, and just as one attempts to identify it, to explain it (away), to assimilate it into a world picture, it disappears.[37] This detail lacks a function and creates uncertainty, doubt, anxiety, and unsettling. The attempt to assimilate the unassimilable leads to the paradoxical moment in mourning when loss cannot be adequately incorporated by the ego. If we understand that a certain punctuation may actually represent loss, then we have begun to find a way to rethink cultural and media studies away from analytic descriptions of media; instead, cultural action becomes a method of research. It is this use of Barthes's later works, his suggestions about a tactics of surprise in media studies, that the chapters of this book take up in various ways. The political formations make use of "paradoxical mourning's" signs (or what Bhabha refers to as "melancholic revolt"); that is, they makes use of anxiety over loss and the resulting destabilization of reception. In cultural action, the unassimilable impasse around loss creates mourning. In this punctuation of mistakes a politics of mourning appears as a fleeting intervention.

The problem for such a politics is still one of power and powerlessness; in this case, it is about a sort of flaunting of a lack of knowledge and power. The position of not knowing, of passivity, does not fit into the prevailing discourses of the Left or Right or even of the entire discourse of rights. For, as Leo Bersani writes, patriarchy is "not primarily the denial of power to women, but above all the denial of powerlessness in both men and women."[38] The tactical intervention into situations I have described in this chapter corresponds, in terms of patriarchy, to the "long nose" taunt. This ancient German gesture of putting your thumb to the tip of your nose and stretching out your hand (as in "nah-nah, you can't get me") was the sign for an erect penis and the *social impotence in spite of it*. This logic of the phallic inversion appears when the demonstration of power starts to function as a confirmation of a fundamental impotence.[39] Try as we may, something gets in the way of knowing. And to admit that the news, and criticisms of the news, gets in the way, displaces the world, and marks our ignorance forces us to face the lack in the phallic signifier, a lack in the Other; and this recognition is too difficult to face. It would be easier to face a powerful enemy than this mark of discontinuity. We cannot bear to look at the television. And when it shows itself in/as a displacement in the smooth flow of discourse, we turn away; the surprises discussed (e.g., melancholic revolt, flash of hilarity, or analytic surprise) here can replicate (with a twist) the lack of power we usually ignore. Of course, tactics will always depend on waiting for the right moment—the moment the archer knows the arrow will have enough momentum to penetrate:

> The play of the punctum as described by Barthes, once reactivated as a form of writing, folds reference in upon itself to place reality in a kind of chiastic symmetry with death . . . this disturbance is anticipated by Barthes in his original definition of the punctum, where he supplies a further sense for the Latin word that we have not yet mentioned: a cast of the dice.[40]

The strategic punctuation, different from a description, helps to define the situation in terms of mourning and melancholia instead of as either "just a mistake" or as "indicative of the system's pernicious lies." The Gulf War is already ancient history in the television's mobile memories. What spectacle is next? What embarrassment will go unreported to the melancholic delight of those watching history unfold supposedly without much participation?

3 | Multiculturalism and Identity Politics in Photography and Film

> There is a block of becoming that snaps up the wasp and the orchid, but from which no wasp-orchid can ever descend.
> GILLES DELEUZE and FÉLIX GUATTARI, *A Thousand Plateaus*

In this chapter I respond to recent efforts to include multiculturalism in media studies. I examine photographs included in Barthes's later experimental works and interrogate these photographs in terms of multiculturalism. Barthes's interest in the interactions among different cultures often depends on his use of artificial mythologies that challenge our conceptions of otherness, and especially Orientalism. His implicit multiculturalism confronts the problems involved in reducing the particular to the universal, the individual to the stereotype, and the singular to the norm. It includes a resistance to the "arrogance of discourse" to systematize the world. In the concrete examples discussed in this chapter, the multicultural photographs provoke a laugh both at the expense of our own desires to make everyone the same and simultaneously at the superimposition of one way of looking on another incommensurable way. Cultural and media analyses have often used Barthes's earlier essays on photographs for a method of analysis. In the later works, he explicitly and repeatedly claims to use the photographs as something more than illustrations. The method grows inductively from the specifics of each photograph. He uses them as a situation rather than as examples to think about larger cultural and media issues. In analyzing one particular set of photographs used in *Empire of Signs,* I speculate on the larger methodological implications and cultural significance of the peculiar use of these photographs.

After this analysis, I go on to examine creolization as a methodology. I examine the "primitive cinema" as the invention of a history-making machine, not merely a history-recording device. A major myth in contemporary culture, that media report history instead of manufacturing it, has come under repeated and sustained attacks from scholars of film and culture. They have repeatedly demythologized the Hollywood realism of movies, the accuracy of news programs, and the objectivity of documentaries. Instead of challenging what Barthes called the "reality effect" found in fiction and strengthened in cinema and television,[1] this chapter works through the myth of the invention of the cinema in order to interrupt its naturalness, not its seductiveness. The artificial mythology highlights aspects of the myth of cinema's power that usually have only aesthetic relevance: the sensation of physical movement, the ability to combine images, and so on. The experiences of the early and proto-cinema have broader implications for historiography and the methods of cultural historians. The most important implications of conceptualizing the primitive cinema differently include demonstrating historical research as a form of brainstorming. That is, instead of understanding the cinema as a monolithic mythmaking machine, this chapter explores the possibility that the cinema functions as an artificial mythmaking machine that produces creole cultures instead of producing a singular ideology.

Multiculturalism has grabbed the attention of the press and the public as well as educators interested in curriculum reform. It has angered critics fearful that adding new dimensions to education will dissipate the foundational skills and universal truths necessary for cohesion in an ever more fragmented society. In addition to curriculum reform, multiculturalism has led to changes in book publishing, art, theater, dance, performance, philosophy, and fashion. By emphasizing its hyphenated structure, it has influenced many ethnic groups with unique heritages, and that hybrid structure has rekindled old animosities against any hyphenates in a supposedly inclusive American culture. In spite of the claims that multiculturalism does not merely indicate the inclusion of more ethnic groups in cultural productions, nor more studies of other cultures, it often names the practice of teaching tolerance for other people and other customs. In that limited understanding, multiculturalism represents a convoluted way to reify both *other* people's cultures and *our* own.

Artificial Mythology and Multiculturalism

The very mention of the term multiculturalism sets off intense debates among politicians, educators, and cultural historians. It has become one of the key issues in the emergent discipline of cultural studies even as the multi- threatens to supersede the cultural. Anger and resentment from reactionary critics have fueled the enthusiasm of those advocating expanding the curriculum and the boundaries of a shared culture. Multiculturalism represents one of the most pressing concerns in both scholarly and political forums. All the attention to the term has persuaded the public and educators that the problem of either too much inclusiveness or not enough is both real and severe. While this issue provokes curriculum reform and angry insistence on returning to the "basics" or the "classics," a multicultural scholarship usually simply means studying non-European cultures or ethnic groups. Those within the emerging field of multicultural studies have argued that the field not limit itself to merely studying more cultures, as in Orientalist studies of the past. Academic research calls for new methodologies even as it continues to merely describe, for example, an ethnic group's art or films. Multiculturalism must engage in novel methodologies as well as new topics. That is, the methods should reflect the change in focus. This chapter suggests a multicultural *practice* rather than a description of some supposedly alternative or marginalized cultural practice. The multicultural appears in popular hip-hop music as well as in electronic browsers, and this chapter examines a specifically multicultural photographic process and its implications for a multicultural identity.

Although this chapter does not directly address the questions posed by Queer theory, some similar confrontations have begun to appear in that discourse. That emergent area of cultural studies requires fuller treatment elsewhere; the theorists need time to distinguish it from gay identity politics, as Judith Butler has done in her work. D. A. Miller has argued that appreciating Barthes as a gay writer would add a dimension always overlooked in studies of Barthes's works.[2] It seems that would reduce Barthes to a mere instance of an identity that shapes the work in predictable ways. A more interesting approach would place

Barthes with Butler in using queerness as a way to destabilize identity and the relationships between a biographical study and the oeuvre of an author. That work will have to wait for another essay or series of essays on Barthes's Queer theory as a guide to polymorphous identities and reading strategies.

Although theorists have discussed racial and ethnic identity, few have suggested the possibility of a multicultural identity. The problem of getting from a sense of a traditional Occidental notion of identity, which many critics have demythologized, to an alternative occurs because scholars do not have the adequate tools to move beyond exposing myths. Multiculturalism promises to move beyond the criticisms to a positive agenda. Posing alternative paradigms for understanding the odd and novel predicament of hybridized cultures, Barthes's later works went beyond describing how cultural myths worked to describe and demonstrate how an artificial mythology can open the door to a multicultural identity. Barthes used the popular form of a tourist guide as a pretext to examine the cognitive maps or paradigms for understanding used by cultural critics. He was specifically interested in examining a multicultural identity. The particular artificial mythology he produced, a pastiche and parody of tourist guides, travelogues, and scrapbooks, challenged critics to reexamine their biases and preconceptions about multicultural issues.

Focusing on the double exposures and disruptions that do not fit neatly in other models of identity, this project uses Barthes's discussion of trick effects to suggest an artificial myth. The photographs used here become a platform, in this essay, for inventing alternative solutions to the multicultural dilemma. This type of multicultural analysis does not exclude everything one learns in school about other cultures. Instead his later projects, like this chapter, demonstrate an interaction between analytic knowledge and pragmatic practice, between descriptions of other people and a multicultural method of understanding and of identity. Starting with a naive view of otherness, this artificial mythology finds the novel approach to looking multicultural—both literally and figuratively.

The challenge of a Barthesian study of culture is not to ignore the later work whenever one engages cultural politics and to merely understand the late Barthes in terms of the absolutely confessional and personal nature of autobiographically inspired meditations. Yet, the politics of a work like *Empire of Signs* seem at first too "Orientalist" to work as a model of multiculturalism. It is a book that seems to reify the Japanese as an exotic people in a strange and foreign land. Yet, in describing his visit to Japan, Barthes repeatedly recognizes his own inability to navigate through the foreign meaning system. He finds himself at a loss to capture semiotic meaning. In a previous article on space and cognitive mapping, I began by describing Barthes's situation upon arriving in Japan and his record of his journey in *Empire of Signs*. His inability to navigate through the meaning system offers a clue to the possibility of a methodology. Lost in a tangle of streets without names, unfamiliar with language, customs, and rituals, and guided only by a map that resembles an illegible palimpsest, a middle-aged Frenchman wanders around a crowded Asian city. He finds only the Japanesy instead of Japan. If we were to add a robbery to this scene, then we might expect Karl Malden to appear from an alley, telling us not to forget our American Express traveler's checks. That infamous commercial plays on our greatest fears about otherness. Indeed, as the commercial teaches us, unless we can hope to reduce chaotic foreignness to a series of commodities, unless we can, that is, incorporate the threat of difference, we probably should not leave home at all. As this description suggests, Barthes's attitude toward the task at hand, a book on Japan, is far more ironic and self-deprecating than reading the book merely as an Orientalist tract might suggest. In fact, his travails and tribulations detour consumerist tourism as well as Orientalism.

The Authentic Oriental

From the most general perspective, this chapter explains how *Empire of Signs* implicitly criticizes ethnographic Orientalism and the romanticization of the primitive by problematizing, instead of perpetuating, "persistent tropes by which Europeans and Americans have visualized Eastern...cultures."[3] In an effort to disrupt Orientalism from within, Barthes ironically comments on "a Western style for dominating, restructuring, and having authority over the Orient."[4] In Orientalism the "Orient, occulted and fragile, is brought lovingly to light, salvaged in the work of the outside scholar...[and] confers on the Other a discrete identity, while also providing the knowing observer with a standpoint from which to see without being seen, to read without interruption.[5] These descriptions of Orientalist discourses sound much like a footnote to the American Express commercials mentioned earlier. Those advertisements seek to help the tourist "make the world a series of accessible sites, equivalent as markers for goods."[6] In order to open the world to commodification, the credit card promises to reduce the threat of different cultures and customs and, paradoxically, maintain those differences as authentic. Working in tandem, credit cards and Orientalism seek authentic differences, and, paradoxically, they also seek to make different peoples and cultures more familiar and universally relevant—in short, more like home.

This tension between the same and the different can be seen in the experiences of Romantic travelers in the nineteenth century, who found a creative inspiration or reaffirmation of their (same) way of knowing the sublimely *authentic*. They looked inward to return to an innocent self. This other self was no more than a projection of negative elements from the everyday self of the world. They learned how to return home to their true souls by traveling to remote and primitive settings. This returning home, which motivates Orientalist discourses, also occurs more comically in what Kristin Ross calls the "complex dialectic of mass tourism." She explains this as "the vestiges of the romantic ideology of the solitary explorer, who, seeking virgin territory, uncharted worlds, suddenly notices he has brought his whole world along with him in a tour bus."[7] In this way, the modern mass discourse both continues and parodies Orientalist and Romantic discourses about otherness. Its vulgarized and kitsch versions of seeking authentic difference in a simulation inadvertently disrupt the notion of authenticity. Those tacky tourist sites "overexpress" the underlying structure of Orientalist discourse and mock the search for innocent and pure truth and beauty:

> [T]ourist settings, like other areas of institutional life, are often insufficiently policed by liberal concerns for truth and beauty. They are tacky. We might also suggest that some touristic places overexpress their underlying structure and thereby upset certain of their sensitive visitors: restaurants are decorated like ranch kitchens; bellboys assume and use false, foreign first names; hotel rooms are made to appear like peasant cottages; primitive religious ceremonies are staged as public pageants.[8]

Certainly, Barthes is not this sort of tacky tourist. Certainly, the description of his visit to Japan does not fall prey to the simulations, the Japanesy instead of the "truth" and essence of the Orient. It seems that Barthes poses as a tourist who finds the authentic inaccessible and discovers an otherness invading the familiar. Instead of the categories of authentic exotic otherness and reassuring familiar self becoming more clearly delineated, the self begins to blur with the other; more importantly, the method of discovery and investigation begins to find itself disarmed by the object of study. The detached observer becomes increasingly embedded. Barthes's European eyes start to look more and more Japanese.

The effort to return to origins, both fueled and disrupted by tourism, also suggests particular conceptions of history, temporality, and cultural change. Marianna Torgovnick explains that Western notions of time remain "fundamentally evolutionist," and the primitive shows us a state before differences (e.g., sexual preference, economic life, religious beliefs, humans and nature, etc.). For the primitive "charm" to work, the foreign society must represent a "common past—our past." On the other hand, it must remain "eternally present" in a place we can visit these primitive peoples. For the origin to remain a common past, the ethnographer must deny these peoples "pasts" of their own. More importantly, the foreign society can have no authentic development of its own. It must remain a place for us to "go home" to, "eternally present and accessible."[9]

The structure occurs in Orientalist discourse with the "they" functioning as a foreign "us" in a similar evolutionist temporality. Barthes's pseudo-Orientalist discourse upsets this evolutionist temporality by suggesting that the "Orient" is neither accessible nor common to our own past. He cannot return to a common past of a simpler, more innocent life. Yet, neither can he capture the essence of the singular and monolithic Other that, in the end, will restore, revitalize, regenerate, and reassert the values of the West and the true self. Instead, Barthes's *Empire of Signs* more closely resembles the adventures of Bouvard and Pécuchet, who "move through fields of learning like travelers in time and knowledge, experiencing the disappointments, disasters, and letdowns of uninspired amateurs."[10] Indeed, Barthes, admittedly more inspired than Flaubert's comic characters, does not even speak Japanese let alone offer anything but anecdotal evidence. He writes something like a tourist's parody of Orientalism to call into question the search for (deep) meanings and to investigate the relationship between a language of surfaces and invention. Those surfaces include precisely those elements excluded from traditional ethnographic science: rhetoric (in the name of "plain," transparent signification), fiction (in the name of fact), and subjectivity (in the name of objectivity). In *Empire of Signs,* the specific techniques of Oriental- ism (e.g., lexicography, grammar, translation, and cultural decoding) not only fail to adequately describe the "Orient," they begin to show their inherent shortcomings. They show their flaws because the tourist attraction (the "Orient") decodes them rather than vice versa.

The Orientalist scholars and off-the-beaten-track tourists alike share a faith in positivism. That faith creates their prejudice against those pseudotourists or postanalytic scholars who would seek anything less than the absolutely authentic. The social construction of these truth- seeking tourists and scholars emerges during the nineteenth century. Our conceptions of tourism have as much to do with critical and lit- erary discourses as they have to do with merely traveling to exotic places. For example, the use of the guidebook quickly stigmatized "its bearer in contrast to all that was indigenous, authentic, and sponta- neous."[11] In literature and criticism the tourist became the dupe of deception and crass manipulation. In a contemporary version of this mythic deception, one researcher describes how "a Turkish respon- dent of mine, whose job it is to divert tourists off the main thorough- fares of Istanbul to a back street leather coat factory, described the language he uses in his work as 'Tarzan English, you know, the kind one reads in comic books.'"[12] In Puerto Rico, a popular joke tells of a man who in his dreams dies and goes to hell; he finds hell contains dancing girls, gambling, and booze, and he has a wonderful time. Upon awakening, he makes a covenant to live his life in sin and try for hell instead of heaven. When he dies, he goes to hell; Satan gives him a pitchfork and tells him to start shoveling the hot coals. In protesting, he recounts his dream and asks, where are the dancing girls, the booze, the gambling, and all the rest? Satan replies, "Oh that! That's for the tourists."

In this context of the degraded activities of tourism, this chapter returns to the pragmatic consequences of reading Barthes's cultural work in light of the later works. The opening comment to *Empire of Signs,* "Orient and Occident cannot be taken as 'realities,'"[13] suggests Barthes identifies his project less with analytic scholarship or authen- tic-seeking tourism than with a usually degraded alternative. He finds only the inauthentic, the reproduction, the "Japanesy" instead of the "Japanese." Instead of the pure, innocent essence of Japanese culture, he goes home with a simulation or, worse, nothing at all. Like a typical tourist tale, one of Barthes's anecdotes describes how he follows a map in vain, telling the taxicab driver when to turn. Finally, he asks the driver to stop at a phone booth so that he can call for new directions. We never learn whether he reached his destination. There is nothing peculiar about this story; everyone has experienced the frustrations of following "bad" directions. He never arrives at his destinations figuratively or literally. So, it comes as a surprise when Barthes affirms his experience. The pragmatic consequences, therefore, are twofold. First, the analysis must account for the problems involved in reducing the particular to the universal, the individual to the stereotype, and the singular to the norm. Second, the analysis must appreciate the resistance to the "arrogance of discourse." The multicultural resists systematizing the world.

Composite Identities

In a postcolonial world, national identities continue to flare up in ethnic warfare, hate crimes, and prejudice, but already these forms of identity seem dated and show signs of strain. Barthes examines the challenge to identity in a series of photos he collects from a local Tokyo paper. One photo shows Barthes's eyes Japanned, while another companion photo shows a well-known Japanese actor with rounded European eyes. This quaint juxtaposition seems, like much of *Empire of Signs,* to smack of a tourist's delight rather than a comment on multicultural and postcolonial discourses. Recent work by Nancy Burson helps to highlight how these composite pictures function. Burson uses the technique of composite photography, invented in 1877 by Francis Galton. She uses digital computer graphics and software developed by Richard Carling and David Kramlich to create various works that composite images.[14] By amalgamating and manipulating images of, for example, world leaders with nuclear arsenals, she makes a startling visual argument about the image of these literal/figurative war heads with features weighted according to who has the most nuclear warheads. The photo looks like a hybrid cross of Reagan and Brezhnev, with a touch of François Mitterrand. In other work, she combines images of models and actresses from America in the 1940s and 1950s and compares this composite image with a similar composite of models and actresses from the 1980s. The differences are both striking and strangely appropriate: the composites picture a typical mythic beauty of both eras. In a similar comparison with images of male ideals from the 1940s, 1950s, and 1980s, one notices similar effects: changes in the look of ideals of masculinity and a familiarity with these images. The viewer wants to nod in agreement, "Yes, that's the look of the 1980s, I recognize it although I have never actually thought of it as a look." The viewer knows that certain faces fit the current idealized images of beauty but rarely considers the image as a literalized abstraction. The result is to defamiliarize the viewer from what we know implicitly: the current image and conception of beauty is historically determined and changes as a matter of fashion. These images literally demonstrate how these standards change and the historical specificity of that change. Her technique was later used by the FBI to update photographs of missing children, and by *People* magazine to project the effect of age on celebrities. Her own "Age Machine," an arcadelike installation, allows the participant to sit down and look at images of herself aging.[15] It takes a still image of the participant's face and then begins to manipulate it in various ways according to the instructions the participant gives the machine. Her other composites include many interesting theoretical combinations, including an image of an Oriental/Caucasian/Black with features weighted according to current world population statistics. It is the mythologized image of the ideals and realities of multiculturalism. The arguments about the correctness of the picture (e.g., its exclusion of many ethnicities, its lumping together of different Asian groups, its choice of a particular shade of black pigmented person, etc.) resemble similar arguments about multiculturalism (e.g., which cultures are included, how are they compared, who looks at whom, etc.).

When we examine Barthes's use of photographs in this context, the Europeanized Japanese actor's picture and Barthes's Japanned picture both appear as *composite* news photos. In that sense, taken together they suggest some of the broader issues evident in Burson's work and in other parodic work using composites of celebrities. They suggest a composite identity—this time the identity is not ideal beauty (and the problems or questions involved in a composite image of the historically contingent look of this ideal). This time the composites parody harmonious mixes of races even as they hypothesize literally about the possibility of such a representation. The composites, like Woody Allen's film *Zelig*, poke fun at the belief in a solid unchanging identity—especially national and racial identity. With the same snapshot, Barthes parodies identity politics *and* ethnocentrism; he does not merely get lost in Japan's foreign sign-system; his identity loosens, and the self seems to lose some of its essential characteristics, even if only in a newspaper representation. This composite identity parodies strong boundaries between self and other even as it *also* pokes fun at efforts to create harmonious interracial mixes. Pointing out the importance of these photos for Barthes's project, D. A. Miller writes that the photos and analysis are the most directly "provocative of our thinking about the inscription of the body" in Barthes's work (Miller, 36). It is these photos that allow Barthes to, as Miller writes, "look the Japanese in the *eye*, the eye that has been the referent of racist insult," without giving in to the liberal tendency to refrain from "taking any notice whatever of the racially other's body" (Miller, 36). These eyes are about bodies: hyphenated bodies.

Hyphenated Identities

In response to calls for a more homogenizing education, Randolf Bourne, a literary theorist of sorts during the early part of this century, argued that "Americanism" all too often resembled a "forced chauvinism." T. S. Eliot's complaint against foreign influences, in *The Criterion*, illustrates how the "forced chauvinism" appeared in discussions of higher education. The "source of weakness and instability" in the curriculum arrives through the seductive power of foreign ideas:

> In America, where education has for two or three generations responded to the whim of any modern theory... where the divergent tastes and ideas of scholars variously trained in Germany, France, or England, have been a source of weakness and instability, every vagary has had its opportunity, and successive scholastic generations have only suffered from successive experiments.[16]

Although this statement appeared in 1933, similar sentiments appear now in the *New Criterion*, where the "whim of any modern theory" describes Barthes's French postmodernist influence. For Bourne the defense of Americanism meant the promotion of Anglo-Saxon culture over more recent immigrant groups.[17] That is, Americanism usually means Anglo-Saxon, "merely the first immigrants" (274). Bourne's analysis of the situation seems even more appropriate for a defense of multicultural education today than in the first quarter of the century. He believed that efforts to Americanize the immigrants had failed, and that "the Anglo-Saxon now in his bitterness to turn upon other peoples, talk about their 'arrogance,' scold them for not being melted in a pot which never existed," and this attitude "betrays . . . the possession of a racial jealousy similar to that of which he is now accusing the so-called hyphenates" (276). Bourne's analysis directly addresses the contemporary debates about the appropriate role for Afro-American or Mexican-American ("hyphenates") cultures in shaping educational policy. For example, Daniel Boorstin argues, in the very language Bourne criticizes, that "the notion of a hyphenated American—whether Polish-American, Italian-American or African-American—is Un-American."[18] Bourne saw the danger not in a fragmented populace but in the probability "that these distinctive qualities should be washed out into a tasteless, colorless fluid of uniformity" (276). In this sense, the much discussed recent "failures of the melting-pot" are "actually good because they promote a stimulating environment instead of boring homogeneity" (276). At its best a multicultural curriculum at universities would encourage "an intellectual internationalism which goes far beyond the mere exchange of scientific ideas and discoveries and the cold recording of facts. It will be an intellectual sympathy which is not satisfied until it has got at the heart of the different cultural expressions, and felt as they feel" (291).

The Right considers these ideals to be on the road to fascism and anti-American curriculum. A careful consideration of the current conflict does suggest a more nuanced complaint against multicultural curriculums. For example, Boorstin's conservative views and opposition to bilingual education also include a defense of a more open immigration policy and a sympathetic view of "speaking broken English— perhaps the only thoroughly American language."[19] Holding a view similar to Bourne's, Cornel West writes that the challenge is "to articulate universality in a way that is not a mere smoke screen for someone else's particularity."[20] On the other hand, Simon Frith, the rock critic, and Henry Lewis Gates, hardly in the same camp as conservative critics, both find serious problems with identity politics. Frith explains that the overreliance on identity politics in rock criticism leads to an "implicit distinction between insider and outsider knowledge, a distinction that makes some sociological sense but ignores what is most interesting about music—its blurring of insider/outsider boundaries."[21] He goes on to explain how reading songs only in terms of identity misses the crucial value of music. He argues that "the best studies of popular music don't try to pin down sounds according to

existing social maps, but rather allow the music to make its own political argument, to re-draw social contours. Aesthetics, that is, determine identity in more interesting ways than identities settle taste."[22]
Frith's suggestion opens up a territory separate from the conflict between Americanism and identity politics. His eloquent portrayal of
the power of aesthetics to determine identities "in more interesting
ways" than relying on existing social maps, whether reactionary or
progressive, alludes to an alternative to traditional notions of politics.

Mixed-up Identities

Perhaps the most significant development in the current conflict over
identity politics concerns the new category of "multiracial." Not surprisingly, many Americans feel uncomfortable identifying with one
side of the hyphenated racial or ethnic category or the other. Barthes's
inclusion of the composite snapshots demonstrates visually the uncanny sense of becoming other, becoming mixed. In music and in cultural politics, the *mix* is more interesting than the singular identity.
Barthes's mix, his composite photos and stolen languages of Orientalism and tourism, outlines the start of a multicultural politics. This
politics reverses the direction of the Orientalist voyeurism, allowing
for a way to allow otherness to comment on epistemologies of knowing. In a discussion of an often cited educational film, which Western
relief workers attempted to use as a teaching tool to explain to a group
of indigenous people the importance of boiling water for sanitation,
Barthes describes how that which exceeds our efforts to capture an
essence or meaning also suggests an emergent multicultural politics—
nothing we have seen before:

> When a film was shown for the first time to natives of the African
> bush, they paid no attention to the scene represented (the central
> square of their village) but only to the hen crossing this square in one
> corner of the screen. One might say: it was the hen that gazed at them.[23]

This bothersome hen pecks at our conceptions of visual images, in
this case, photographs and films. It tells us as much about our interpretive practices, our habituated perceptions, as about the amusing
miscommunication between these people and the outsiders. Perhaps,
we laugh neither at the Peace Corp workers nor at the villagers but
rather at the expense of our own desires to make everyone the same,
and simultaneously we laugh at the superimposition of one way of

looking with another incommensurable way. We laugh at and for the potential possibility of seeing representations from two incommensurable places. We laugh at the composite of differences collapsed momentarily and ridiculously into sameness. As Miller writes about Barthes's use of the two news photos, those eyes promise a "certain détente." The word *détente* suggests not only an easing of tensions between feuding groups but also literally a slackening or loosening. The composite of these two meanings represents Barthes's strategic politics. He recognizes, as Miller writes, that "every utopia secrets signs of the conflict that it fulfills the wish to abolish" (Miller, 39). It is this recognition of conflict in a utopian practice that characterizes what one might call the Barthesian Laugh. This is the joyous and ironic hope of Barthes's multiculturalism as an artificial mythology. Composites could be generated for top-selling books, movies, or influential scholars, weighted according to popularity or theoretical significance. Composites could mix scholars with entertainers or politicians with idealist rock stars, or show other poignant combinations. The endless potential and significant implications have yet to be explored by those seeking cultural change. Imagine Roland Barthes and Oprah.

Creolization

The ethnographic film *Trobriand Cricket* depicts how a group of islanders have modified the English version of cricket. The film begins by describing the evolution of the game up until its introduction to the Trobrianders during World War II. Through interviews with villagers and voice-over narration, we learn how the game functions much like the fetishized materials of the "cargo cults." The cargo cults would use refuse for religious purposes (e.g., damaged machinery, crates from supply shipments, and other discarded supplies left by the British and American troops). For the Trobrianders, cricket functions in an entirely different context, and for different ends, than the British intended. Most of the film depicts an actual Trobriand version of cricket, which functions as part of an elaborate ritualized (and violent) battle between different villages. Because they use a game left behind by the British colonizers for entirely different ends, the Trobrianders resemble groups of colonized Indians in South America who used Spanish symbols in unexpected ways. Michel de Certeau describes this specific type of use and its apparent effects:

The ambiguity that subverted from within the Spanish colonizers'
"success" in imposing their own culture on the indigenous Indians is
well known ... the Indians ... often made of the rituals,
representations, and laws imposed on them something quite different
from what their conquerors had in mind; they subverted them not by
rejecting or altering them, but by using them with respect to ends and
references foreign to the system they had no choice but to accept....
they escaped the dominant social order without leaving it.[24]

In the sense that the Trobrianders alter the British version of the game
to fit within their own symbolic system, the game functions as a kind
of creolization, a hybrid form created out of the "contact situation"
between two very different cultures. In apparent contradistinction to
this creolization of the game, the documentary looks and sounds rather
traditional. It seems to repeat an invisible style, now widely criticized,
that suggests a complete unproblematic access to all the relevant facts.
It contains interviews, films of events, photographs of historical development, drawings, and a consistent voice-over that definitively anchors
the diegesis. Neither the film's form nor style calls attention to the
labor involved in *making* meaning. The film, like many traditional
documentaries, appears to simply record an extant reality. The images and sounds we encounter appear natural and given rather than
constructed and contextualized by the filmmakers. Scholars of documentary film have pointed out the problems in this type of realist organization in filmmaking. The filmmakers of *Trobriand Cricket* metic-
ulously planned a realist depiction, which the critics might dismiss as
naive in its form of presentation. Yet, something undoes all this planning, all these efforts to naturalize the images, and all these techniques
that assure us about our fixed and transcendent perspective. The disruption does not appear in the film's form but in the cricket match-
battle depicted.

During the match, a mock tourist appears on the playing field re-
plete with a faux carved wooden camera and Bermuda shorts. He has
a formalized role in the Trobriand cricket match as a kind of mascot
and appears, at some point, during all of the battle-matches. That
mock tourist plays off the spectator's ethnographic urge to "see the
natives as they really are." Masquerading or burlesquing the tourist's
position allows the natives to comment obliquely on the drive for
authentic artifacts. The native-becoming-tourist (rather than a native
seen without seeing us) suggests an alternative to the opposition be-

tween tourists (and ethnographers) who look and the natives who act authentically.

On one level, the film does not call attention to its signifying structure, nor does it ever let go of the objectifying power of the scientific narrator. In this sense, the film fails to make us question our ethnographic urges. As a "good" ethnography, this film attempts to depict the "ensemble of social relations," the unself-conscious rituals, any spontaneous reality, the opinions of objective and detached experts, and the dialogue of trustworthy informants. These elements often come packaged in the anthropological bias toward valorizing a "primitive" culture untouched by the troubling differences of Western societies: sexual and linguistic. A number of critics, most notably Jacques Derrida in his reading of Lévi-Strauss's *Tristes Tropiques,* and Torgovnick in her essays on "primitivism," have exposed this bias.[25]

On another level, the mascot-mock-tourist pokes fun at our parochial voyeurism. The film might be understood as almost ritualistically using what is left to it by the Western ethnographers (the intellectual cargo, one might say). Rather than presenting a formal criticism of ethnography with a more sophisticated self-reflexive style, the film depicts the staging of ethnographic situations in the cricket match-battle. All the roles of the ethnographic situation are played out implicitly in terms of the film's traditional presentation and, also, parodically on the playing field! The players pervert, mock, or creolize standard ethnographic situations. For example, the "ensemble of social relations" now appears as players acting like airplanes flying to the Trobriand Islands, bringing cargo and cricket. This dance of the "contact situation" leads into an erotic charging (or fetishizing) of the ball and bats. The supposedly objective and detached judges derive their authority from their personalities rather than from access to facts or expertise. Reality, controlled by magicians' spells, remains susceptible to counter-spells. A sponsor stages and funds the supposedly unself-conscious ritual-match for his own prestige. The old, apparently trustworthy informant never plays in the match (as opposed to the players who never speak to the filmmakers). The viewer becomes a tourist-spectator with camera in tow. And the belief in a pure asymbolic primitive culture untouched by differences gives way in the face of a scoring system for the match based on puns rather than achievement. For example, the score is always announced as "six" when the sexually charged ball is "lost in the bush." Usually the ethnographic urge pushes us to say, "if only we could return to a culture so untouched by the 'written' clichés of our corrupted society." The punch of this film comes from its literal playing out of the "contact situation" and a playing with ethnography's attempt at access to authentic artifacts.

In the study of "tourist art," the problem arises of how to account for more than one symbolic system, and for "the fact that the arts may be produced by one group for consumption by another."[26] The special relationship that exists between tourists and the natives (implicitly charged with the task of producing the authentically different) creates an effort to mediate differences in a peculiar way. As Nelson Graburn explains, tourist art is "important in presenting to the outside world an ethnic image that must be maintained and projected as part of the all-important boundary-defining system ... symbols of their internal and external boundaries" (5). In this sense, what Graburn calls "ethno-kitsch" functions as an "arts of acculturation," which synthesizes, for example, native and European forms; these artworks are "innovations created out of the unique contact situation" (8). The innovation arises from a social interaction. And here we can see the specificity of the discourse borne out of the mediation of differences. Again, although the tourists seek the authentic, the very interaction (i.e., tourism) produces something entirely different. For example, Graburn explains that the "Hopi Kachina *dolls* are probably imitations of the apparently magic *santos* that the Spanish Catholics brought to the Southwest" (11). The natives modify existing forms, or invent new forms, in order to sell the objects to tourists.

In the Pueblo "turtle dance," an example of a dance of the "contact situation," a clown sometimes borrows a spectator's camera, reversing the usual photographic process: "The clown became the tourist with camera while the tourist became the photographic subject."[27] This situation does not merely portray an imitating or identifying with someone. Instead of providing an evolutionary perspective, where the Indians function as innocent and primitive, the situation functions as a symbiotic relation found in the "contact situation": mixing, hybridization, contagion, or creolization. One cartoon often printed in Native American newspapers depicts a Japanese tourist taking a picture of three totem poles. On the back of one of the poles, unbeknownst to the tourist, we can read "Made in Japan." The demand for the authentic actually produces the inauthentic until the distinction between the "Real Thing" and the staged no longer holds. In these indigenous cultures, parody allows the tourist to become a part of the group. In Native American descriptions, tourists often fall into mythical categories like "tourists from back East," "tourists from Texas," "hippie tourists," and "save-the-whales tourists." Burlesquing the characteristics of the mythical tourist foregrounds the relationship between strangers and natives or the anomalous and the familiar. As Constance Perin explains, "every anomaly and 'stranger' announce that they cannot be accounted for by concepts that organize a familiar field of meaning."[28] This sign of difference is not easily assimilated without distress. Perin notes that "familiar meaning systems are lodes of conservative energies, mined to provide the visceral comforts of equilibrium. They can be contested successfully, from within or without, only gradually when changes are more attention- than fear-arousing."[29] On one level, these cartoons and parodies function to mediate the threat of difference. In mediating difference, something else happens. Not only do the natives ultimately give up authenticity in their efforts to present it, but the tourist finally captures only a simulated difference.

Particular ways of mediating difference suggest an alternative to both authentic and simulated history. In ritual dances, the Hopi kachina functions as a "person" who travels and mediates between realms: *hopi /kahopi* (Hopi/un-Hopi), living and dead, liquid (e.g., rain) and flesh (i.e., life).[30] The kachinas function as "cloud people" wandering through the sky and raining upon the earth. The literal translation of kachina as "a sitter" suggests how these masked figures mediate among gods and people. The kachina "comes to sit and listen to the petitions of the people."[31] Usually the Hopi pray to these cloud people for rain, but these messengers can bring any needed resource (e.g., money). The kachinas do not appear directly from the gods but appear in the masked dancers who channel the kachinas. During the dance, the masked participant loses any personal identity. The Hopi have modified these kachina masked dancers into dolls by borrowing the Spanish form of the *santos,* a religious doll. One of these Hopi kachina dolls is the "Koshare Tourist." The doll is of a balding man with dark hair and a ridiculous grin, wearing Bermuda shorts. He wears three cameras around his neck and carries four camera cases. The empty fourth case suggests that someone is taking his picture. The person looking at the doll occupies the place of the photographer. A visitor who buys a tourist doll owns a *mise-en-abîme* of his or her own tourist's position. Obviously, the doll helps the natives to cope with the tourists as strangers, and it might allow the tourists to recognize their position in the natives' social structure. Out of that mediation something else happens. As a souvenir that mirrors the myth of the tourist who brings needed resources, the doll goes beyond a mere repetition of the clichés of inauthentic native artifacts and ridiculous tourists. It functions as a third term in the interaction precisely because it stages or detours both native artifacts and touristic activity. In this sense, the doll functions as a passage between frames of reference (native and tourist, object and looker, history and historian). As a *mise-en-abîme*, the doll represents not a tourist nor a Native American but a boundary or passage between different ways of looking and understanding: a mixed history, a creolization.

Sergei Eisenstein implicitly theorizes this creolization in terms of the cinema. In the famous intellectual montage sequence from the film *October*, he edited together a series of spatially unrelated images: a baroque Christ surrounded by a semicircle of golden rays, the many-armed Hindu god Shiva, the mosque on Kamennostrovsky Prospekt in Leningrad, a mask of the Japanese goddess Amaterasu, the beak of one of the minor deities of the Nipponese Olympus, a religious mask from Yoruba, Eskimo shamans with hanging swinging wooden arms, and a Giliak hollow wooden idol. This sequence functioned within a larger sequence titled "For God and Country," which contained images of the provisional government leader Aleksandr Kerensky, the White Russian General Lavr Kornilov, a small plaster Napoleon, and Czar Nicholas II's statue miraculously reassembled. He described this sequence of figurines in terms of a passage to an alternative way of thinking:

> [T]he "method" of my intellectual cinema consists of moving
> backward from a more developed form of expression of consciousness
> to an earlier form of consciousness; for the speech of our generally
> accepted logic to a structure of speech of another kind of logic.[32]

This intellectual cinema, a relatively well-known practice among film scholars, is usually described only in terms of the formal structure (e.g., the non-narrative editing) or the conceptual meaning (e.g., criticisms of deism, Kerensky's centralization of power, and the White

Russian's religious fanaticism). Few commentators have discussed the specific objects filmed except as they relate to the larger conceptual or intellectual argument. If one studies the list of items, it soon becomes clear that Eisenstein has filmed a series of souvenirs. Eisenstein described his montage technique as creating the circumstance where the combination of images would actually come together in the spectator's perception. In discussing the spectator's creative process, he directly connects intellectual montage to travel and the presentation of past experiences:

> [I]t includes in the creative process the emotions and mind of the spectator. The spectator is compelled to proceed along the self-same road that the author traveled in creating the image. The spectator experiences the dynamic process of the emergence and assembly of the image just as it was experienced by the author.[33]

Eisenstein explains in this description of the effects of montage how the spectator shares not only the trace of the journey in the souvenirs but also the experience of the intellectual movement. The sequence edits together cultural commonplaces, a collection of souvenirs, to create an intellectual montage *and* an allegory about writing history with cultural artifacts. The souvenirs not only stand for a particular deity but also represent the contact situation between many cultures. Eisenstein's intellectual montage does not visually argue that there is no deity, but rather his series of images simulate the appreciation of many deities, many cultures. Kornilov fought for "God and Country"; Eisenstein parodies this religio-patriotic fervor by intellectually traveling around the world, collecting images of visually incommensurable deities.

One theorist who has undertaken a similar project, Paul Virilio, uses a history of cinema to make an argument about how "the logistics of perception" function as the epitome of the modern war machine. He does not merely describe the historical evolution of an idea but links two histories, war technology and cinema, to make an argument about the connection of vision to weapons. He argues that now

> the fusion is complete, the confusion perfect: nothing now distinguishes the functions of the weapon and the eye; the projectile's image and the image's projectile form a single composite.... Ever since sights were superimposed on gun-barrels, people have never stopped associating the uses of projectiles and light, that light which is the soul of gun-barrels.[34]

As this quotation indicates, Virilio charts how film technology and war technology advance along similar and intertwining lines of development. In uncovering these connections, he explains the history of the cinema as a war machine and the staging of war as cinematic. Yet, unlike most other historians of the cinema, he uses history to make an argument about how we should understand vision in general. As in my argument here, he uses historical artifacts to change our frame of reference. If we take his argument seriously, then historiography would have to, at least, account for the problems inherent in pinning down and verifying in visual accuracy the facts, for those efforts at exact verification may in fact have more to do with a war machine logistics than with innocent fact-finding. Unfortunately, Virilio never accounts for the effect his theory of vision has on his own theorizing and history. He theorizes how the cinema and, even more so, electronics and video diminish space and time, but he does not go on to suggest how his descriptive interpretive project avoids the dynamic surrounding visual sightings common to cinema and war technologies. How do shifts in perception, which Virilio carefully describes, affect models of history and change? Virilio's description of Hale's Tours, which I describe as a tourist attraction, highlights the similarities and differences between these two projects. Virilio sees the tour as "setting the audience up as aggressors" and notes that "the whole performance was usually financed by transport or arms companies, which were to lose no time in distinguishing themselves during the First World War."[35] The interdependence between cinema and tourism is neither dominant, determining, nor absolute, but useful.

Just as ideological concerns and technological changes (e.g., improvements in printing pictures) allowed traveling to shift from an auricular practice to sightseeing, the need for democratic ideologies and technological changes made new types of tourism possible. In that sense, the early cinema functioned in large part as an extension of the tourism industry, and read in terms of creolization, the origins of the cinema suggest an artificial myth about the link between technological travel and a becoming other, which Barthes explores in *Empire of Signs*, for example. While many have noted that Étienne Jules Marey's early effort at designing a moving picture camera resembled a sawed-off shotgun, the stereoscope's marked resemblance to binoculars has apparently gone unnoticed. The magic of these scopes may have to do as much with the positioning of the viewer as a tourist (rather than as a soldier) as with the visual illusion of a three-dimensional image. The proto-cinema contained many instances of a cine-tourism. Many early peep shows contained views of tourist sites. And the nickelodeon professors, who toured America with "magic-lantern" shows, would typically show a series of slides from Africa or India and explain their pseudoethnography about the amazing sites they saw on their travels. Never mind that they never actually went to these locations and that the slides were shared among many "professors," they still created the tourism effect. Technology had already brought the other into the homeland, and the various cultures collapsed without time or space to separate them. Even if only for a fleeting moment, these multiculturalist experiences suggest how technology opened the senses to an otherness that could not turn off.

Marey's efforts to capture movement for analysis led strangely enough to efforts to experience literal and figurative travel. He searched for a method to prove Darwin's theory of evolution by natural selection. Having invented a graphic instrument for the recording of pulse and blood pressure, he applied that work to the recording of organic functions, especially the function of movement. Marey argued that the graphic recording of these functions would reveal over time how variations in function led to organic changes (i.e., evolution). He went beyond these descriptive goals to claim that by understanding how, for example, birds fly, one could build a machine that would fly according to the same structures and principles. He began his experimental work by modifying his graphic monitoring instrument to indicate movement. In one experiment, a man's walking was graphically monitored with an apparatus attached to his body. The graph was then represented with drawings capturing each progressive stage of the movement. The drawings (usually around sixteen), placed on the circumference of a *phenakistoscope* (a round wheel that would spin), not only produced movement but also allowed Marey to slow down movement to analyze its precise structure. In 1878, he saw Eadweard Muybridge's experiments in which a horse would trip a series of threads and the resulting series of pictures captured the precise movement of the horse galloping. Muybridge, at Marey's urging, tried to use a similar method of photographing birds in flight, but Marey found the experiment inaccurate and imprecise.

Out of his frustration with the Muybridge method, he looked for a camera that could move to follow the flight of a bird and take many pictures rapidly at precise intervals. He was already familiar with Pierre Janssen's *revolver photographique* (a cylinder-shaped camera with a revolving photographic plate), which Janssen had used to take pictures of Venus moving across the sun. The camera had the advantage of taking pictures at short intervals, and it could follow movement rather than wait for movement to cross its path. Marey built a *fusil photographique* (a photographic gun) to "shoot" a bird in flight at split-second intervals. He tried Janssen's method of using one photographic plate but later switched to strips of photographic paper, and he learned to project the result on a screen. The entire films lasted only two or three seconds. He made a number of important improvements to his mechanism including transparent film, longer strips of film, a more mobile camera, and a projector that used celluloid film and had an endless belt. In 1889 he invented a gear to allow for the intermittent motion necessary to project strips of film. In 1894, Marey met Thomas Edison, who soon took these experiments from science to show business.

This story of the early experiments in motion pictures is well known among film historians. History, however, is not merely a collection of facts; it has to have a theory to connect those facts. And this particular history has an impact on how we make histories and artifacts. Marey himself did not like the cinema, because it did not freeze movement in order to analyze its sequential units. Instead it created an effect of movement that could not serve Marey's efforts to document physiological change. In a sense, therefore, cinema offered *a different model of change,* a model based on a fascination with movement and travel and a techno-evolution. "Then came the film," Walter Benjamin writes, "and burst this prison-world asunder by the dynamite of the tenth of a second, so that now, in the midst of its far-flung ruins and debris, we calmly and adventurously go traveling."[36] Tom Gunning has explained how the early cinema documents this fascination with movement. For example, in the film *Panorama of the Flatiron Building* the camera shows "the base of the then tallest building in New York City with the traffic and pedestrians moving around it. [Then] the camera tilts up somewhat jerkily until it views the top of the building. The film then ends."[37] Writing the history of camera movement from the perspective of later narrative cinema, one might suppose that it began as a subsidiary to narrative action. As Gunning explains, we might mistakenly assume that "the camera moves when something in the shot moves." He explains that

camera movement began as a display of the camera's ability to mobilize and explore space. The "content" or purpose...is as much a demonstration of the camera's ability to tilt as it is the Flatiron building. We find a plethora of such films in early cinema, based on camera movement from a variety of vehicles as well as from the camera's moveable tripod.[38]

The emergence of the cinema (as a fascination with movement) corresponds to the growth of modern tourism. The early movies often consisted of travelogues from far away lands, and the Lumière brothers sent many cameramen all over the world. The Lumière brothers' and George Méliès's films appear at about the same time as early tourist guidebooks like Baedeker's became widely popular. These filmmakers offer two different models of tourism. The Lumière brothers show a behind-the-scenes look at the authentic (e.g., *The Workers Leaving the Factory*), while Méliès creates an obviously staged fantastic adventure (e.g., *The Impossible Journey*). All three filmmakers consciously and explicitly catered to the touristic drive. In film history, many have used these filmmakers as the division between realism and the fantastic that still characterizes the cinema. Whether real or fantastic, the desire to go someplace helped create the cinematic apparatus. The fascination with travel in the early cinema relates to both other media, still photography, and vaudeville, and, by extension, to temporal questions about past and present. Histories of cinema often consider Méliès as staging vaudeville-like entertainments by stressing the proscenium and offering magic shows and "arranged scenes" facing the camera. And these histories explain that the Lumière brothers imitated a photographic-like tradition by recording historical events and posing family members. Rather than call these widely accepted schemata into question, this brief history supplements the prevailing notions by noticing a similarity between these filmmakers. The Lumière brothers present the movement of objects like walls falling down or water flowing from a hose. These simple films make the movement-oriented events appear to happen again in, what Virilio or Baudrillard would call, a virtual reality. Similarly, Méliès presents acting and filming in order to provoke or cue a sense of movement. He provokes this sense by using the mechanical movements of nineteenth-century acting and magic-show conventions that force a reaction in the spectators. The stereotypical cues for specific emotions had more of a visceral charge than mere recognition. The films cue a physical reaction. The magic-show conventions startled or "took your breath away." These cues functioned like the kicks in a Kung Fu movie, which often move the spectator physically. In Méliès's films, the camera tricks (both stop-action editing and optical printing) surprise the spectator with discontinuous movement. This discontinuity suggests the same surprise encountered by rapid communication and travel: "How did you get here?" "Where are you calling from?" "You sound so close?"

Thomas Edison's early film productions share this fascination with reproducing the actual movement of travel. In the film *The Panoramic View of White Mountain Pass*, a camera fastened to the front of a train records its movement through a tunnel and around a mountainous turn. The sequence is continuous and lasts only for a few minutes. In this rather literal tracking-in or dolly-in shot, we approach the end of the tunnel and then the edge of the turn. After the train emerges from the tunnel, the scenery moves toward the edge of the frame, rushing into the spectator's peripheral vision, creating a sense of movement. A similar effect is created in amusement parks like Disney World. One ride, "The Wings of Man," ends with the little cars actually moving very slowly toward a hole in a large movie screen, while at the same time the film of a landscape rushing by toward the edges of the wall creates a powerful sensation of a fast motion forward and falling. Not only does Edison's film combine a travelogue with a spectacle of movement, it also suggests an important temporal consideration. To understand how the early cinema posed an important temporal question for historiography, one can compare the mise-en-scène of a hypothetical photograph of the White Mountain Pass to the film version's mise-en-scène. What would the scene look like? What would the photograph depict? It would document the event. It would simply depict that "this happened." What does the film, on the other hand, depict? It shows us what happens.[39] It depicts that "this is happening." Film's movement creates a temporal effect. The early cinema is a presentation in two ways, part of vaudeville acts (i.e., shown as a presentation in, and as part of, vaudeville shows) and *a making the past present*. Not actually (or even phenomenologically) present, the past functions as a virtual presence with currency; that is, it moves us:

> [T]he thrill of motion and its transformation of space...gave the spectator an almost uncanny feeling. An early reviewer...described Biograph's moving camera film of the Haverstraw Tunnel in this way: "The way in which the unseen energy swallows up space and flings itself into the distances is as mysterious and impressive almost as an allegory."[40]

Hale's Tours took that allegorical effort one step farther. Hale's Tours used the realism of the motion picture to take the passengers on impossible and fantastic journeys. One would enter the pavilion and buy a train ticket. In the entertainment pavilion, a railroad car open on one side ran on tracks in a dark tunnel. The wall facing toward the open side was a continuous screen. As the train began to move, the films showed the countryside or city streets passing by. Often a tour guide would lecture during the adventure. The unevenly laid tracks heightened the illusion, which was so overwhelming that frequently passengers would yell at pedestrians to get out of the way. One passenger who went to the same show week after week was quoted as saying that he was waiting to see if the conductor would make a mistake so he could see a train wreck. Strangely, the films were shot from both the cowcatchers and from other locations on the train; these different views were then edited together without regard for a continuous point of view. The metonymic fragments are linked by the spectators. The tour confuses the distinction between the *actual* and *virtual,* the *then* and *now,* and *absence* and *presence.*

The important historiographical question that arises from studying the early cinema in terms of the fascination with movement, travel, and presentation has to do with the mediation between different, but interrelated, domains (e.g., tourism and cinema, war technologies and cinema, other and self, technology and human evolution, etc.). How one understands that relation changes the theory of history one develops. Understanding creolization in terms of the *mediation of change* underscores the peculiar way artifacts can have a currency (both current and useful for an exchange among cultures or symbolic systems as well as a mediation of differences). If we take facts as frozen in the past, then we can analyze development in discreet units, as Marey wanted. That stop-action photographic history would work well with a macroevolutionary approach (i.e., evolving systems theories of creativity). The early cinema suggests a different relationship among frames. And it also suggests a different relationship to the foreign, native, or Other. A creolized history of cinema makes artifacts current rather than markers of a past without currency. The interplay among symbolic systems, domains of knowledge, and ways of understanding (e.g., foreign, native, personal, public, expert, common, true, fictional, etc.) suggests a model of history premised on proliferation of possibilities rather than merely the evolutionary selection of ideas. The use of artifacts need not serve descriptive proofs or convincing arguments. The mediation of differences and change need not settle on one symbolic system over and above others. Rather, making artifacts relays of change or (intellectual) movement allows these artifacts to function in a creolization or a language of combinatory inventions rather than a language of arguments and proofs. Artifacts do not wait for (definitive) interpretations; they *mediate* change. Michel de Certeau makes a similar claim in *Heterologies*.[41] By making the past an objective fact, history becomes a taxonomy; chronology converts history into nature, what Barthes in *Mythologies* calls an "alibi."[42] Jonathan Culler connects the effort to discount this alibi to the tourist's practice: "The tourist is not interested in the alibis a society uses to refunctionalize its practices."[43] When time functions to categorize events as, for example, a cultural movement that occurred during the first quarter of the twentieth century, it does not function to remind us of the possibility of other conceptions and the mortality of our own. The principle of death in the field of knowledge reminds us that our truths are metaphors or models and that other models may replace our current conceptions. As Certeau argues, time can have repercussions on our reasoning only if reason does not "renounce what it is as yet incapable of comprehending."[44] Even the notion of what will probably occur uses a rational taxonomic system. This use of probability might function quite well in certain circumstances; it does not encourage invention. Creolization, a temporary solution, constantly changes the mix involved and encourages future modifications. It represents a way of using mythologies as the basis for artificial myths. In that sense, this type of inventive practice has a profoundly political dimension: the creolization offered in these experiments, like *Trobriand Cricket*, offers a method to intervene in changing the way one plays the game, not merely the way one describes it.

Multiculturalism need not limit itself to descriptions of ever broader groups of previously unacknowledged literatures and cinemas. It need not function only as a category for something resembling an Orientalist project of describing the otherness of exotic literatures and marginal national cinemas. This chapter has argued for a multicultural practice and demonstrated an artificial mythology for multiculturalist research. Just as the older mythologies of a singular community and shared culture begin to show serious signs of wear and an inability to stretch to fit the changing demographics of contemporary societies, the mere addition of more and other kinds of literature and films does not go far enough. The real novelty and excitement of multiculturalism arises from its ability to function as a methodology and a system of research. This chapter has demonstrated how to analyze the history of film in terms of creolization rather than just study multicultural films. It demonstrates how otherness already exists in the familiar cinematic practices as long as the viewer changes the focus of the situation. As soon as cultural critics begin to see double and to blur the distinctions between them and us, then the possibility of a multicultural practice begins. For Barthes, this practice depended on a parody of Orientalist discourse and a literal going Japanese even as the other becomes Europeanized. Humor seeks to disrupt our assumptions about the exotic that prevail as much in newfangled inclusive curriculums as they did in the older Orientalist scholarship. As long as the position of the scholar remains transcendent and purely detached, no multicultural creolization can occur. If the literal and figurative miscegenation of multiculturalism occurs, then the artificial mythology of creolization will change the face of scholarship forever. Those literal photographic distortions used in Barthes's *Empire of Signs* have a figurative dimension as well as being the more obvious spoof on narcissistic recognition. Instead of seeing his photo and exclaiming, "it's me!" he says, "it's not me" or "I'm not me." Using this mixed-up identity as a research model not only disrupts the mythology of the traveler who always confirms his own self as different from the natives but also implies an artificial mythology where mixed-up identity becomes the very basis for the photographic image and the cinematic experience. The historical facts remain the same. The focus changes. It begins to look like a pop-art installation on out-of-self experiences. Of course, multiculturalism as a research methodology wants to challenge the self-complacency of a culture that admits no mixing. American culture, the ultimate mix, still seems frustrated with the possibility that the invasion of the aliens entered with the emergence of photographic and filmic representation even before the invention of the camera. The pop-art travel machine, intensified with the cinema, promises a "becoming-other" called multiculturalism.

4 | Urban Decay and the Aesthetics of Social Policy

Proposal and Policy

In this chapter I examine a major social problem, urban decay, using the method of artificial mythology. Contemporary films and media reports picture urban decay as the epitome of a Spenglerian decline of civilization. Drug and psychosis-induced violence, as a symptom of high-density urban spaces and anonymous neighbors, for example, has a visceral impact that helps naturalize the myth of decaying architectural urban spaces as necessarily violent, dangerous, and hopelessly fated for condemnation. Even the tele-urbanity of television brings violence and absurd social decay into the sanctity of the home. Movies, especially the film noir of the 1940s and 1950s, have helped to reinforce and create these myths. Instead of trying to expose some real underlying structure for urban decay, this chapter works through the myth to highlight aspects of the common conception of the decaying *noir city* usually overlooked by social scientists and urban planners. Examining the representations of urban decay while masquerading as a solution to the problem à la Jonathan Swift, the chapter challenges cultural and media scholars to interrogate studies of modern and urban experience.

Academics and the popular press both consider urban decay one of the most important and serious problems confronting contemporary culture. Politicians point to it as a symptom of decadence or neglect, journalists mention it as a backdrop for crime and drug dealing, and suburbanites hold it up to justify their move out of the city. Urban decay has provoked research in many academic disciplines including but not limited to urban planning, sociology, and restoration architecture. Although the Right and Left disagree about its causes and effects, both sides agree that it remains a pressing problem. Big-city mayors meet to chart its course and costs. Commentators always seem to link the topics of crime, poverty and unemployment, drug abuse and use, and the decay of responsibility to inner-city urban decay. The association of these problems with, for example, young Black men or Chicanos always has the naturalized assumption that these problems appear in, and grow out of, urban decay. The association of immigrants with inner cities in the early part of this century resembles the more recent association of African-American culture with inner cities. Both liberals and reactionaries take for granted or naturalize the assumption that these problems always take place in the context of urban decay. For liberals, the urban decay causes the social problems; for racists, the people cause the urban decay; and for neoconservatives, liberal policies cause the urban blight. Conservatives often anthropomorphize cities, use them as metonyms for liberal social policy, and then insinuate a dislike for the city. It is acceptable to hate "inner cities" as the code for areas of urban decay. It is no surprise that social scientists and urban planners alike consider it only as a problem to alleviate. In fact, it might seem heretical or reactionary to suggest that in spite of well-reasoned social programs and adequate funding, the urban decay problem will never disappear. It might seem like a dismissive comment by Rush Limbaugh that urban decay might be inherent in the very structure of urbanity and what it means to live in an urban area. Yet, most researchers recognize that the efforts to solve the problem by effacing it with "urban renewal" have all too often led to an exacerbation of social problems. City governments now often view the "renewal" as part of the urban decay problem. This chapter does not attempt to intervene in the important questions of how governments allocate funding. Rather, it asks a more basic question about *how we frame social policy issues.*

Part of the difficulty in researching urban decay concerns how problem solvers conceive of, or represent, the situation to themselves and others. Little scholarly work has suggested how theories of representation might help to deal with large social problems facing our society. Although relatively recent studies in critical legal studies, anthropology, and architecture have attempted to explore questions of representation, and although the social-scientific paradigm has come under attack because of its inadequate reflexivity and archaic positivism, few studies have focused constructively on a specific socio-architectural problem using contemporary theories of representation. The aesthetic dimension of living conditions usually drops out of the social-scientific approach even when the issue concerns urban aesthetics (that is, literally crumbling buildings, boarded-up windows, graffiti, clumps of makeshift not-quite-dwellings, etc.) as it bleeds over into social upheaval. In architecture, aesthetics or questions of representation continue to have a prominent position, except when planners consider urban contexts. Then, architects demur to the supposed wisdom of social scientists instead of continuing to consider aesthetic issues. It seems that either architecture falls into an "art for art's sake" or, conversely, acts like a slave to efficiency. Architecture, torn between public construction and personal expression, seems unable to ever adequately decide between artistic autonomy and social commitment.

One prominent social scientist, typical in her conclusions and exemplary in her careful research, explicitly describes representations of violence with a "medical model." Using the medical metaphor, she seeks to purge representations of violence and cure society of this disease, especially in films and television.[1] She generalizes from her citation of "good research" on children's responses to make claims about the effects of representation in general. The effect of these representations moves along a linear line from "small effect" to "large effect." This approach, typical of social-scientific research, does not allow for a contradictory or nonequivalent response; that is, she cannot account for a so-called violent representation producing something besides violence each and every time, or for various different levels or types of violence. On the other hand, contemporary theories of representation examine precisely the difficulties in determining universal effects or limiting interpretations to a singular meaning. Under the weight of pressing social issues, even to ask if these violent film images give people *pleasure* would not merely meet with dismissal as a moot point but would also appear as a dangerous distraction (from the more important issues) that may fuel the "epidemic" of violent representations. Pleasure and aesthetics play little part in determining the value of representations in discussions of urban problems. Of course, pleasure could play a crucial role in discussions of architecture, urban planning, and policy. For example, Bernard Tschumi argues that the "greatest architecture of all is the fireworker's: it perfectly shows all the gratuitous consumption of pleasure."[2]

The fireworks used in the Australian Invasion Day celebration convey precisely this economy of pleasure. Preceding that celebration, there was a widespread public outcry about the inappropriateness of building a monument to the invasion of Aboriginal Australia. Not only was the invasion a tragedy for the Aborigines, but the monument was a giant birthday cake located in the worst urban ghetto in Sydney. The plan was scraped because of the protests: the cake would conjure Marie Antoinette saying "Let them eat cake" for both the current disenfranchised inhabitants of the area and the Aborigines. Other equally absurd architectural solutions were considered, and the fireworks celebration was finally chosen. The Aboriginal people staged huge protests of the event. The television broadcast of the event played "the popular 'Power and the Passion,' a famous song by Midnight Oil (Australia's favorite polemical rock band), which is utterly scathing about public as well as 'popular' chauvinist culture in urban white Australia."[3] The day after the event, graffiti and political cartoons punctuated the ironic joke: "Let them eat fireworks."

As discussed earlier, in spite of the event's organizers' intentions, the fireworks had taken on a new tactical importance. The song, fireworks, and slogan gave the otherwise mortified viewers of the invasion festival a "flash of hilarity and encouragement." The "tactical" use of the fireworks produced this corrosive laughter and consumption of pleasure. Simply through *felicitous timing,* polemical significance insinuated itself into "the place of programmed pleasure."[4] This pleasure depends on an *arts of timing* rather than on colonizing space as in urban renewal programs. To understand timing, the participants must have something like an aesthetic appreciation for the right moment; they must have repeated exposure to the representation of urban decay to understand the ironic tensions, contradictions, and ridiculous solutions.

The rule for the social scientists is simple: the "more exposure, the worse the impact." These researchers appear to assume that poor people cannot afford aesthetic considerations: more pressing and primary issues demand priority. Yet, as every architect knows, the solutions to social and practical problems always have an aesthetic dimension. Even the most practical solution, the most concerted effort to make form follow function, will have an aesthetic dimension. Marshall Blonsky, in *American Mythologies,* describes an important aspect of social-scientific solutions. In a chapter titled "A Tourist Guide to a Nightmare," he describes his visits to the New York City subway sewers, and how these visits made him reconsider his *idea* of the "subwayland." What is more important, Blonsky discovers how social solutions often involve efforts to control representation. He explains that "an experimental program called Outreach...sought to convince underworld homeless to go to the universally despised shelters.... The aim of the program wasn't hortatory, however; government urging a regime of health on its citizenry. The aim was intelligence."[5] The government wants to know who these people are; they want to fit them into an aboveground system of representation. Social control begins with representation and accounting.

Besides keeping an eye on the filthy swarm, other "solutions" to urban decay suggest relocating the "undesirables." In the movie *Sister Act,* Whoopi Goldberg's version of Catholicism saves the inner city with (Catholic?) gospel revivals and a few coats of paint. During one scene, a regular at the local biker bar says, "If this turns into a nun's bar, I'm not coming here anymore." Hollywood's version of chasing the undesirable people away to make way for "gentrification" does little for the current inhabitants. Although the term *gentrification* has a negative connotation within bohemian subcultures, its association with Young Upwardly Mobile Urban People (Yuppies) sometimes makes the issue a class-based prejudice instead of an urban policy. In economic terms, the current dwellers want to stay in their apartments without an increase in rents. On the other hand, subcultures often associate gentrification with an unbearable preciousness. That association suggests an emergent policy that carefully considers aesthetic issues beyond nice versus dirty. Questioning ways of understanding urban decay and change ultimately depends on examining how social policy represents urban decay. These efforts to ask questions about representation present a specific dilemma. How can a study of how we represent or imagine a problem, in this case urban decay, lead to specific pragmatic solutions? In answering this question this chapter does not merely criticize social-scientific "solutions." Instead this chapter offers a guide to thinking through urban decay as an existing situation, to working with it instead of against the representation. This chapter does not propose a moral statement, nor does it advocate one particular style over another. It does not offer more plans for "good" works.

Social scientists, cultural historians, and politicians all focus on the construction of social space as a key problem. Among the issues and problems examined in terms of social space, urban decay represents the most pressing concern in both scholarly and political forums. While this issue provokes studies and policies, the emergent academic discourse called cultural studies has provided mostly descriptive readings rather than speculative suggestions or experimental models for alternatives. Because the descriptions further persuade the readers that the problem is both real and severe, the need for solutions seems ever more pressing. The emergence of neighborhood associations, block-party groups, squatters, house-building charities, and even well-organized gangs suggests alternatives to previous solutions to urban decay like projects and urban renewal. Academic research usually describes these various changes in sociological terms. The engagement of urban universities in surrounding communities continues to increase as both groups realize their mutual interests. With these "community partnerships" arise calls for pragmatic solutions. As these pragmatic solutions travel back and forth between a popular culture and an expert culture, informing each other's assumptions and actions, the course of scholarship begins to change from description to proposals, at least in this one area.

Practice

Beatriz Colomina, in her editorial introduction to *Architecturepro-duction,* explains how architecture refers to interpretation and criticism, not merely to buildings. She goes on to explain that "a building is interpreted when its rhetorical mechanism and principles are revealed."[6] With the mechanical reproduction of the image of the city, the size of the audience increases. As that image influences the audience, the cognitive maps of cities change. The audience (the tourist in front of a building, the reader of a journal, the viewer of an exhibition or a newspaper advertisement) "increasingly become[s] the user, the one who gives meaning to the work."[7] The organization and meaning of urban spaces is a "product of social translation, transformation, and experience."[8] The urban-artist-activists, the situationists, who used the city as their palette for experimental wandering or *dérives,* sought to give the special moments of everyday life a language in order to make invention the basis of a social formation. Those moments of rupture suggested the possibility of "reinventing everything everyday."[9] Taking this situationist attitude and applying it to urban decay suggest both an alternative research paradigm and a pragmatic approach to the situation. The situationist research paradigm would research the elusive urban decay, a collection of architectural and social forces, as a tension between the passerby and the buildings and surroundings. Instead of merely describing the situation in empirical terms, the research would stress something like an aesthetic response. The use of the situation reinvents it every day. The urban dwellers reinforce and suffer through the decay every day. The pragmatic approach stresses an alternative route for a literal and figurative stroll through the "inner city." The situation becomes an explicit site for invention rather than a neutral benign background. Commentators connect the growth of particular cultural forms to urban situations. The situationist practice makes this use of the environment more explicit. Besides provoking the situation of urban decay, the strategy described here also challenges the framing of the issue. If the framing of the situation constrains and encourages particular readings and interpretations, then altering or *détourning* the prevailing interpretive paradigm will lead to inventive novel solutions and sometimes down a blind alley. The situationist strategy does not pretend to have the single correct solution to the problems facing urban culture. The pragmatic strategy seeks only to broaden the potential solutions, the possible routes, and the emergent models for understanding the situation. In this sense, proposing an artificial mythology based on a situationist strategy of *détourning* the prevailing interpretations of, for example, leaking buildings will challenge both those living in urban decay and those interpreting its meaning to, at least, consider the apparently absurd solutions.

Designers interested in the situation of disorientation in cities have noted the importance of a conceptual image or cognitive map. Way finding depends more on cognitive maps and on what one knows about a situation than on what one sees. The recognition of a cognitive-textual aspect to space conceives of space as a textual translation. Feminist work on cities also points to the importance of contextual factors in mapping a city. In a discussion of detective fiction, one critic asserts the difference between the way female detectives conceive of a city and the way men do:

> The tradition of the detective novel clearly deals with the questions and darkness of the city, but from Williams' description, it seems to do so in a particularly masculine way: the rational abstract intelligence, elevated and separated from others, which isolates and differentiates until it identifies a single cause.[10]

Women writers of detective novels, on the other hand, "see light and change in the city as well as darkness."[11] This rather pat contrast does highlight an alternative to the film noir city. This chapter focuses not on the solution of the dark city crimes but on those elastic intersections and confusing boundaries that provoke both male and female detectives with unsolved enigmas. What the comparison of male and female writers does, perhaps unintentionally, is suggest that the city is a textual system, not merely a neutral setting. For example, Paul Rabinow explains how, in the mid-1960s, an enormous effort at urban planning began in France. He writes: "In addition to including the latest technological and functional advances, the urbanism teams were directed to create a symbolism of urbanity and micro-spaces of sociability embodying the values of comfort, ease, and centrality."[12] He goes on to quote the authors of the "authoritative *Histoire de la France urbaine*," who conclude their discussion of this urban planning project by saying, "the material to be worked on is as much human behavior as the physical environment."[13] Rabinow's thorough exploration of the norms of modern life addresses how the image of the city became "an object to be harmoniously ordered" and organized according to "an urban parallel to Bentham's *Panopticon*" (211–12). Urban architecture can be read as an effort to enact "universal norms for humanity," and "three universal needs—shelter, boundaries, and signaling—provided the grid of intelligibility" (244). Michel Foucault uses such plans and schemes as "strategic exemplars," "as a means of illuminating not an entire age but particular nuclei of knowledge and power" (212). Like the project undertaken here, Foucault's *Discipline and Punish* finds a way of thinking with an image (e.g., the Panopticon).

Computer technology gives a precise model for combining information as well as combining educational values with entertainment values. An experiment with a merger of entertainment values with educational goals appears at Disney's EPCOT. The Disney fantasy of urban life, EPCOT (Experimental Prototype Community of Tomorrow), has an obviously fictional character to it. How does the illusion work as a generative device rather than as a veil over some reality? We might dismiss Disney Land or even Disney World as merely "quaint" entertainment. The explicit educational and political goals (a "World of Nations" without black African nations) make the experimental city a far bolder construction. With its underground workers, its techno-global-village of amusements and robo-guides, its perceptual-architectural games like fountains that throw sausage-size globs of water over passersby, smell machines, and its rooms that make music when one walks over the multicolored floorboards, this city resembles a number of other narratives. Its techno-architectural emphasis falls somewhere between the ominous cartoonlike futuristic sets in films like *Metropolis* or *Brazil* and Jacques Tati's film *Playtime* with its whimsical view of modernity's absurdities. Its familiar or supposedly comforting social control falls somewhere between the homebound thrills in Huysmans's *Against the Grain* and Leni Riefenstahl's *Triumph of the Will*. It has always been an undecided fantasy between hallucinogenic excitement and hegemonic panopticonic pleasure. This dialectic of delirium and control is precisely the mix theorized by psychoanalytic film theorists during the 1970s. In those theories, the cinematic apparatus allowed for delirium, but only in the confines of a patriarchal-humanist social order. The gaze of the viewers was carefully guided, and through that guidance, social control sutured subjects into a hegemonic ideology.

We can appreciate the relation between the punctum (private) and the combination system (public) by referring to the city as a nexus of public and private. For example, Walter Benjamin writes that we are currently "building houses with glass walls, and patios extending far into the drawing rooms that are no longer drawing rooms...in other words, private life...is dismantling itself, openly shaping itself."[14] Avital Ronell compares Benjamin's description of houses to

> those that can be viewed in Southern California, with large curtainless windows into which you can look, if you want, and see a man walking around in his underwear, beer in hand, the television on, doubling public diffusion in the radical translucency of a private space, the television communicating with the window, the outside looking inside.[15]

In this sense, one kind of living, private life, is thrown, or projected, out to another kind, public life. Ronell makes the connection explicit when she writes that "rumor belongs to the ec-static."[16] As we follow the system, wander through the city, we make the rules. In his discussion of Tokyo, Barthes explains that that city's address system "is apparently illogical, uselessly complicated, curiously disparate," but this alternative system requires that the knowledge of a city "usually managed by map, guide, telephone book" gives in to a system not based on the abstractions of printed culture but on the "gestural practice":[17]

> This city can be known only by an activity of an ethnographic kind: you must orient yourself in it not by book, by address, but by walking, by sight, by habit, by experience; here every discovery is intense and fragile, it can be repeated or recovered only by memory of the trace it has left in you: to visit a place for the first time is thereby to begin to write it: the address not being written, it must establish its own writing. (36)

In this urban territory, streets have no names, neighborhoods have train stations as relays rather than squares as centers, cooks cook "nothing at all," "emptiness is produced in order to provide nourishment," and a "central emptiness" forces traffic into "a perpetual detour" (24, 24, 32). That emptiness provokes the detours of invention. Barthes's travel guide offers a kind of rhetorical way-losing, a lost sense (head in the clouds?) necessary for invention.[18]

As a guide to losing one's way, Barthes's text resembles the *mystère*, the nineteenth-century French novel genre. In these novels, "everyone is an unknown, is lost, and soon loses" themselves.[19] Gerard Nerval's *Journey to the Orient* functions, in this sense, as a model for Barthes's *Empire of Signs*. The adventure produces an "increasing delight and astonishment," Nerval writes, "as I discover myself a thousand leagues away from my homeland and let my senses slowly absorb the confused impressions of a world which is the perfect antithesis of ours."[20] Of course, Nerval's "Orient" is Arabia not Japan. And while Barthes's version corrodes any privileged ethnographic position, Nerval often falls into the problems that Edward Said identifies with "Orientalism": essentializing a supposedly unchanging and peculiar society, often to reassert Western values. These tales of wanderings develop through Baudelaire's "The Stranger," who loves "the clouds... drifting clouds... there... over there... marvelous clouds!"[21] Novels of urban wanderings like André Breton's *Nadja* and *L'Amour fou* come quite close to Barthes's poststructuralist version. Breton focuses on the small discovery and the apparently gratuitous encounter in his "eagerness to wander in search of everything" in order to make "a mockery of what would have seemed most probable."[22]

In examining urban decay, strategies will have to deal with unpredictable, unstable, and ephemeral situations, and these situations depend as much on the spreading activation as on any particular origin. So, for example, in the case of urban decay, the decay is often not visible as "decay" until that notion catches on; that is not to suggest that the effects are not painful or serious, but that the decay depends on more than loose bricks or garbage on the sidewalk. It depends on a more general "sense of a situation." In that sense, the reception of ideas determines the event *retroactively.* This works in a similar fashion to any idea catching on and changing the way we think; for example, when we learn the word "God" and some meaning for that word, it begins to change the very structure of our mental processes. The spreading activation of a single word has an enormous influence on how we frame many problems. In a similar way, "urban decay" helps to frame our perceptions. Richard Dawkins, the eminent biologist who has suggested a theory of cultural evolution, calls the unit of spreading activation a *meme.*[23] His term applies to those words-as-ideas that affect our talking-as-thinking species. Different from memes, the substances examined here have disparate and nonevolutionary effects. For example, if the situation of "urban decay" catches on in your community, it will depend on spreading activation, but it may not lead to an evolutionary progress, and it may have disparate effects. Instead of having a unidirectional (or evolutionary) development, the representation may spread out in numerous and unpredictable ways. A chart of this particular spreading activation would resemble the rhizomatic growth of weeds rather than the silhouette of a tree. To suggest the regressive potential, and annoying consequences, of this peculiar type of spreading activation, I have coined the term *allermeme.* The term combines Dawkins's *meme* (which denotes something copied) with the word *allergen* (the element that sets off an allergic reaction). The allermeme only appears retroactively when it sets off an allergic reaction. It does not exist apart from spectators, city dwellers, and so on. What is more important, it functions retroactively, in a way similar to prejudice. As Slavoj Žižek, the influential Lacanian cultural theorist, explains, prejudice does not give negative traits to the oppressed group. Instead the meaning or signification occurs après coup. Žižek uses anti-Semitism as an example. He explains that one might encounter the term Jew in racist literature as

> connoting a cluster of supposedly "effective" properties (intriguing spirit, greedy for gain, and so on), but this is not yet anti-Semitism proper. To achieve that, we must invert the relation and say: "they are like that (greedy, intriguing...) *because they are Jews.*" This inversion seems at first sight purely tautological — we could retort: of course it is so, because "Jewish" means precisely greedy, intriguing, dirty.... But this appearance of tautology is false.[24]

He goes on to explain that

> Lacan's emphasis is precisely on this retroactive character of the effect of signification ... the effect of meaning is always produced backwards, *après coup.* This therefore is the fundamental Lacanian thesis concerning the relation between signifier and signified: instead of the linear, immanent, necessary progression according to which meaning unfolds itself from some initial kernel, we have a radically contingent process of retroactive production of meaning.[25]

Using this example as a model to understand urban decay and the function of allermemes suggests that the cluster of signifiers associated with urban decay (i.e., crumbling buildings, etc.) appears only after we designate (rightly or wrongly) the area as afflicted by urban decay. The traits appear because they are part of urban decay. This suggestion (that naming something urban decay produces the effects associated with it) seems, at first, absolutely ridiculous. We might retort that the situations of racism or anti-Semitism concern prejudiced mental representations, not any real attributes in the physical environment. Of course, this claim is correct. One might protest that the analogy does not hold because urban decay concerns actual effects in the physical environment. This claim is also correct, except, of course, that the mental representations of those physical attributes determine how we understand, at the most basic level, what we see and experience. For example, when a tourist visits Roman and Greek ruins, the experience is thrilling. Because no one lives in ancient ruins, the crumbling buildings and peeling paint mark the site as old and authentic rather than as an example of urban decay. These crumbling buildings generate sorely needed funding. Dean MacCannell has noted that tourism is often better than other forms of unequal development.[26] Instead of building factories, some underdeveloped areas now use tourism to generate economic resources. Before a site becomes an attraction, the area must first have markers indicating that the site has significance. Marking an area as "urban decay" gives it an obviously negative significance; instead of proposing to change that marking, it may prove more productive to investigate the phrase and its effects more closely.

Noir City

The notion of urban decay is not new. "Urban decay" finds its most eloquent modern representation in Oswald Spengler's *The Decline of the West* (1918).[27] Spengler sees social and ecological decay and entropy as corollaries to modernity and advancement. He states modernity's "destiny-idea" as an "unsurpassably intense Will to the Future." Instead of the optimistic future envisioned by Rockefellers and revolutionaries alike, Spengler saw an implosive end to culture and, ultimately, to the world. Not surprisingly, this image of an imploding destabilized world resembles the gloomy world of film noir, which try as the characters may, will engulf them, swallowing up not just their hopes but their lives. As Žižek explains, the narrators often find themselves reconstructing an intricate plot only to find "set in motion the investigative machinery which, sooner or later, will point its finger at him" or her. Žižek explains, that "the *noir* flavor pertains to this position of the subject who can only observe helplessly how the trap set by the investigative—i.e., discursive—machinery, nominally led by himself, tightens around him."[28] In short, the crucial aspects of Lacanian psychoanalysis demand a noir sensibility or appreciation. On a trip to America, Lacan was discussing the translation of *The Four Fundamental Concepts of Psychoanalysis* with Alan Sheridan, the translator. As they came out of the plane, they were discussing the difficulty of translating the term *jouissance*. Sheridan suggested using the word *enjoy*. At this moment, Lacan looked up and saw, in the distance, a billboard advertising Coca-Cola; it read, "ENJOY COKE." Lacan turned to Sheridan and said, "No, not enjoy." The term *jouissance*, literally related to sexual bliss, connoted an element of pleasure, but Lacan wanted to stress the destabilizing aspect. Enjoyment, a peculiarly American tyranny, expressed in the salute "Have a nice day," had no place in the noir sensibility Lacan wanted to engender in his students. Urban decay is the *jouissance* of architecture and modernity. In that sense, one can read Spengler's essay on the "unsurpassably intense

Will to the Future" as a discussion of the inevitable confusion between sexual desire and urban malaise found in film noir.

The birth of the modern city created not only peculiarly urban problems but also the motivating force linking a noir sensibility with urban desolation, malaise, and destabilization. A noir sensibility emerges as a function of, and response to, the modern city. Benjamin finds this connection eloquently allegorized in Baudelaire. As Benjamin explains, Baudelaire's *flânerie* "surrounds the approaching desolation of city life with a propitiatory luster."[29] And, in another context, Benjamin continues with a discussion of how the *flâneur* functions like a detective in a Poe story. Yet, just like the noir detectives, the *flâneur*, as Alexander Gelley explains, "testifies to the constitutive impenetrability of the city mass to mere spectatorship. The *flâneur* is himself caught in the mystery that he presumes to master—both the labyrinth of the city and the faces of the crowd."[30] *Flâneurs* and noir detectives alike find themselves ironically swallowed up because of their own efforts to investigate and escape. There is in this sensibility a melancholic's revolt: an ironist's twist that progressive liberal solutions never quite recuperate. Neither celebration nor condemnation of urban decay, the noir *flâneur* winks with a tactical flash of perverse pleasure and wry humor.

In this chapter I explore the urban decay of representation and suggest how work by architects may involve an alternative (even situationist) picturing of the concept urban decay. It seems fitting to set up certain guides, constraints, and parameters in order to facilitate applications. As Tschumi explains, in regard to the Manhattan Transcripts project,

> In architecture, concepts can either precede or follow projects or buildings. In other words, a theoretical concept may be either applied to a project or derived from it. Quite often this distinction cannot be made so clearly: for example, a certain aspect of film theory may support an architectural intuition, and later, through the arduous development of a project, be transformed into an operative concept for architecture in general.[31]

One could end this chapter with an optimistic outlook for the future, as in a comedy, or by invoking the tragedy of our crumbling cities. Certainly everyone has heard these scenarios applied to the situation of urban decay. The big-city mayor always represents the situation as a comedy, while the news often portrays the streets as a depressing tragedy. The apocalyptic rhetoric shared by the naive and cynical alike portrays the city as a battleground with powerful antagonists and severe impending doom. Noir city does not contain a sudden grand downfall, nor noble opponents. Silly pathetic villains bumbling after feckless heroes in bad situations make film noir a model for the kind of sticky situations usually associated with hopeless love affairs. The city itself looks more and more like Walter Neff's obsession in the film *Double Indemnity*: "She was a red-hot poker, and I couldn't let go." Noir city constantly confuses the apocalyptic with uncontrollable desires: not just a time to die, but a time to die a little death, *la petite-mort, jouissance*. For the heroes of these films, death awaits. For the viewers, that death has a certain pleasurable conclusion. In examining representations like movies, critics often fail to recognize that the hero's fate does not necessarily mean the audience will suffer vicariously. Instead, the audience experiences the death differently. Obviously, the audience does not die, even in the most violent films. Instead they translate the deaths into something else. Falling apart without hope, noir city always suggests something beyond the requirements of rational planning and modernity, something beyond complacent pleasures and the need to cure ourselves of pain and anxiety. Wallowing in foolproof fate, the heroes of noir city know the *jouissance* in desolation, destabilization, and decay. The social scientists can only make statistical pleas for cures to this hysterical reaction. Just as the film noir gives the audience a contained experiment in hysteria, the contemporary urban situation has similar elements of hysteria and seduction. Focusing only on the rational solutions to urban problems ignores the aesthetic elements of social policy and urban planning. Later the project may fail because it is "unlivable," and the current situation may appear as too dangerous for anyone to live in. The noir-city approach does not claim to solve the problem. Rather it highlights the element that makes the social-scientific solutions appear inadequate. Those elements include the seduction of the seamy, the pleasures of watching decay as a changing, evolving force rather than as an end in itself, and the hysteria of living in a contemporary city as almost pleasurable in its unpredictability. Surely the threat of death, rape, harm, armed robbery, and vandalism do not warm us to the marrow. Urban areas have an element of unpredictability and excitement that exceeds the needs of a rational corporate market. Those excesses do not necessarily always involve death and destruction. The decay does not always lead to apocalyptic downfalls nor should it lead to merely rebuilding from the ground up.

One could make a list of noir city's ingredients: bittersweet irony, gritty realism with a wink, simple assertions spiked with startling metaphors, obsessive planning and rationality falling prey to fate's unlucky contingencies, and dark ominous urban settings peppered with suspicion and seduction. Flashbacks, low-key lighting for shadows and silhouettes, wide-angle focus to put the viewer in the middle of the action and intrigue, askew camera angles, the ever present venetian blinds and metal bed frames, and "choker" or extreme close-ups juxtaposed with high-angle shots all to intensify the claustrophobia and paranoia. You better throw in some mirrors, guns, and silk stockings to keep tricking and seducing vision's detached certitudes.[32] In constant play with these visual elements, a voice-over narration often heightens the voyeuristic effect by suggesting the style of a documentary on urban decay or the internal monologue of someone looking back with 20/20 vision at what went wrong.

One could discuss those other similar representations of cities: *Open City, Naked City, Atlantic City.* Roberto Rossellini's *Open City* (1945) pictures Rome under Nazi rule. It is undamaged but strangely forlorn. That imperceptible tainted quality makes the film a strange corollary to *On the Town*'s (1949) idealized version of urban life. What if the sailors had stepped off the boat in Fascist Rome? They might sing something like: "Roma, Roma it's a wonderful town; the façades go up and the people go down...in a hole in the ground." No such luck. Hollywood had not yet rediscovered its origins in, for example, Mack Sennett's evil sensibility. He cast the LAPD as the Keystone Kops and greased actual intersections in order to film unwitting drivers skidding out of control. Hollywood had not yet returned to D. W. Griffith's extravagant *Intolerance,* which seemed to blur the distinctions among decadence, decay, progress, and prosperity: the set looked like industry had finally become an expensive image of its own waste behind the veneer of production.

With the Italian neorealist's rejection of the "white telephone" artificiality of Fascist cinema, filmmakers began looking at cities as sets once again. In the United States, *Naked City* (1948), and those other low-budget, postwar noir films, transformed the *flâneur* with speed into the hard-boiled detective swept up by an often *fatale* muddle he had wanted to avoid. "What we call noir," as Mike Davis explains, is "a fantastic convergence of American 'tough guy' realism, Weimar expressionism, and existentialized Marxism, all focused on unmasking a 'bright, guilty place' (Welles) called Los Angeles" or maybe any city USA.[33] This world looks like a "'Dream Dump'...a hallucinatory landscape tottering on apocalypse" (38). All too eager to "mine Los Angeles's barrios and ghettoes for every last lurid image of self destruction and community holocaust," Hollywood cannot help itself (87). It continues to find an uncanny tragedy right in the middle of our happiest fantasies.

Recently, Hollywood has tried to protect itself by proclaiming films like *Boyz in the Hood* as progressive political realism—sounds like "socialist realism" to me. Paradoxically, with little formal censorship and increasing explicit sexuality and graphic violence, decadence has little place anymore in Hollywood. Urban decay becomes one more personal problem to overcome or fall victim to. Sex and violence become another set of special effects (with stand-ins and body doubles) to increase realism. In noir, the insinuations of sex and violence trace and intensify modern urban life's unresolved contradictions and tensions. They speak of ominous potentialities rather than a singular reality. While the progressive realism of films like *Boyz in the Hood* seeks to contain and control the excesses of decay with moral messages and a lack of visual expressionism, the models for noir heighten and charge the intense spilling over, falling apart, and decay. These models provoke an intense allergic reaction by infecting both architectural solutions and urban problems with a bodily enervation, something between laughing, crying, and sneezing.

During the early 1960s, a group of affiliated artists began examining the pleasures of decay in the contemporary world. They named their loose affiliation FLUXUS in part because of its denotation of a medical term for a violent attack of diarrhea. This group's work often referenced this sudden evacuation of the bowels in their literal inclusion of feces in their work and in their figurative allusion to an anti-art practice that would get beyond all the "bull shit" associated with high art. The suggestion of flux or change in the group's name also connected the defecation and decay to a creative spirit. A few of the associated experimenters (to avoid the term artists) specifically examined urban issues and urban decay. Wolf Vostell's "Happening is architecture, Dé-coll/age Architecture" (1961) offers an example and model for future work in this area. He photographed the demolition of a housing project. The title refers to the demolition as a Happening of architecture. The neologistic portmanteau word "Dé-coll/age" both suggests a breaking apart of the collage, the décolletage of a low-cut dress, and the collage practice of sticking pieces together with the seams obviously showing. His risqué practice attempted to show the seductiveness of the obverse of construction and putting the pieces together. His photographs poke fun at architecture's grand schemes for modernist housing projects as well as at the entire ideology of construction as a positive value. His photograph illustrates his witnessing and capturing a falling to pieces. Carolee Schneemann's caption for her "Parts of a Body House," in *Fantastic Architecture*, edited by Wolf Vostell and Dick Higgins, applies equally well to Vostell's work and noir city in general:

> Should not all future architects and environmental scientists be required to study Urology, not just in the narrow sense of the gastric tract, but in the larger sense of the movement of all liquids and liquid-behaving solids and masses within our bodies? Are these not working models for the flow of all kinds of traffic? Concentrations of people and social engagements? Flows of information and social change?[34]

This figurative use of the study of the urinary tract is definitely meant to have a parodic quality. Just as the pop artists, like Oldenburg who was also associated with FLUXUS, associated the lowest forms with the grandest schemes, Schneemann associates urban planning and pissing, to use the vulgar term, for both parodic and inventive effects. Her analogy shocks with a satirical humor that resembles an artificial mythology as well as suggests a new context with which to understand older issues and problems in urban and cultural studies. Schneemann's caption also serves as an introduction to other similar noir-city architectural installations. Her connection of flows of liquids in the body to information and social change not only alludes to FLUXUS's preoccupation with defecation of all kinds both literal and figurative but also to how prominent aspects of urban decay, leaks and plumbing problems, connect to cultural flows. Out of the leaks and sewer system something figurative besides killer alligators might spring.

Ilya Kabakov's installations offer particularly poignant examples of this flowing noir city. Kabakov, a Russian artist who focuses on the decline, decay, and fall of the Soviet Union, has constructed a number of installations that examine life in the Soviet Union both literally and figuratively. His installations have appeared in the United States in prominent venues like the Hirshhorn Museum in Washington, D.C., and major New York galleries. His *Ten Characters* focuses on a "communal" apartment created after the 1917 efforts in the Soviet Union toward "consolidation" and "settling." Large apartments were resettled with many individuals and families. Each individual or family had only one room. As the influx in to the cities continued, more and more members of the family and their relatives lived in these small apartments (10 3 12 meters).[35] Myths and rumors arose out of the crowded conditions, the rubbish and debris, and the constant "babble of voices from every side which never falls silent day or night" (52). Living in the midst of this urban decay, Kabakov develops an architectural solution. An architecture with the flow of noir city. He constructs an installation of a number of rooms in the apartment filled with trash, clutter, and myths. These installations make concrete, for example, the situation of overhearing a neighbor in the next room and wondering, what in the hell is going on over there: it sounds like our neighbor just flew into space from his apartment; or guessing that another neighbor "never threw anything away" (42). There is something very troubling, sad, and frustrating about these installed myths. The fantasies of finding a way out, or inventing fetishistic rituals of collection, not only speak of the inhabitant's fears, anxieties, and utter desperation but also suggest the fantasies of neighbors forced to endure the maddening strangeness and noise of neighbors who never become close friends — just people in close quarters. These installed myths speak about the unresolved contradictions in a socioeconomic system that seeks to create community but instead merely helps fester unreconciled differences.

If Kabakov's installed myths merely spoke of these troubles in an inadequate communal system, then they would need neither installations nor myths. Instead, Kabakov uses these installed myths as a twist to the more straightforward social-scientific messages about living conditions. He does not replace one empirically verifiable message with another newer version. Rather, he puts a spin on the evidence — a spin that social science never accounts for in its efforts to catalog and picture the concept of urban decay. The installed myths show a world and a sensibility: bittersweet irony (these installed myths mix humor with the realization that some people actually live in these conditions), gritty realism with a wink (the situation is both desperate and fabulous), simple assertions spiked with startling metaphors (a neighbor would do anything to get out—the installed myth shows his plans and contraptions to literally fly into space), obsessive planning and rationality falling prey to fate's unlucky contingencies (when you look through the hole in the ceiling of the room where the man flew into space from a flimsy catapult seat, you cannot help but wonder how far up he went before he fell fatally back to earth), dark ominous urban settings peppered with suspicion and seduction: "Sometimes it is a wicked world of unstoppable fights, hatred, enmities of many years" (52). It is a dark vision of life in an apartment, but these concrete or built images of rumors, scandals, and concepts of urban decay create a perverse pleasure, a *jouissance*—that fleeting laugh when the figurative becomes literal and the singular reality is forever shaken. The social scientist would merely explain that the people wanted out of these tense and cramped quarters. Kabakov builds the concept of the (im)possibility of escaping. His installation alludes to the obsessive planning involved in these vain efforts. By suggesting the absurdity of the effort to escape by flying into space, he also projects a potential perverse pleasure. Kabakov makes the unseen seen. The visitors to these installations take with them the allermeme "shoot the moon."

In the description accompanying the installation "The Man Who Never Threw Anything Away," Kabakov describes how in an effort to find the man, a plumber who supposedly lived in one of the rooms in the communal apartment, some workers trying to fix the heat opened the door. The tenants got to examine the contents of the room but never found the plumber. Again, up to this point, the story illustrates in Kafkaesque fashion the frustrations of not finding the plumber when you need one. That small bittersweet joke only begins the story. When they look through the belongings, they find various tracts and statements explaining the accumulation of junk in the small room. Most of the tenants shuffle back to their corners of the apartment, but the narrator's Uncle Misha pokes around a little more. And he finds something: "Near the door, struggling through dozens of cardboard boxes filled with innumerable papers, documents, certificates and the like, and on which were scribbled: 'Book of life,' volumes 18–26, Misha stopped near an enormous pile of manuscripts." He began reading a chapter in the manuscript titled *A Dump*: "The whole world, everything which surrounds me here, is to me a boundless dump with no ends or borders, an inexhaustible diverse sea of garbage." This is not a pretty place filled with pretty buildings; neither amusing nor hopeful, this place sounds bleak. The description goes on:

> In this refuse of an enormous city one can feel the powerful breathing of its entire past. This whole dump is full of twinkling stars, reflections and fragments of culture: either some sort of book, or a sea of some sort of magazines with photographs and texts, or things which were used by someone. . . . An enormous past rises up behind these crates, vials, and sacks; all forms of packaging which were ever needed by man have not lost their shape, they did not become something dead when they were discarded. (45)

He has added a twist, and later the manuscript adds, "this feeling of a unity of all of that past life, and at the same time this feeling of the separateness of its components gives birth to an image . . . it's hard to say what kind of image it is . . ." (45). One image seems particularly appropriate: "it's an image of a certain civilization which is slowly sinking under the pressure of unknown cataclysms, but in which nevertheless some sort of events are taking place" (45). Kabakov shares Kafka's sense of humor in more everyday settings: the world of these installed myths crumbles slowly, sadly, and with a wry wink, a fleeting joyous flourish in accounting for the image for the dump.

Kabakov's more recent work "Incident at the Museum or Water Music"[36] goes farther in illustrating the concept of noir city. And it does so in ways difficult to describe in print. In fact, it forces this participant to describe the experience not in objective terms of what happens, when and where, but in terms of one particular visit. I had come to New York in October 1992 on a rainy day to visit three or four galleries with special exhibits on FLUXUS (including work by Vostell, Oldenburg, George Maciunas, and Schneemann). Having seen *Ten Characters* a year or two before, I was excited to see the new exhibit, and to get out of the rain. When we entered the Ronald Feldman Fine Arts Gallery, there was an anteroom, where we left our umbrellas. On the wall before the entrance to the main gallery rooms was a description of the exhibit. I dutifully read the description quickly without much thought and entered the first room. It was a sumptuous gallery. Darkly painted walls, old ornate trim, waist-high wooden paneling, and plush maroon divans. The room had an elegant cast, and I felt a bit intimidated by its respectability, in the way certain museums make one whisper in respect. As I came into the room, I noticed these beautifully executed, large, socialist-realist paintings. Their very ornate, wide golden frames added to the museum quality of the gallery. There was a leak in the roof, so I quickly went into the other rooms in order to not let the unfortunate leak ruin my experience of bathing in the aura of the whole scene—beautiful paintings, luxurious gallery. Unfortunately, the other room's ceiling had sprung a leak as well. I began studying the paintings more closely, trying with increasing difficulty to shut out the sound of the leaks filling pots. I thought for a moment how this old and glorious building might even fall down soon; a little voice in me said we should probably leave, but simultaneously I thought I would have time to look at a few more paintings before the ceiling gave way—the leaks were that bad. My friend caught up with me, and I made some quizzical comment about the leaks—how funny they seemed in this context. She said, "I think it's intended." "No, it can't be," I insisted, looking more carefully at the ceiling. "Yes," she said politely, "that's the exhibit; you listen to the sound of the rain filling the various buckets." "No!?" I said again, this time with an increasingly intense rush of perverse pleasure. Socialist-realist paintings in an old, leaky gallery staged at the moment when the former USSR was crumbling—a somewhat sad irony. Again, if that were the whole message, then we could have stayed home and listened to it on NPR. Kabakov set the pots up in a way to make what he calls "water music"—to find the pleasure in the decay and change. The pleasure of flux(us) was here, but now thought through on an entirely new level. We sat there and listened and smiled, and walked around the gallery laughing and talking, and we listened in on others laughing and talking. This seemingly luxurious but decrepit place regained some of its imagined luster—now with a new ring: ding, plop, flupta, flupta. Those leaky ceilings and tin pots excited me to propose a practice (which this chapter describes). The coda for this new practice could come from Kabakov: "in the world of the slightly sad, but at the same time, high and flourishing harmony that is so unexpectedly resounding here." As the leaky roof at Frank Lloyd Wright's appropriately named "Falling Water" illustrates, the flux and leak are not ornamental. The signs of decay are the *jouissance* of architecture and modernity.

5 | The Role of the Public Intellectual

> The only thing worse than being talked about is not being talked about.
>
> OSCAR WILDE

With the publication of Barthes's autobiography, bookstores in Paris filled display windows and catered to the public's interest in this academic celebrity's story. In the United States, such fascination with a scholar in the humanities is rare. Scientific experts may appear on news programs or in a PBS series, but news programs rarely discuss issues relevant to the humanities. That situation of benign neglect changed, perhaps for the worse, for a few years during the late 1980s and early 1990s. Right-wing critics of the humanities and higher education jettisoned themselves into the limelight and into the public's imagination. Surprisingly, questions about the relevance of Plato, the strategies of French poststructuralism and deconstruction, and feminist literary criticism took center stage in public policy debates and had the aura of national significance. Considering that humanities texts usually sell embarrassingly few copies, all this attention should have satisfied the wishes of academics eager for public recognition and influence. Of course, anyone who lived through those years knows that the humanities became infamous, not revered and respected. Unexpectedly, bookish English professors found themselves publicly attacked and mocked by media-savvy critics until the public began to distrust the entire pro-

117

fession. The debates inflected terms like "desire" and "sexuality" with ominous suggestions of social control.

Unfortunately, before these challenges to new disciplines like semiotics reached the public, Barthes died. If he had lived to participate in these publicized challenges, his approach would certainly have drawn on his work on love as well as his autobiographical methods. His contribution would have included arguments about the importance of pleasure in academic scholarship and a third position that favors neither ideological analyses nor classical rhetoric. More importantly, he would undoubtedly have played the unfashionable pose of the whipping boy for critics like dominatrix Camille Paglia and tough-guy Allan Bloom. In doing so, he would have created an artificial mythology around his own celebrity. Instead of the conservative critic acting out the naturalized myth of the hard-boiled detective, for example, to challenge the academic mob, the Barthesian critic wears his often masochistic desire on his sleeve, upsetting the neat opposition set up by the conservative critics and reinforced, unwittingly, by the strong defense of the academics. With these contributions, the debates about social demeanor would have shifted to focus on academic demeanor in the face of the changes in higher education (e.g., the use of new technologies). Instead of a witch-hunt with acrimonious exchanges, the situation would have resembled a challenge of modern-day media-savvy courtiers. Each round would have used the media for quick wit and hilarious, if subtle, comebacks. If Barthes had lived, then the last laugh would have been his. Who would have thought that the debates about academic demeanor could have been so much fun?

The spate of best-selling books by conservative critics of academics and mainstream educational agendas continues to create an enormous controversy about the relationship between universities and the general public. This book has focused on issues that intersect the interests of cultural studies scholars and the public's concerns and interests. Unfortunately, the most attention lavished on academics' writings and arguments by the public occurred as an outcome of strong and persistent attacks on those arguments and approaches. The critics condemned the views and interests of academics, especially those that overlapped with general social and cultural concerns. In fact, the other chapters in this book could easily serve as a laundry list for critics looking for areas not suited for academic intervention. Issues like multiculturalism were interpreted as a scheme invented by teachers and professors rather than as a particular cultural formation now facing America. Critics accused teachers of leading students down a dangerous path, of taking advantage of their unaccountable tenured positions, and of neglecting their duties to pass down the achievements of Western civilization.

In regard to media aesthetics, the conservative critics of American higher education have taught teachers and activists an important lesson. These critics' great achievement and innovation have nothing to do with the content of their arguments or their apocalyptic tone. They have an uncanny, and carefully researched, ability to use aesthetic techniques for powerful effects. They use narrative in the portrayal of the conflict and a lampooning strategy borrowed directly from TV (e.g., *Saturday Night Live*'s parodies), movies (any teen movie about school with a boring, prim, and correct teacher), and popular magazines (most notably *National Lampoon*). The *Saturday Night Live* skit, which mocked *60 Minutes'* weekly staging of the Left versus Right conflict, presciently summarized the tone and strategies of the later cultural conflicts over higher education. When the Shana Alexander character, "Jane," concluded her remarks, the obnoxious James Kirkpatrick character began each week's response with, "Jane, you ignorant slut," to the audience's great delight. The Right, adopting the *Saturday Night Live*'s parody version of Kirkpatrick as their model, correctly assumed that a nasty lampooning strategy would win more favor among the general population. The academics under attack all too often tried to appeal to calm reasonableness and merely accused their critics of gross distortions and inaccuracies. The Left had forgotten the effectiveness of their own use of name-calling (e.g., sexist pig) and *scandalography* (e.g., Abbie Hoffman throwing dollar bills onto the floor of the New York Stock Exchange). Dinesh D'Souza's editorship of the *Dartmouth Review* often used parody as a weapon. For example, in the infamous article "Dis Sho Ain't No Jive, Bro," a reporter parodied African-American dialect in order to mock affirmative action programs. Not coincidentally, the movie *Animal House* was based on a Dartmouth fraternity. One Princeton history professor characterized D'Souza as having "a remorselessly adolescent sense of humor." It was precisely that sense of humor that won such a large audience for the otherwise stiff and boring conservatives.

This lampooning strategy, borrowed from movies, showed how much D'Souza and the radical Right owed to their own study of media and what I call *scandalography*. The conservative critics taught academics little about the importance of classical education. They demonstrated that parody and aesthetic decisions in general have an enormous power to instruct and persuade. Perhaps the leftists' concerns with authentic identity and unmasking deceptions made them deaf to the importance of media aesthetics not as mere symptoms of underlying sociopolitical forces but as a new form of criticism. Instead of demythologizing the conservatives' criticisms, an artificial mythology will read the critics as guides to popularization and find the untapped potential of these criticisms using Barthes's suggestion that "it is within speech that speech must be fought, led astray."[1] Artificial mythologies lead the debate astray in order to appreciate an alternative to the binary oppositions currently limiting the debates about curriculum reform and the role of the humanities in American culture.

Popularizing Intellectuals

Barthes was no stranger to celebrity. As one of a group of unusually famous French intellectuals who together initiated the structuralist and poststructuralist revolutions in humanities scholarship, he had an international reputation and influence with less of the controversy and contentiousness surrounding his compatriots Lacan and Derrida. The enormous influence on scholars of these theorists' works and the increasingly wide popular audience for their works incited the conservative criticisms in the United States. In fact, the celebrity of these French intellectuals allowed for the attack to have an ethnocentric component claiming contamination of American minds with foreign ideas.

The more important issue brought to the fore by the debates about these intellectuals' influence concerns the popularization of humanities scholarship. Whether one agrees with Barthes or the conservative critics, they both taught one important lesson to academics seeking a more relevant curriculum and a wider popular appeal. They demonstrated the popularizing of scholarly thought and debates as well as the seductiveness of their prose and theories. Although conservative and liberal critics alike note the estrangement of academics from popular forums, the emergent academic discourse called cultural studies describes these problems rather than speculates on models for popularizing research in the humanities. Efforts to have scholarly books cross over into popular markets using everything from packaging and layout to racy topics and speculative approaches, the emergence of academic celebrities with followings outside their disciplines, and even the growth of World Wide Web home pages and list servers for large and amorphous groups of interested parties have already changed the intellectual landscape dramatically.

Understanding the new roles for academics will take time in spite of the urgent need to answer continuing attacks on humanities research and theory. Narrowly cast messages will also, in an apparent paradox, make scholars' research more widely available. Again, Barthes's work holds a clue to this development. His work appealed to a very specific audience, which grew into a large popular, but not mass, following. If Barthes's works imply that artificial mythologies function as recipes for cultural innovation, then the third, seemingly absurd position, between the opponents in the cultural debates suggests new questions and novel solutions to problems confronting higher education. Instead of an innovation born from the struggles of creative geniuses, this artificial invention allows for new combinations to occur, in this case, the combination of radical conservative and radical feminist thought to suggest a model for popularizing scholarly work. The particular conceptions of these culture debates, curriculum reform, and higher education's relationship to sociopolitical power can sometimes stymie innovation. How cultural studies, conservative critics, and "the silent majority" conceptualize the function, workings, problems, and issues surrounding the culture debates inevitably will close down other conceptualizations. The scholarship proposed here suggests that academics use their knowledge differently, neither as a tool for aggressive attack nor as a building block for further descriptive knowledge. This practice uses the scholarship in a way that strengthens a contingent performance rather than in the way a modern student expresses clearly and quickly the "correct" answer; that is, instead of merely adding more knowledge by curriculum reform, the method proposed here uses knowledge to allow the student to follow personal fascinations as well as to appreciate the importance of media savviness.

What's All the Fuss About

The charges that a politically liberal slant to university curricula will have a strong, and adverse, effect on students took hold of the critics' imagination. When researchers conducted sociological studies to examine these issues, they found that universities have had little impact on students' beliefs, actions, or political positions. For example, Alexander Astin, who carried out large-scale studies of college students' attitudes and cognitive development in the early 1990s, explains that "unlike earlier generations of college students, students today show little evidence of the 'liberalizing' effect of the undergraduate experience. . . . In other words, the liberal-conservative balance shows little change during the four years after students enter college."[2] Educators and critics alike probably do not want to hear that message. The efforts at curriculum reform as well as the calls for a return to moral education both assume students will change their attitudes and beliefs as well as their knowledge base. However, these findings probably fit well with the research of scholars of media and cultural impact. Film and television theorists, for example, have long argued that media reinforce, rather than create, attitudes and beliefs. Of course, at some point the accumulation (of particular types of messages) does begin to have a great influence over how the majority of people in any culture view a situation. As messages reinforce each other, mythologies appear on specific topics. Out of these myths general worldviews or ideologies arise. The conservative critics claim that humanities professors conspire together through publications and conferences to present a specific ideology. The critics call for a return to an ideology-free education with open advocacy of particular moral imperatives and truths. The sociological studies indicate that the attacks apparently target the wrong antagonists. Even students seem little swayed by professors' opinions or ideologies. The apparently misguided attacks on educators have less to do with the naïveté of the critics than with the sophistication of the media-savvy handlers and advocates of these conservative critics. The critics' attacks will have only limited impact on American university agendas. Economic crises and technological changes will have a much greater and more profound impact. In trying to understand why a well-funded appeal would focus on what most members of the public view as a war of words, an analysis of the situation would have to understand the conflict in narrative and representational terms. The critics stage a moral tale not for the task of routing out evil in universities but to capture the imaginations of the public using mass media. The critics have, perhaps unwittingly, noticed what those involved with the information superhighway now realize: the key to disseminating knowledge in the twenty-first century may involve going directly to a large public audience and narrowly cast demographic groups simultaneously by using electronic media. Even the best-selling books depended on the electronic spectacles. The critics' message has less to do with higher education than with an artificial mythology: a way to popularize intellectual arguments by wrapping them in narrative, spectacle, and aesthetic strategies.

Strangely enough, professors of literature became major targets of the critics even as those educators understood better than anyone the methods and strategies used in the attacks. Again, the critics reached out to a kind of peer-group pressure. They sought to make their message a populist appeal to students as well as parents. They know what most students, professors, and parents already knew: "*the student's peer group is the single most potent source of influence on growth and development during the undergraduate years*" (emphasis in original).[3] Not to overstate the case too much, this sociological study did find that the general liberalizing changes that do occur among students in college include acceptance of feminism, support for legal abortion, and a more accepting attitude toward alcohol consumption. The conservative critics will no doubt point to the abortion issue, but it is the peer group that appears to create that change in attitude rather than anything learned in courses. In fact, one could imagine a narrative involving the most conservative students getting drunk, having sex, spending time with the opposite sex as equal partners rather than in sex-segregated high-school cliques, and finally having to deal with an unwanted pregnancy. With all these changes in college students' lives, the messages of liberal and radical professors probably have little impact. The most powerful messages from both liberal and conservative sources find their way into mass media and into the cocktail conversation of students. Lectures and homework may, in fact, no longer offer the best method of disseminating information to students. The critics of higher education inadvertently taught the public and the professors a lesson: make the messages function equally well in printed analytic forms, in media forms, and by word of mouth. In short, the attacks took the form of something like an oral cultural form more fitting to a television-electronic culture than analytic print forms alone. Those new forms of information packaging do not discount the importance of written analytic communication. Rather they combine these more traditional scholarly methods with media forms.

The furor over "political correctness," which first appeared in the press during the fall of 1990, accused the *teachers* (the partying stu-

dents were innocent dupes) of trying to repress free speech by obses-
sively focusing courses on the oppression of women and minorities
rather than on the liberation of people in general.⁴ According to the
right-wing criticisms, these so-called postmodern professors presented
Western culture as a mere symptom of sexist and racist prejudices and
class conflicts. And worse, they fanned "the flame of ethnic and sexual discontent among the students."⁵ It appears that the critics understood two key factors. The educators needed only to encourage the
existing discontent and channel it into particular ideologies. The critics also understood the importance of focusing on the same issue
that the professors had highlighted: difference—sexual, ethnic, and
racial differences. The criticism of higher education advocated assimilation and unity rather than identity and difference. The attack needed
to dismiss this emphasis on difference without making that more complicated issue the ground for battle. To displace the battle from a
group's rights versus assimilation and unity to some other overlapping issue, the attack needed a titillating and provocative issue easily
packaged in the media's electronic culture. The issue objected to by
the critics became the perversion of sexual desire. In other words, the
attack claimed that postmodern polemicists sullied what some might
call good, old natural desires. In these professors' classes, the "weird
concern with sexual questions" tainted (male hetero-) sexuality with
suspicion. In their courses, artworks and literature became psychoanalytic symptoms of a lurking pernicious (white male) desire. These
usually unnamed professors also insisted on "imposing official speech
codes," and the "prissiness" of the atmosphere supposedly came to
resemble the McCarthy era. The political repression spread to museums, journalism, and public-school curricula. To contain and reverse
this domino effect, right-wing critics began a campaign to shame university administrators and to anger alumni over the conduct of these
postmodern professors.

These unnamed professors advocated a peculiar type of scholarship that combined liberal or Marxist politics, French psychoanalysis
and deconstruction, and feminism in studies of literature, art, media,
and culture. Although few of the conservative critics actually seriously
engaged an individual scholar's work, an understanding of the specifics
of the media and cultural theories under attack clearly shows how
the critics framed the issues. The animosity between the parties had no
truces or common ground for negotiations. In this climate, no one

cared to carefully work through the opposition's arguments and theories. Explaining precisely the emphases and nuances of individual feminist media theories would lessen the critic's ability to associate these theories as a group with broader social, cultural, and educational decline. A complicated and narrowly cast theory usually sounds more reasonable and less influential than specific sloganlike phrases and vulgarized assumptions taken out of context. In examining the conservatives' attack on contemporary feminist theories, a brief explanation of those theories from a scholarly perspective will help to disarticulate the rhetoric of the battle from the construction of theories.

In the broadest sociological perspective, film theory, infused with the revolutionary zeal and frustrations of the counterculture of the late 1960s and early 1970s, rejected an explicit aesthetic in favor of a political polemic. It initiated the shift from film-as-aesthetic-object to spectator-as-sociopolitical-effect. To describe subjectivity as conventional, neither universal nor natural, allowed theorists to focus on the social construction of reality. Specifically, it allowed for an explanation of how particular forms of social organization created a manipulated consensus. According to this model, cinema, especially classical Hollywood narrative cinema, creates subjects (i.e., subjects of, for example, patriarchal-capitalism) to maintain and reproduce existing relations of socioeconomic production. Both the critics and the theorists would probably agree with this broad overview.

The psychoanalytic theory tends not to appear in the critics' attacks except in a general dismissal. The theorist argued that through the "misrecognition" of a unified existence separate from others, spectators reconstruct themselves as individuals, undetermined by history and social formations, and free to choose commodities and lifestyles. Both groups agree that the fulcrum of this media theory depends on an epistemological reversal of humanism: from subjects-as-cause to subjects-as-effects. The theory stresses the machinations involved in reinforcing individual subjectivities as consumers rather than producers, while the critics' version stresses the supposed discounting of individual creativity, self-expression, and especially the importance of the contribution of great geniuses through the ages. The theorist wanted to examine spectators, not producers. This shift forms the basis of the conservative criticisms. Efforts to include alternative creative geniuses, women writers for example, were greeted with claims of relativism and abandonment of the Western tradition. Still the major complaint concerned the focus on aesthetic achievement as part of a somewhat pernicious ideology rather than as evidence of human advancement.

Ideology-criticism used an amalgam of Lacanian psychoanalytic feminism, Althusserian Marxism, Barthesian cine-semiotics, and Derridean deconstruction and demystification and resembled the earlier Frankfurt School's pessimistic criticisms of both mindless conformity and the hegemonic power of the consciousness industry.[6] The ideology-criticism argued that creating conformity, or making someone an unwitting subject of a social order, involved a complicated and tenuous process. To understand that process, scholars needed to study how aesthetic form (for example, editing techniques and other filmmaking conventions) interacted with visual comprehension, personal desires and identifications, and political processes. They not only studied how the system worked smoothly, but they also exposed the tensions and failures in the otherwise "invisible style." Although this ambitious set of goals has provoked constant and vehement opposition since its emergence, first in *Cahiers du Cinéma,* and then in *Screen,* it gained wide and enthusiastic acceptance in American media studies. By the mid-1980s, theorists began examining problems and solutions to forming new disciplines, like cultural studies. Theorists did not want merely to extend ideology-criticism's scope of explanation beyond cinema studies. They wanted to find a more stable and powerful institutional home in American universities. During the 1970s and 1980s, film scholars often legitimated their discipline by reference to a specialized "school" of theory. In doing so, they inadvertently made the value of cinema studies depend on the relevance of foundational theories (e.g., Lacanian psychoanalysis). Once scholars reevaluated and criticized how theorists *applied* psychoanalysis and poststructuralism, some scholars merely abandoned any effort to theorize film, while others sought to patch up the obvious problems. Film studies, threatened institutionally by its own offspring, cultural and especially television studies, and theoretically by widespread dissatisfaction with its methods of research and scholarship, also had to contend in the late 1980s with conservative attacks on its importance for college students. For media and cultural theorists themselves, the productive enthusiasm surrounding ideology-criticism had faded by the early 1990s. Indeed, as the right wing began their dated attacks, many media scholars had already moved on to other theoretical approaches. While media theorists began writing about the cracks in the edifice of ideology-criticism, vulgarized versions of media theory spread throughout the humanities, into museums and public schools, and into the angry minds of conservative critics.

The critics focused on the larger assumptions rather than the specific readings of aesthetic forms and textual practices. The contemporary feminist media theories initially adopted what film scholars called a cine-semiotic approach. This approach combined Christian Metz's analysis of textual practices with an appreciation of the crucial importance of gender differences in spectatorship. Of course, the conservative critics saw this claim of the fundamental importance of gender in interpretation as a challenge to appreciating the production of great works rather than to the reading of great works. Once the theorists opened the door to two opposed readings or interpretations, then the singular greatness and achievement of the work was called into question. It was great for white male European audiences, for example, but not for women of color. Again, the inclusion of new readers did not bother the critics as much as the sense that art reflected an ideology that benefited only one group in a society. Just as the critics initiated these attacks, the theorists had moved on to more complicated appreciations of reading and spectatorship. They no longer advocated interpreting aesthetic works in terms of a monolithic ideology.

Another important rhetorical issue concerned the "generation gap" in the United States between those who came of age during World War II and those who came of age during the height of the Vietnam War. While the conservative critics vaguely allude to the authors of these theories as baby boomers, the theories actually did begin appearing in the late 1970s, when the generation born between 1948 and 1953 entered the professions and began publishing. For example, Laura Mulvey's "Narrative Cinema and Visual Pleasure" appeared in 1975. Camera Obscura, a very influential journal focusing on feminism and film theory, began publishing in 1977, and m/f, another important feminist theory journal, began publishing in 1978. The attack on a generation became a crucial rhetorical ploy used in the critics' arguments. Portrayed as 1960s radicals with power, the academics found it as difficult to challenge this attack on their age as the conservatives found it to challenge the "don't trust anyone over 35" attacks during the late 1960s and early 1970s. As in other instances, the conservatives borrowed the same rhetorical strategies used to such advantage against them only fifteen years earlier.

Another aspect of the dispute concerned the proper methodologies for studying the humanities. The feminists sought to "unsettle" the epistemological assumptions of traditional empirical studies of cinema, media, and culture. And like the cine-semioticians, they argued that the empirical model found its complement in classical realist narrative cinema. The feminists employed semiotics to demonstrate how classical realist cinema depends on the illusion that in the cinema the gap between sign and referent barely exists at all. What we see does not look constructed as much as captured by the camera. It is difficult to actually see the process of filmmaking while watching a Hollywood movie. They relocated feminist cinema studies away from analyses of "images" of women to analyses of the way media organize vision and hearing in predictable ways. The conservative critics tend to blur this important distinction. For example, in arguments against political correctness, the older analyses of negative images of women are associated with deconstruction, psychoanalysis, and contemporary feminist theory. The later theories focused on optics, while the earlier theories focused on sociology and attitude formation. The two groups of feminists rarely agreed on an appropriate approach to feminist analyses. These groups tended to describe themselves either as theorists or as cultural historians, but rarely as both. The theorists employed the psychoanalytic theories to explain that women's self-images in films often functioned as a being-for-another (a being-as-being-seen). Men looked at women as objects. The critics collapsed the criticisms of empirical studies of media with the emphasis on images of women in media. In doing so, they attacked these readings as politically motivated by special interests rather than empirically accurate descriptions. In fact, scholars interested in images on television, for example, increasingly used empirical research devoid of any theoretical or political analysis. On the other hand, the critics of empirical research began exploring alternative media practices and advocating new forms of scholarship. These new forms of scholarship were ignored in the attacks on academics because the new forms had more to do with new technologies and new institutional demands on publishing more and making research more relevant or accessible to a general public. In some ways, the critics of academics had focused on an earlier moment in media and cultural studies. That moment in feminist ideology-criticism occurred in the late 1970s, not in the late 1980s. The critics never named Mulvey's writings of the late 1970s as the epitome of everything they opposed, but they could have easily chosen her work as a prime example of feminist attacks on mainstream culture and great aesthetic achievement.

Mulvey built on and adapted Christian Metz's psychoanalytic film theory. Metz rethought formalist analysis, favored by the conservative critics, by adding the dimension of how formal aspects allowed for specific spectator positions. Mulvey examined and stressed the importance of specific types of pleasure in spectatorship. According to these theories, why we go to the cinema and why we enjoy going has as much, if not more, to do with the position from which we see (or hear) films as with any particular content. The story is not as important as the visual style. That is, if the movie does not fulfill those expectations of continuity and seamless views of the action, then the spectators will call the film "bad." On this account, the critics and the theorists agreed. And, according to Mulvey and Metz, certain films (especially films from classical Hollywood cinema) encourage particular spectator positions. In her recent work, Mulvey recognizes that "the either/or binary pattern of her earlier theorization left the argument trapped within its own conceptual frame of reference, unable to advance politically into a new terrain or suggest an alternative theory of spectatorship in the cinema."[7] The picture of spectatorship and subject positioning she offered in her earlier work functions as the target of the attacks on media studies. In Mulvey's earlier conception of spectatorship, the "male gaze" regards Woman as a "to-be-seen" object. Her application of psychoanalysis constructs an image of male desire in which men derive sadistic pleasure from creating and seeing women as objects. For Mulvey, Hollywood narrative films allow men to eroticize the objectification of women's bodies. The male viewer identifies with the male hero and sadistically acts out vicariously voyeurism, fetishism, and narcissism. In this explication of the male gaze, Mulvey reevaluates and extends Metz's conception of the "transcendental signifier" by examining the specificity of the cinema's system of address according to gender. In this rereading of Metz's psychoanalytic theory of film, patriarchal discourse defines the gender category of Woman as lack and as lacking; Woman must be lacking in order for the patriarchy to appear abundantly powerful, but Woman's lack threatens to destabilize the patriarchal order as a castration threat. So, the patriarchy must first flaunt women as lacking and then try to contain that lack. Spectators watch films like masculine protagonists watch and control feminine characters. In this sense, the "transcendental subject" is a position usually only open to male-identified viewers; the male protagonists function as ideal egos, while the male-identified spectator (mis)recognizes the character as a stand-in for "his" ego. Captivated by this image of the self (Imaginary signifier), the male spectator identifies with the omnipotent male protagonist; the woman-as-spectacle becomes either demystified (punished) or fetishized (disavowing the threat of lack). For example, Mulvey reads Josef Von Sternberg's films as encouraging the sadistic fetishization of Marlene Dietrich's body. In sum, for Mulvey, both plot and production depend on the effacement of difference in the (dis)placement of women and reality as mere objects or images to be seen. The Hollywood cinema teaches us that women are meant to *look* beautiful, presenting a seamless image to the world so that men, in confronting difference, can avoid the recognition of lack. Mulvey connects this to-be-seen quality to what she calls "the male gaze," because the images (of women) supposedly exist only as images for the male scopic drive. In this sense, any apparently unsullied view of reality in the cinema holds in place the opposition between male sadistic lookers and female objects.

The feminist theorists devised ways to understand this mechanism as well as offered alternatives. The critics again saw this methodological change as a dangerous development. From a brief summary of the feminists' positions, one can easily see why the critics and the theorists could never find a common ground. The theorists used the opposition of coded visual constructions versus the deconstruction of these codes in a feminine writing practice. This *feminine écriture* could ruin representation and ultimately lead to a differential articulation of subjectivity. The new practice could dismantle the Western episteme, dominated by patriarchal logic. A feminine discourse could articulate the "unrepresentability" of the body in patriarchy by attempting to apply deconstruction as an opposition to the patriarchal "social code." Annette Kuhn's description of "deconstructive" cinema focuses on films that break down and possibly analyze the modes of signification (or meaning construction) characteristic of dominant cinema.[8] Significantly, she adds that within the film itself, deconstructive cinema departs in content and form from the dominant mode. It renders impossible the kinds of spectator identification typically set up by "realist" cinema. And it engenders a critical attitude. She explains that "in the final instance" deconstructive films acquire their deconstructive force only from their context. Deconstructive cinema needs to focus on only a few general discursive codes—it problematizes these codes but does not exhaust them. Her notion of deconstruction offers an implicit critique of Noël Burch's use of the term *deconstruction*. It does not merely foreground codes essential and specific to film, as in Burch's model of deconstructive cinema, but it also offers a critical approach to meanings and messages. Burch's model offers an ahistorical "deconstructive cinema" that remains outside the conditions of consumption. Kuhn's model of deconstruction has a more anti-illusionist agenda than Burch's deconstruction as the "parametric play of codes."[9] Although the conservative critics would probably lump Burch's formalist Marxism with the feminist deconstructions, the distinctions again show the important aspect and contribution of feminist analysis. Feminists stressed the importance of historically contingent and gender-specific readings over the achievements of production. This aspect of the argument tends to get muddied and lost in the rhetorical battles. Even Burch shifts the ground from production to the process of an institutional practice, including how spectators learn to read films.

Burch explains that theorists cannot reduce the institution of Hollywood cinema to the film industry. It also includes the mental machinery involved in how spectators interiorize the codes of the cinema: everything that makes the spectators "accustomed to movies." The "deconstructive" cinema of experimental filmmakers returns to the conventions of the early cinema to challenge the Institutional Mode of Representation's linkage of cinematic codes with ideological frames. Although Burch stressed the ideological dimension of media, he did not completely engage with gender issues.

The feminist theorists had two competing positions about how gender influenced reading and spectating. The earlier essentialist theories argued for a pregiven, innate, natural, biological basis for gender differences. The feminists criticized essentialism in the general shift away from humanistic interpretations of ideology toward structuralist models, as described earlier. During the late 1970s, calls for political change required rejecting essentialist theories.[10] From the early 1980s, leading British feminists adapted Lacan's psychoanalysis into the broader nonessentialist structuralist arguments.[11] Lacan's formulation allowed for a structurally constructed, rather than biologically determined, notion of gender.

Again, the very premise of these theories can never find agreement with the conservatives' positions. The conservatives, however, tend to see the battle as monolithic, while the theorists have many competing views. One of the most productive changes has been to read cinema (or culture in general) not in terms of a masculine gaze or a sadistic gaze. Gaylyn Studlar's *In the Realm of Pleasure: Von Sternberg, Dietrich, and the Masochistic Aesthetic* takes a different approach.[12] In another context, I took the book too harshly to task for its manipulations of psychoanalytic theory. The real achievement of the work is Studlar's nuanced use of the masochistic aesthetic. She analyzes "many of the psychoanalytic assumptions that have provided the foundation of feminist film theory's consideration of the role of sexual difference in spectatorial pleasure and [suggests] new directions for understanding the interplay of spectatorship, gender, and identity formation" (3). She focuses on six films by Josef Von Sternberg as anomalies "to show how these films are informed by pleasures that cannot be accounted for in current theory" (3). She rejects "Freudian-Lacanian" film theory and builds a psychoanalytic model based on Gilles Deleuze's rethinking of masochism, which applies to cinematic pleasure in general. That is, we can read cinematic pleasure according to a masochistic aesthetic rather than as a catalyst for sadism. Like Mulvey, Studlar rethinks Metz's imaginary signifier, but instead of extending his notion to include the cinema's system of address according to gender, Studlar explains that the disavowal essential to maintaining the spectator's position depends on the perception of separation from the film's illusion of reality. Metz's famous phrase for describing disavowal is "I know but nevertheless . . ." But, Studlar says,

> the voyeuristic separation of subject/screen object does not automatically align the spectator with sadism, as Metz implies in *The Imaginary Signifier*. . . . Contrary to Metz, sadism is the one perversion in which separation of object and subject is neither required nor maintained. . . . Masochistic desire, by contrast, depends upon separation to guarantee a pain/pleasure structure. . . . Like the masochist, but unlike the sadist, the spectator must avoid the orgasmic release that destroys the boundaries of disavowal, takes him/her outside the limits of normal spectatorship and into the realm of the true voyeur, and disrupts the magical thinking that defines the infantile use of the cinematic object. (27)

In the cinema, masochism, not sadism, functions as the analogous perversion of looking. In regard to that looking, Studlar explains that

Mulvey neglected the role of masochism in the structure of the gaze. She cites David Rodowick, who writes, "Mulvey defines fetishistic scopophilia as an overvaluation of the object... but [Freud] would also add that this phenomenon is one of the fundamental sources of authority defined as passive submission to the object: in sum masochism" (37, quoting Rodowick). From this, Studlar explains that the "logical conclusion" of Mulvey's article is that masochism should be paired with fetishistic scopophilia (37). In other words, visual pleasure is not necessarily an action of control and mastery; the look maintains a tension between control and loss of control not only "in the *act* of the look, but also in the *return* of the look" (37, quoting Rodowick). Studlar associates the film's relay of looks with something besides an active, sadistic gaze and connects fetishism to a masochistic aesthetic. She argues that pleasure for the male spectator need not be achieved "exclusively through a controlling, essentially sadistic gaze. Control is turned across to the female; pleasure is found in the renunciation of domination" (49).

In her rethinking of spectatorship and visual pleasure away from the sadistic male gaze and toward a bisexual masochistic engagement with looking, Studlar makes two important claims about the structure of the gaze. First, she argues that to claim that women do not fetishize the bodies of characters in films promotes "the general cultural sanction against women's public right to sexual looking" (45). Instead, she says:

> All film spectators can be said to watch a "fantasmatic gone awry," a fantasy disengaged from the body and no longer serviceable as a purely masturbatory object.... Scopophilia, like fetishism, originates in precastration complex development and predates Oedipal conflict and genital sexuality. In "Face-Breast Equation," Renato Almansi traces the origins of scopophilia to the oral phase and the relationship of the child to the mother. (47)

And, Studlar continues, "The imaginary fusion with the cinematic dream screen results in a loss of ego boundaries analogous to the child's pre-sleep fusion with the breast" (184). That is, masochistic scopophilia is based on a pre-Oedipal and pregenital fusion between face and breast, where the child willingly loses control at the dream screen of the mother's breast. In reference to the possibility of using a sadomasochistic feminist practice as a "deliberate, premeditated erotic blasphemy," Studlar explains that her use is more analogical and based on a symbolic likeness between spectatorship and masochism — in that sense she argues for a masochistic aesthetic instead of masochism per se (215, n. 8). So, in terms of the masochistic aesthetic, the spectator's gaze resembles a bisexual loss of control; therefore, vision need not be associated with control and mastery. This description of a masochistic gaze has much in common with Barthes's punctum, which returns the gaze and wounds him in a moment of fascination. He cannot turn away nor does he want to turn away from the painful encounter. His mastery fails throughout the later works as he uses this masochistic aesthetic.

Studlar explains that the characters in film return the gaze of the audience: "The Von Sternberg/Dietrich heroine is the object of male desire, but she is not the passive object of a controlling look. Dietrich looks back or initiates the look" (48). From this observation, Studlar argues that the object can function as a subject; the disrupting gaze comes from, for Studlar, the characters in films. Again, this description can easily describe the workings of Barthes's later works, where the objects and situations around him comment on his failed metalinguistic efforts at transcendence and his unhappy journeys through love, otherness, and even his own subjectivity. With Studlar's masochistic aesthetic, one can cast Barthes as a masochistic acting out with the attackers of academics. Instead of arguing for a mastery over the rhetorical playing field, he demonstrates a different strategic encounter with the critics. Their claims against the antihumanist attacks on aesthetic achievements as ideological usually meet with strong humanistic counterattacks that claim that the broadening of the curriculum can only benefit the students. These claims miss the important stress on interpretation and reading positions that the feminist theorists introduced. A Barthesian punctum practice, a truly masochistic aesthetic endeavor because it leads to a loss of mastery and an unsettling of subjectivity, that leads to an artificial mythology about the debate would change the framing of the situation instead of arguing within the given positions and topics. A clue to where the Barthesian *dérive* would begin comes from the more moderate conservative attacks on academic media studies.

The complaints have come not only from shrill, angry old curmudgeons like Allan Bloom. Robert Hughes, like the more bombastic conservative critics, condemns professors' cultural theories as well. He argues that these theories supposedly frame "natural" desires and stifle the "creative passionate energies of aesthetic output." He shares the Anglo-American distrust of "French thought," and the suspicion of terms like "phallocentricism."[13] As Henry Lewis Gates notes, this "book-length complaint about complaint" repeats the same arguments we have heard before about how "particularisms on parade (ethnic, racial, sexual) threaten to fragment a once unified polity."[14] Because Hughes focuses on an already high-profile issue (and gets reviewed in the most prominent book reviews), one cannot help but wonder if he avoids the "annoying" habits of right-wing critics. For example, although he avoids Bloom's wholesale condemnation of feminists and advocates a woman's right to choose to have an abortion, Hughes attacks "Baby Boomer academics, members of a moralizing and sanctimonious generation both left and right" (25). This rather strange chauvinism against a whole generation of scholars might suggest that the underlying conflict has to do with the transition of power, prestige, and visibility between Hughes's generation and those academics and intellectuals now in their forties and early fifties.

Like other conservative critics, Hughes objects to "PC" language and, unfortunately, never comments on a more appropriate way to allow for language to change (24). Politically correct or not, language in America changes constantly and rapidly. Do these changes create a conflict because they suggest an academic intention? In trying to place the blame for these changes, Hughes argues against the teacher's correctness. In American populist rhetoric and movies, rebelling against the teacher's rules of correctness has a long and proud history and wide social acceptance. Anti-intellectualism is as American as apple pie — and as conventional. Yet, Hughes objects to the conventional and boring repetitions found in so much politicized art and media theory.

On the other hand, Hughes's genuine ambivalence distinguishes his complaints from other, shriller conservative critics; he condemns right-wing critics for promoting the same "Us versus Them" opposition they accuse the academics of advocating. Gates notes that this book is not merely "another installment in the series that includes Allan Bloom's *The Closing of the American Mind*, Roger Kimball's *Tenured Radicals*, Dinesh D'Souza's *Illiberal Education*, Charles J. Sykes's *A Nation of Victims*, Martin Anderson's *Impostors in the Temple*, and Thomas Sowell's *Inside American Education*. And Hughes's subtitle — *The Fraying of America* — calls to mind Arthur Schlesinger's

The Disuniting of America" (Gates, 113). Hughes points out that the "loss of reality by euphemism and lies was twenty times worse and more influential in the utterances of the last two Presidents and their aides than among *bien-pensant* academics, although you didn't find any complaints about that in *Commentary* or the *New Criterion*" (27). And much like Scott Henson and Tom Philpott, who researched how right-wing funds "credentialized" conservative cultural critics, Hughes sees the irony in "the choir of conservatives denouncing 'well-subsidized left academics' as bludgeoners, whilst taking their own subsidies from various right-wing foundations" (80). As Gates notes, "The paradox of the cultural right, as Hughes perceives it, is to contribute to the very fragmentation that it decries" (Gates, 114). Picking up on the apocalyptic tone and Nazi motif of the conflict, Hughes mentions that Pat Buchanan's "Patriotic Correctness" would not appear "out of place in the Reichstag" (44). Most importantly, instead of calling for a "return" to studying classical texts on art and culture as the only foundation for higher education, Hughes advocates "aesthetic intuitive criticism" (202–3). And his own aesthetic achievement as a writer bodes well for his argument. His clear and eloquent prose flows smoothly through many of the issues that hopelessly tangle Bloom, and too many other best-selling conservatives, in a morass of incoherent rantings and turgid prose. Gates notes that Hughes's prose "issues apothegms at a spitfire rate, as if it were written with one eye toward the next edition of Bartlett's. The result can be exhilarating [which] means that the book is more fun to read than it has any right to be. After all, most of its complaints have been made before" (Gates, 114). Hughes is entertaining.

Different from the conservative critics, Hughes does not have a particular fondness for teaching ancient, "eternal," and "universal" truths of Western culture. Therefore, he does not call for eliminating courses on contemporary culture and media. And he advocates shaking up conventionality and, in that sense, implicitly supports curricula that challenge traditional approaches to the arts and humanities. In general, Hughes has a more nuanced approach to the crisis of higher education than any of the right-wing critics. The criticisms of "left-wing academics" often simplify political issues, even as academics complicate issues of race or gender. The last twenty years of scholarship has shown us nothing if not the fluidity of identities. Identity politics and conservative attacks on those politics usually involve cookie-cutter approaches. For Hughes, too many commentators about higher education forget that education should startle and shake students out of their habituated complacency. Art and education gain nothing from handy formulas about social control and oppression or, on the other hand, from a rote memorization of Aristotle's *Aesthetics*.

At once seduced, and repulsed, by the flow of contemporary media-saturated culture, Hughes unwittingly adopts a televisual style of writing. Although he (dis)misses contemporary popular culture, his prose style betrays his intuitive affinity for contemporary media. He combines many cultural allusions in each paragraph for dizzying effects similar to channel surfing. His aesthetic sensibility freed from the idealism of the conservative critics offers an excellent model and guide for the academic theorists he slights. His lessons have less to do with his arguments and opinions than with his craftsmanship and skill.

Hughes's work demonstrates and justifies the importance of media aesthetics for a new form of criticism born out of the conflict over postmodernism. The earlier right-wing versions of media aesthetics used broad, low parody to great effect. Hughes illustrates how a less obvious and less contentious use of aesthetic strategies might work. He leads the way to a new (postmodern) media theory. Unfortunately, he might lead the way kicking and screaming. In Barthes's terms, we need to steal Hughes's language and techniques and use them not as part of cynical attacks on higher education but to theorize the connections between love and knowledge, not just the pleasures but the problems as well.

This reading of kicking and screaming critics of American higher education inevitably reminds me of the risqué acting-out of Camille Paglia. She does not fit nicely into the right-wing critics' camp with which she is often identified, nor with other advocates of using media in higher education. On the one hand, she urges academics to adopt media technologies as a component of teaching and scholarship — something the critics of curriculum reform usually condemn. She argues,

Word-worship has made it difficult for scholarship to deal with the radical cultural change of our era of mass media. Academics are constantly fighting a rearguard action. . . . The humanities must abandon their insular fiefdoms and begin thinking in terms of *imagi* nation . . . There is neither decline nor disaster in the triumph of mass media, only a shift from word to image.[15]

On the other hand, she argues that "feminism has been simplistic in arguing that female archetypes were politically motivated falsehoods by men.... By such techniques of demystification feminism has painted itself into a corner. Sexuality is a murky realm of contradiction and ambivalence. It cannot always be understood by social models" (12, 13). Here she sounds like a less shrill version of Bloom's advocacy of a return to an eternal natural order. In fact, throughout her work she often forgets her own championing of (unnatural) mass media and conjures a murky world of Olympian gods, earth cults, and, most importantly, eternal Nature. She connects this Nature to Woman's biology and argues, much like Bloom and others, for an eternal image of femaleness. For Paglia,

> Nature's cycles are woman's cycles. Biologic femaleness is a sequence of circular returns, beginning and ending at the same point. Woman's centrality gives her a stability of identity. She does not have to become but only to be. Her centrality is a great obstacle to man, whose quest for identity she blocks. (9)

Paglia's sound-bite style of almost disjointed slogans has an incantatory effect in spite of the fact that her conclusions verge on parodies of arguments. Admittedly, this passing allusion to Paglia's ambivalence about identity and media does not analyze her work in any depth; it merely uses it as an important marker in a debate about desire, (media) technology, and culture.

For the purposes of this chapter, Paglia's essentialism in the supposed nature/culture debate suggests just how culturally loaded nature looks when we begin writing books and essays about "Woman's essential nature." For example, to make her point, Paglia discusses Woman's "centrality," a metaphor, and "beginning and ending at the same point," a figurative description of menstruation. She discusses a supposedly transcendent truth as if the "radical cultural change in our era of mass media" has had little effect on sexuality and even "biologic femaleness." To see how biology has changed in our era of mass media, one need only discuss the radical transformations to Ivana Trump's face, Mariel Hemingway's breasts, Phyllis Diller's liposuctioned stomach, or even the changes in female bodies and cycles due to radical mastectomies, delayed menopause, and so on. And beyond these everyday occurrences, how does one account for transsexuals, or, in terms of media, body doubles. Paglia implicitly argues against postmodern feminism's concern with manners by suggesting that those questions are beside the point, and that radical techno-bio-cultural changes under way will have far more significant implications than new norms of behavior. Much in the way that Hughes supports his arguments using media aesthetics, Paglia, in spite of herself, understands the necessity of studying technology for potential clues to designing more appropriate college curricula and scholarly practices. In order to "teach the conflict" as Gerald Graff advocates, we may need to precisely locate the conflict: Is it a matter of manners or media? Barthes's later works answer this question by suggesting that our manner of loving or caressing knowledge produces a new way to handle media. His efforts to think through the body produce his peculiar form of experimental writing. If only Barthes had lived longer, then he might have played the submissive body to Paglia's dominatrix. *A Lover's Discourse* would then become a script for a Deleuzean masochistic contract toward a smooth space where eroticism is no longer ghettoized in genital maturity. This recipe book would have a series of instructions to spread eroticism throughout the body-politic while foregrounding and disrupting power relationships. It would function as a manifesto of an asexuality beyond the binarism of essential versus culturally determined sexuality. It would suggest a different relationship between sexual desire and knowledge. Oh, if only Barthes had lived to see the day.

To understand how desire and knowledge operate in the Barthesian masochistic aesthetic model, we need only turn to those unfortunate situations where desire and intellect are rigorously separated. With the repression of any personal investment in the production of knowledge, desire returns from the repressed in a distorted form as sex scandal or harassment. When James Mark Baldwin criticized William James's model of creative evolution for ignoring the social aspect of knowledge and for not having any constraints on the production of mental variations, he suggested the importance in the early years of the twentieth century of discussing knowledge not as an abstract entity but as embedded in social values and desires. To describe this evolutionary process of the dissemination of knowledge, he used the phrase "social heredity." His definition of truth included "social confirmability," which required other people to agree and similarly understand variations. The "social confirmability" chose "fit ideas" according to the "fitness for imitative reproduction and application."[16] This theory allowed Baldwin to explain how society continues to evolve in spite of the fact that physical selection might no longer play the crucial role in human evolution. Unfortunately, Baldwin's own fate seems to confirm his theory that social context plays a crucial role in determining the truth value of ideas. If "fitness" depended on imitation and application, then an unpopular theorist may doom creative variations. The scandal that sent Baldwin from the ranks of the "most important psychologists" in America, and from his position at the Johns Hopkins University, also appears to have buried his theories in an eighty-year hibernation. Behavioral and then humanistic theories would dominate explanations of creativity and learning during those intervening years. Baldwin's unfortunate personal history appears to have played a role in determining the course of the selection of ideas. Indeed, most psychologists know little about this previous leader of American psychology.[17] Anyone who might guess that desire does not play a role in the evolution of thought may find his story instructive. For after the scandal that sent Baldwin to Europe, his name was literally erased from psychological theory. Many of the major academics in the field quietly denounced him and made sure his theories would fade away. The sin that Baldwin committed against society consisted of an alleged visit to a "house of Negro women" in 1908. His behavior was unacceptable particularly because it involved an interracial encounter in addition to adultery and prostitution. Promiscuity and mixing doomed Baldwin's social explanations of creativity and learning for years to come. It would take more than a strong dose of Barthes's pleasures to allow the connection between desire and knowledge to resurface. Baldwin failed to use his own theories; that is, he failed to recognize the connections between the social scene and the production of knowledge.

The story about Baldwin's particular sexual dalliance would certainly play differently today in the academy. Nevertheless, the debate around curriculum reform still focuses on the issue of correct behavior and proper desires. In the conservative's portrayal, the academic arbiters of taste claimed that students and teachers should make a concerted effort to respect each other *out of a political necessity*.[18] The new sense of decorum demanded, for example, that even if a male professor found the term *girl* acceptable, he should use tact and defer to the prevailing sentiment of female students by using the term *woman* instead. For both academics and the reactionary critics, manners took on an ominous political tone. The particular use of the phrase "political correctness" suggested to critics a climate of prudishness and prim respectability. Correctness connoted something out of a Jane Austen novel rather than care or rigor. One was to be correct, stiff, overly polite. Politics was effaced by a twentieth-century version of *bien-séance*. For example, Stanley Fish explains that a conservative like Benno Schmidt skirts the issue of the community context of speech on campus by "reducing the content to an offense against sensibility. This is the work done by the word 'obnoxious' when Schmidt urges us to protect speech 'no matter how obnoxious in content.' "[19] The conservatives set out on a campaign to defend the "obnoxious" against the "correct." And Americans enjoy identifying, for better or worse, with rough obnoxiousness over prim correctness. Still, Baldwin would no doubt find himself with few allies among conservative critics. These critics are less concerned with the referent of "obnoxious language" than with its place in a metonymic series in culture: it plays well in the media. Baldwin's crime against propriety, that he had inappropriate sex partners (in his case, black women), sullied, even as it proved, his theory of social heredity of ideas. Whether we like it or not, easily seduced and manipulated social forces produce knowledge. Barthes suggests a way to change knowledge, not by abstract reasoning alone but by allowing other forces to promiscuously mix with his systems of thought.

This combination of loving and knowing does not teach us how to know something; it teaches us how to know *of* something, to appreciate the relationship with thinking. Barthes suggests that readers have a light touch that allows the heaviness of theories to dissipate. This light touch introduces pleasure into the academic discourse. Is this the problem that the critics of American higher education have condemned repeatedly, that academics allow their own desires to interfere with students' understanding of the world? Yet, Barthes does not suggest that knowledge function to produce a mastery. Instead, the body functions as an interference to this mastery; it sets in a masochistic aesthetic. As Barthes explains, the body functions "not from the point of view of pleasure, but in relation to what we romantically call love and death."[20] He savors a problem and counteracts the usual indifference to the fate of knowledge. Taken as a guide to this aesthetic, *A Lover's Discourse* reveals that masochistic sentimental lover, discussed earlier in terms of Paglia's dominatrix pose. Revealing desire in the classroom in this way dramatizes, almost caricatures, his personal vulnerability. Admitting his intense stake in the works he examines, Barthes does not merely wallow in a personal confession. He attempts to intervene against the alienation from knowledge. This alienation allows for the belief that social desires somehow exist separately from the progress of thought. This alienation also leads to the inevitable repression of desire and the return of the repressed. Again, Barthes takes great pains to point out that this move does not suggest a transcendent position outside the bounds of institutional sanction or power. He explains that

> to teach or even to speak outside the limits of institutional sanction is certainly not to be rightfully and totally uncorrupted by power: power (the libido dominandi) is there, hidden in any discourse, even when uttered in a place outside the bounds of power. Therefore, the freer such teaching, the further we must inquire into the conditions and processes by which discourse can be disengaged from all will-to-possess.[21]

He acknowledges the implications and makes those interferences part of his lesson. He recognizes that the study of signs, meanings, and cultures depends on social and personal values. He does not stop there but also insists on a loosening or lightening of these relationships in order to increase the flow of knowledge. This loosening he accomplishes by leading the texts astray — scandalizing through fragmentation, digression, and excursus what we took for granted. This activity is not done in a mean-spirited resentment but, again, as a loosening in order to produce new knowledge. And this strategy involves the students as well and suggests the particular link between masochistic love and knowledge that Barthes advocates. He writes in *Leçon,*

> I should therefore like the speaking and the listening that will be interwoven here to resemble the comings and goings of a child playing beside his mother, leaving her to bring a pebble, a piece of string, and thereby tracing around a calm center a whole locus of play within which the pebble, the string come to matter less than the enthusiastic giving of them.[22]

His work sets love in motion wandering around discourses. He abandons both the eternal truths of the conservative critics and the demythologizing of ideologies of the theorists.

A *Lover's Discourse,* for example, appears to study *the* discourse of love-as-passion and romantic love as epitomized in Goethe's *The*

Sorrows of Young Werther. From that calm center, he produces a whole locus of play. His method of dramatization, of making it "a" lover's discourse, prevents one from assuming that Barthes intends to apply a descriptive system to his data. Instead, the lover struggles with the inadequacies of a general rhetorical taxonomy. What can we learn from connecting the most intimate pleasure principle with institutionalized social relations? What kind of knowledge can we gain in professing desire in the classroom? The answer to this question is not only in the connections between PC and PR but in the relation of Barthes to the PP or Pleasure Principle. Freud, in *Beyond the Pleasure Principle* (1920), tells the famous story about the little boy who compensated for his mother's frequent absences by inventing a game where he could make her return at will. Barthes invokes this much discussed fort/da game to explain his strategy in *A Lover's Discourse.* The lover invokes the insecurities of the child who stages the traumas and travails of everyday life by structuring these anxieties in the fort/da game. Barthes writes that as a child he could not forget those "interminable days, abandoned days" when his mother was working far away. In the evening he would wait for her at the bus stop. He recalls that "the buses would pass one after the other, she wasn't in any of them."[23] He explains this "scenography of waiting" by describing how he organizes and manipulates it. He "cut out a portion of time" in which he mines the loss of the loved object and provokes all the effects of a "minor mourning. This is then acted out as a play."[24] In short, Barthes transforms anxiety into a play activity by staging the utterances—in our case, discourses about love, knowledge, and academics—as a fiction with multiple roles (impatient, jealous, infatuated, enamored) and figures (doubts, reproaches, desires, depressions). Who would have thought that Hughes, Paglia, and others would find themselves remotivated in this scenography of mourning the death of the University as we know it. Who would have thought that these characters could move in such strange and wonderful ways. Who would have thought that the debates about academic demeanor could be so much fun.

As we leave the seminar space, as Barthes collects his notes and partially erases the chalkboard, we pause one more time to wonder about his naked pathetic sentiment with its hints of bathos (those statements that suggest a series of interpretations from naïveté to irony). What will our report say about his strategy of singing a love song without looking at the ones he loves, about his demeanor, his desires, his sense of decorum? Perhaps the conclusion of an article written more than ten years ago on this Professor of Desire suggests a way of acting and responding to the new demands:

> When, in the Symposium, Socrates states that love is the one thing in the world he understands, he is immediately desired by those who believe mistakenly that to possess the Master physically would be somehow to possess the knowledge to which he claims. What Alcibiades takes to be a jilting by Socrates is also the only way to assure that he might eventually proceed toward self-knowledge. Only by refusing Alcibiades can Socrates prevent him from accepting a subservient role in a social hierarchy of marked class differences. The final entry in the *Fragments* invokes a similar act of refusal which, following Socrates, is less a simple refusal than an *aphophasis*: "So desire still irrigates the non-will-to-possess by this perilous movement: I love you in my head, but I imprison it behind my lips. I do not divulge. I say silently to who is no longer or is not yet the other: I keep myself from loving you." Only by acknowledging desire in the very moment of denying it can the professor of Desire teach the knowledge of love and love of knowledge, thus fulfilling the nurturing function essential to the learning process as a continuous affirmation of joyful wisdom.[25]

This description of the pedagogical situation seems relevant to professors and universities learning finally to deal with sexual harassment cases. It also sheds light on an artificial mythology of the current debates on curriculum reform. Instead of rejecting the critics' claims, Barthes explains that one must learn the art of seduction and the power of restraint in order to enter into the teaching of a popular audience. The conservative critics understand the first lesson, using every media-savvy technique to seduce and delight their audiences. Professors understand better the sense of limits and the power of listening with an empty, passive receiving mind, the mind of the maternal, the mind that gives and gives without wanting anything in return. Together, the personal fascinations and manias that overwhelm and the media-savvy techniques suggest an emergent discourse that combines the strategies of conservative attacks (the myth of eternal noncontingent truths) with liberal and radical feminist counterattacks (the myth of transcending ideologies) in order to introduce a third possibility: a pop theory that vacillates between naive love and ironic smirks, between masochistic confusion and an unsettling utopian spirit.

Confronted with the accusing gaze of the conservative critics, Pee-Wee Barthes responds by losing all subjectivity: his voice chokes and gags in nonhuman ways, his body contorts, his face suggests a mask of comic horror, he mourns over the death of the University as we know it. Who can argue with this appealing hysteria?

6 | Family Values and Media Technology

Simple

In 1989, former President George Bush visited Amish and Mennonite leaders at a schoolhouse in Lancaster County, Pennsylvania. He extolled the virtues of traditional family values and predictably pointed to the Amish family as a role model. One could easily see through his visit as mere political posturing, especially because the president's men had the hitching rails for horses moved to the front of the school for a photo opportunity.[1] Besides this easy demythologizing of the political uses of family values and the Amish, the question of what family values means if the Amish family functions as a particularly powerful role model usually remains unexamined.

The Amish advocate a simple life and reject worldliness and secular knowledge. They live in isolated, large rural families in small, tight-knit, Christian religion-centered communities that reject national politics as worldly and corrupt.

The renewed interest in returning to a simpler life focused around family values has the same mythic power in contemporary America as the pressing problems of urban decay, the downfall of higher education, the emergence of a multicultural society, and the emergence of the United States as a singular superpower. As they have done to these other myths, many cultural critics have demythologized the nostalgia for a simple life surrounded by a close-knit family with little interference from the outside world. They note that the ethos depends on a time supposedly during the 1950s that in fact did not possess the qualities associated with family values. People were far more anxious, and families were far less stable than many commentators would have the public believe. Family values also come under attack as an empty slogan for a new political marketing strategy to appeal to nostalgic yearnings for a mythic family with more in common with a Hollywood movie than any reality. Just as the nature movement begins to resemble the mythologies surrounding tourism, in which the real traveler or naturalist avoids the eco-tourist traps and goes off the beaten track, the nostalgia for the simple life and authentic family now has a hierarchy of supposed dupes much like the discourses surrounding tourism. Ranging from the family farm owners to hobby farmers in suburbanized rural areas to urban consumers of pickup trucks, simple living glows with sophistication. In this hierarchy, groups that supposedly reject worldliness and secularism altogether take on a special status as both tourist sites of authenticity and sites of nostalgic mourning for a disappearing way of life. In the efforts now under way to "return" to a past way of life, one group in the United States stands out among others as the authentic rejection of worldliness and secular sophistication. That group is not the Christian Coalition.

Amish

That group is the Old Order Amish settlements, especially those in Lancaster County, Pennsylvania. Many commentators argue that these small agrarian communities represent the most successful economic and social tradition in family farming. In spite of their relatively small numbers and very limited geographical expansion outside their initial areas of settlement in the eighteen and nineteenth centuries, their image is well known throughout the United States because of media coverage and tourism.

The Amish exemplify the simple life and the rejection of worldliness and secular knowledge in their own manifestos and explanations, in the tourist's opinion, and in the scholarly literature. Much of the scholarly research, limited to a great degree to those closely and positively associated with Amish and Mennonite communities, uses a sociological analysis to discuss group cohesion. The work of John Hostetler is exemplary in terms of both its thorough scholarship and its typical approach. He combines a sociological approach with scattered personal anecdotes about growing up Amish. His empirical care reinforces his strong advocacy of the Amish way of life with a tone of detached reasonableness. His 1963 study is the standard in the field of studies of this group because of its complete historical background and synchronic analyses of contemporary social customs. Although no one appears to have attempted the task, it would be easy to demythologize the simplicity of the Amish lifestyle, and to challenge the pat opposition between sophisticated lifestyles and simple living. Before the Kraybill and Olshan anthology cited earlier in this chapter, it was surprisingly difficult to find *any* criticisms of this lifestyle as *not* simple. The simpleness is taken as a given, and the difficulty of that lifestyle is then either embraced or discussed in terms of group cohesion. There is no theoretical discussion about the rejection of worldliness or the simple life, perhaps because it seems out of place to make sophisticated speculations about something so simple. This presumed opposition *also* motivates much of the current debates about culture and family values. The lifestyle arguments currently bandied about in political advertisements use this conception of the simple Christian family life. In fact, the argument against taxes for social programs also depends on conjuring up the self-sufficient, religion-centered extended family living apart from sophisticated urban worldliness. The Amish do not accept social security or any form of government tax-supported welfare. They do not attend public high schools. They reject higher education after the eighth grade. They refuse to serve in the military. They avoid settling in urban areas. And they neither vote nor pay certain taxes. These qualities make them a bellwether of the national political agenda's proposed changes to contemporary society. One would be hard-pressed to find all these current issues about education, social security, and taxes in one group. The Amish are the icon for the *new* American Dream: isolated, large rural families in small, tight-knit, Christian religion-centered communities that reject national politics as worldly and corrupt as well as any outside interference that threatens their simple life.

The Amish now actually consist of a number of different splinter groups. Even within each of these groups, local communities have different customs and rules. The most conservative group, the Old Order Amish, arrived in America during the colonial era during the 1700s. The five hundred or so families who came over during that initial migration first settled mostly in Lancaster County, Pennsylvania. They had left mostly German-speaking areas of Switzerland and Alsace because of increasing religious persecution and a lack of suitable farming land in uncontested areas. As part of the Protestant Reformation, the Amish began as a splinter of the Swiss Brethren sect of the Anabaptists in sixteenth-century northern Europe. While Luther and his followers retained the infant baptism ritual, the more radical groups rejected infant baptism in favor of adult baptism. The "rebaptizers," or Anabaptists, believed that only those knowledgeable of sin need the removal of sin in baptism. The church governments rightly saw this change in ritual as symptomatic of economic and political unrest. The infant baptism assured the church-state that everyone was a subject from the start. The new system insinuated that an individual chose to enter the redemption of religion. This small opening for choice was not tolerated. The Anabaptists were persecuted and sometimes executed by drowning. Drowning was the official church-state's cruel joke on the rebaptizers, who used the pouring method rather than the immersion method. Around 1527, the Anabaptists wrote seven articles of their faith called the "Schleitheim" articles, which still form the foundation for the Amish beliefs and separation from modern life. Significantly, in one of these articles they argue that the rule of government functions according to the flesh, while the Christians follow only the spirit. The articles also specify adult baptism and a strong separation from forces of evil, and forbid taking oaths.

The Amish split from a larger group of Mennonite Anabaptists who followed the teachings of Menno Simons. Their founding leader, Jacob Amman, emphatically broke from the less conservative and more conciliatory groups in the Anabaptist sects. Amman argued that those suspended from religious activities because of apparent indiscretions should also suffer complete social censure as well. This activity of shunning those not in conformity to the strict doctrines of religious living (rather than the Catholic church's emphasis on rituals) formed the basis for the Amish isolation and separation from changing social customs. Amman was not a friendly or forgiving fellow; he cornered other religious leaders and demanded an immediate answer to whether they supported the shunning practice completely and wholeheartedly. Many tried to find a suitable compromise or to buy more time for mediation and consultation with parishioners. Amman would hear nothing of it. He expelled those unwilling to yield and then shunned those who did not follow his dictates. He also began a crusade against trimming beards and wearing buttons on clothes. His followers were known as *Hüftler,* "hook-and-eyers," because of their more primitive clothing style. Their uniqueness became more obvious. With Amman's inflexibility, stubbornness, and ambitions for power, his followers were increasingly isolated. When the Amish first arrived in North America with a larger group of German-speaking Mennonites and other people, they began assimilating. Hybrid rituals, begun during the mixing of the immigrants on boats from Europe, increased defections from the traditional Amish customs. During the American Revolution, when the Amish failed to pledge allegiance to the United States, many of their members left the sect to join less demanding religions. After the war, the separation between Amish and non-Amish caused more splinter groups and more families to leave the sect even as the separation also led to a more obviously defined and homogeneous group. Among the distinctive characteristics, the shift from a central moral authority like the Vatican or a national government to strict family and community authorities is the most important factor in understanding the Amish in terms of the national politics of family values.

The liberation from an abstract central church and government authority still characterizes their detachment from the surrounding communities and American government. They do contribute more than their share to local communities' efforts to raise money for volunteer fire departments, but they do not participate in other civic "duties" such as voting or attending PTA meetings. Their schools do not prepare students for "upward mobility" in modern society, and they do not offer any instruction in art, music, acting, or creative writing. Their schools refuse to teach the "new math" or the sciences. The curriculum includes only reading, writing, and arithmetic skills. The schools dismiss the values of self-expression and self-confidence in favor of stressing simplicity, humility, and fear of God. Their education consists of primary skills, values of social responsibility and group cohesion, and liberal doses of play. They have different games than modernized children, sometimes because of their separation from the surrounding communities and sometimes because of the limits on technology. For example, the children can only have scooters, not bikes, because the gear mechanisms of bikes make the riding too easy and suggest other more mechanized forms of locomotion. Some communities forbid rubber tires on tractors, and other communities do not allow certain conveniences of milk production. The Amish in certain areas have different size brims on their hats. When they move from one community to another, they adjust to the new neighbors by trimming their brim or getting a new hat. For those within the sect, the different communities look and live somewhat differently.

Instead of following the democratic laws of the United States, the Amish claim to follow God's law of love and redemption. They are remarkable for surviving not merely in the face of technological and social change but in spite of efforts by the legal government to disrupt their customs. Only relatively recently, during the late 1970s, did they gain the right to ignore laws requiring students to attend at least some high school. Their isolation and intermarriage has led to a clear lineage from the original settlers. For example, on one farm road with three farms and eight mailboxes, all the surnames on the mailboxes are the same, Stoltzfus. Stoltzfus was the name of the family who originally settled in Conestoga valley in the late 1700s. The descendants still live in this same area, and this continuity also creates a strong social cohesion with the group rather than with any larger society.

The stress on family values to the exclusion of individuality in every aspect of life including names and clothing reinforces the Amish belief system. For example, their dolls have no faces, not only a requirement of the prohibition against graven images but also an indication that even dolls should lack individual features. In adolescence, some individuals do experiment with alternatives. Some young men sneak off to New York City, get driver's licenses, cut their hair, or rebel in other mild ways. These aberrations make these individuals' eventual baptism into the religion a choice rather than a rule of law. The members have enormous social pressure to join simply because their entire world reinforces the religious life, and setting oneself apart from that life would mean a radical break with everything one knows. The feeling of choice given to the adolescents assures the young adults that they have tasted the other sophisticated life and chosen to follow the "spiritual" path rather than the "carnal" path of convenience and individual pleasures. Outside the community lies decadence and decay; inside the group is a connection to life and growth. Even the scholarship on the Amish always codes their experience in terms of the "death" of small distinctive communities and family farms outside their communities. The "expanding machine civilization" leads to this death of the surrounding communities.[2] Given this choice, a surprisingly large number of Amish teens still have secret "reunion" parties, and many gradually leave the sect.

Unlike other utopian communities, the Amish believe strongly in entrepreneurial capitalism and do not have any forced communal social arrangement. Each farm has signs outside telling passersby what is for sale. On one farm road in western Chester County, Pennsylvania, very close to the Lancaster County border in the Conestoga valley, the signs read "Chair Caning," "Mums," "Apple Cider," or later in the fall, "Pumpkins," and at the end of the road of three farms, a more elaborate permanent sign with a picture of an egg carton announces "eggs for sale." The grandparents do not retire to another community. Instead they build an attached house onto the main house and move in next door. In their retirement they focus on producing handicrafts for the community and for the tourists. For example, on one of the farms just mentioned, the older patriarch of the family works in a small room in his attached part of the house, caning chairs, while his wife and grandchildren tend to the flowers and doves for sale. His son tends to the cattle, and his daughter-in-law manages the household and farm business.

Family Values as Philosophy

For the tourist trade, the Amish represent a pastoral past as well as an exotic other. The simple lifestyle appeals to a nostalgia for a mythical rural agrarian life centered around family and religion. The effort to visit a myth of a simple past, both fueled and disrupted by tourism, also suggests particular conceptions of history, temporality, and cultural change. As discussed in an earlier chapter in terms of tourism, the myth of this pastoral past depends on an evolutionist sense of history. The Amish appreciation and explicit rejection of this evolutionary sense of progress complicates the situation. While peasants normally might charm tourists into appreciating a common past, the Amish lifestyle and fashion statements constantly change the merely pastoral into dress as protest. Although they do not vote, the Amish practice a form of politics against progress and against efforts to reduce them to a natural simplicity rather than a chosen simplicity. To the desire that they remain always the same, they respond by flaunting a peculiar history of their own. Maybe the tourist's ancestors farmed land with horses, but they did not use weed-whackers, wear polyester clothes, or talk on the phone. Allowing for these conveniences, the Amish still do not resemble peasants-for-show as in a Disneyfied landscape, as many booklets claim in describing their farms as neat and tidy. They are not plastic or sterile enough, and not willing to be photographed as a character in someone else's amusement park. Even as they attract visitors eager to see a simple family life gone by, their oddness and different history disrupts the "family of man" sense of community. Their difference challenges the spectators. On the one hand, their social and sartorial customs function as boundary mechanisms keeping them separate from the world. For example, they speak a distinct German dialect among themselves and speak English only to outsiders. On the other hand, their differences engage directly the mythologies of the surrounding communities. Their costume and customs protest against technological progress, changing fashions, and government policies. The play between these two images of the Amish as both separate from the world and actively protesting against worldliness highlights the importance of how this group represents themselves to themselves and others. Once the image of this group has a number of competing components, for example, the sociologists' image and the tourists' image, then the research depends on appreciating the overlapping terms.

Heidegger and the Amish

As I have already mentioned, the simple life is a recurring theme in both scholarly and other views of this group. Martin Heidegger's philosophy offers the most coherent and complete analysis of the representation of the struggle between worldliness and a peasant's engagement with the soil. He also includes in his reflections a description of technological progress that looks quite similar to the Amish belief system. Because of these analyses, his work represents an obvious and important contribution to understanding the antitechnological basis of the Amish simple lifestyle. Although his work usually appears in discussions of much more worldly matters, and some critics might complain that he offers an overly complicated analysis of simplicity, he does appear to present an extensive, careful, and admiring philosophy of peasant life and folk cultures. Indeed, on the surface it seems as though the Amish epitomize a peculiar reading of Heidegger's notion of engagement with the earth. Of course, no Amish folk claim to have read Heidegger, nor will any of their documents make reference to any philosopher besides the founders of their religious order. Heidegger's philosophy does, nevertheless, illuminate some of the crucial aspects of these self-proclaimed "plain" folks' way of life. And their common Germanic origins also suggest a similar cultural attitude toward earth and nature.

Examining Heidegger's writings on technology and on the engagement with the earth also broadens the issues that preoccupy the Amish to larger cultural and even metaphysical concerns. In an essay on the "Origin of the Work of Art," Heidegger explains part of his theory by alluding to a painting of "a peasant woman's shoes" by Vincent van Gogh.[3] His choice of a peasant's shoes is contested and controversial, as this chapter discusses later. In reading the reason for using these shoes as an example, one suspects the Amish would find this appreciation quite fitting with their own religious beliefs about working in the fields and engaging with the earth. They respect three values above all others: their devotion to religion, the agrarian lifestyle, and a cohesive family and community. Heidegger finds in those shoes the Being of the woman peasant. Her essence has to do with the dirt in the shoes. This dirt represents her engagement with the soil and earth in tending to the fields. The Amish also find their sense of Being in the toil with the earth. Their well-known avoidance of technology and convenience encourages more of a direct engagement with the earth and a stronger dependence on the family and community. Being for the Amish and Heidegger comes from an engagement with the earth, not from a worldly-wise wisdom. As one commentator writes, "Soil has for the Amish a spiritual significance" (Hostetler 1980, 117).

The Amish symbol system depends especially on clothing. As mentioned earlier, dress functions not merely as an instrument of protection against the physical elements but also as a language of protest against worldliness. The coat, for example, does not merely function to keep someone warm; it has a symbolic value that exceeds its practical function. Amish costume was common among medieval European peasants, but now it symbolizes a way of life and family values set against worldliness. The elevation of everyday tools and clothing to symbolic value resembles the "artwork" in Heidegger's writings. The "Work of Art" essay approaches the source of an artwork's essence or nature in order to learn "what it is and as it is" (17). In typical Heideggerian fashion, he answers the question by posing a series of related problems. He discovers that the artist and the artwork depend on each other for definition: "neither is without the other" (17). In a similar fashion, the Amish always insist that merely owning a particular style of clothes or plowing a field with a horse-pulled plow does not raise these tools and objects to a symbolic value. The user's intent and engagement are crucial to this process. The symbolic and the thingness of a tool depend on each other as well. Yet, the art or symbol depends on the "something else" over and above the "thingly." The work may have usefulness but not as an end in itself. The goal of the artist as well as the Amish consists in raising the "thingly" to the level of allusive symbol or allegory. To further explain his aesthetic theory, Heidegger uses the example of the peasant woman's shoes. The equipment part of a useful object is always in relation, always "for something." It is not self-sufficient. Heidegger uses the painting for something, for an example to illustrate his explanation of how the painted shoes suggest the Being of the peasant woman's *engagement with the earth*. The art of the painting goes beyond the mere equipmentality and thingness of the shoes to capture *the way the shoes belong to the earth*. Not merely of the world, not merely useful, the shoes are also *of* the earth (sheltering, concealing). They exceed their use value; they exceed their unconcealed truth or matter-of-factness. Likewise the Amish clothes exceed their use value and matter-of-factness. The clothes and use of tools do not merely represent an efficient and simple way to live and farm. Many modern commentators have repeatedly stressed the bountiful yields and conserving of the soil achieved by Amish farming techniques. These commentators miss the more important aspect of the Amish techniques. For the Amish, the symbolic or allegorical value exceeds the use value. There are many ways to farm simply and efficiently. In fact, the modernized farmer would also claim to achieve higher yields with less labor and expense than the Amish farmer. The debate is not between styles or fashions of dressing and farming. The struggle for the Amish and Heidegger alike centers around the struggle between earthiness and worldliness.

Derrida examines Heidegger's use of the peasant woman's shoes in "Restitutions: Truth to Size," which intervenes in an apparent disagreement of fact between Heidegger and Meyer Schapiro.[4] Schapiro explains that the painting Heidegger refers to in his discussion of the shoes could not possibly illustrate a pair of *peasant woman*'s shoes; Schapiro argues that, in fact, the shoes that Heidegger saw in the painting probably belonged to van Gogh himself, a city dweller. He insinuates that Heidegger's mistake may have more to do with a romanticization of peasant life than with any philosophical argument. Heidegger's participation in Nazism suggests the larger problem with his apparent mistake, and the associations of folk culture with fascist politics. So, from the start, Derrida's intervention takes great care in deciphering the significance of Heidegger's apparent slip and Schapiro's efforts to trip up Heidegger on this point of fact. For the purposes of understanding Amish culture, the essay demonstrates the interdependence of worldliness and earthiness, between the worldly media representations and the authentic Being of a farmer working the earth. In an art historical context, Schapiro focuses on this single example. He writes Heidegger letters, studies lists of paintings from museum exhibits, and carefully analyzes each possible picture Heidegger used as his inspiration for the description of the peasant woman's shoes. He concludes that Heidegger most likely saw the painting referred to at a particular exhibit, and none of the pictures illustrates a peasant woman's shoes. In fact, Schapiro produces evidence to suggest that van Gogh often painted and sketched his own shoes. Heidegger probably saw one of those paintings rather than a painting of a peasant woman's shoes. Schapiro argues that, therefore, the dark patches inside the wooden clogs, which for Heidegger suggest the engagement with the earth, probably represented (worldly-wise) street grime rather than freshly plowed earth. That Heidegger was wrong could illustrate a problem in his philosophical advocacy of a peasant's work as elevated to an engagement with the earth rather than worldly sophistication.

Derrida begins his intervention by investigating why Heidegger uses a painting to describe shoes in the first place. One could just as easily imagine a pair of work shoes. Why does the philosopher make explicit reference to a painting by van Gogh? For Heidegger, the shoes belong to the earth "only in the picture" (Derrida, 34). The essence of the shoes resides not in their thingness. That is, although Heidegger would argue that truth happens in van Gogh's painting, he would not suggest that, therefore, something, some pair of shoes, was correctly portrayed. The artwork leads to a "happening of truth," which always entails the conflict between world and earth (Derrida, 38). Significantly, one can also imagine a particular pair of Amish shoes, but the Amish forbid portraying themselves as individuals. Therefore, the examples must be general rather than specific. In that case, the

Amish as a stereotype depend on the overarching representation of themselves as a nondelineated group: one indivisible group under God. In this case, the artwork entails a conflict between Schapiro's worldliness and Heidegger's earthiness. The conflict functions as a figurative battle of world (what it is) and earth (as it is) or, in contemporary terms, *facts* in the world versus *uncanny general essences* (Derrida, 37). Again, for Heidegger, art exceeds mere reproduction and matter-of-factness. Strangely enough, this is precisely the battle between Heidegger (uncanny general essence) and Schapiro (facts). Heidegger advocates the unconcealedness of Being in the shoes, while Schapiro seeks the truth or knowledge-fact of the shoes. The correctness of representation that Schapiro's essay defends is only part of the story, and taken alone would, in Derrida's argument, get nowhere. In fact, the opponents in this debate belong to one another the way a pair of shoes belong to each other or the way laces tie up an apparent rift (Derrida, 374). The earth (sheltering and concealing) and the world (opening up) represent precisely the battle of the work-Being described by Heidegger as artwork. In trying, perhaps in vain, to return these shoes, to make restitutions, we constantly return to the question, what are these shoes for: equipment, example, symbol, allegory, or frame? In terms of the Amish, what are *Hüftler*, or hook-and-eyers, for?

Heidegger discusses how objects harbor momentous possibilities in addition to their use or beyond their instrumentality. We can read all made objects as something other than functional, as something like an artwork.[5] The essence of technology is nothing technological; it resides in its peculiar character beyond or beside its instrumentality. Technology then cannot merely function as the excluded term in Amish life. Instead, the Amish focus on the essence of technology, not its instrumentality. The symbolic value of a technology tells the Amish more than its newness or even convenience. The question concerning technology occupies much of Amish religious teachings. According to their teachings and their advocates, the Amish resist the supposedly "irresistible" trend for technology to be larger and larger (Hostetler 1980, 369). Heidegger also challenges his all-consuming attitude that technology encourages a reduction of everything to the technological imperative. He argues that the instrumental definition of technology is "untenable" because it does not consider how a technology or technology in general sets out to reveal the world (*QCT*, 21). Modern technology differs from artisanal hand-worked crafts because the former unreasonably demands the extraction of energy and the building up of reserve energy. Sounding much like an Amish tract, Heidegger goes on to argue that "agriculture is now the mechanized food industry" (QCT, 15). Against the modern technology that unlocks, exposes, and orders for profit, he advocates a freedom which is "originally not connected with the will or even with the causality of human willing" (QCT, 25).

Again, this connection of a limiting of human causality and will to an alternative notion of freedom sounds like an Amish belief. Instead of a universal technology that rationalizes and orders everything, the Amish claim to always make a technology "appropriate" to their scale (Hostetler 1980, 369). For example, they use horse power and manufacture their own farm implements if the communities around them no longer use these technologies. It might seem irreverent or inappropriate to ask, how do the Amish know with certainty what the "appropriate" scale is? Once one asks the question and looks for the obvious answer, the question looks more crucial to understanding the Amish communities' relationship to technology and technological change. They do not resist change. In fact, they have made many changes both including and excluding particular technologies according to the particular community's beliefs and according to the historical contingencies. So, for example, the telephone was widely accepted as it appeared in rural parts of Pennsylvania. Later it was limited, and in some communities it reemerged. They use mail order extensively. The Amish in some Lancaster County communities use backyard trampolines for amusement. They accept the use of weed-whackers as long as they have gas engines. Most Amish wear clothes made with synthetics like polyester rather than "natural" fibers like cotton. The rationale for the use or exclusion of a technology depends not on its newness or even convenience, but whether it will interfere with labor-intensive farming practices and decentralized industries, and most importantly on its symbolic value, which exceeds the functionality of the tool. The technology is understood not merely as an instrumental tool but as an all-consuming worldview: "The logic of expanding technology points toward infinite industrial growth and infinite energy consumption" (Hostetler 1980, 371). This statement about Amish beliefs could easily summarize part of Heidegger's argument. In spite of the rhetoric of live and let live exposed in much of the literature about the Amish produced for the tourists, one Amish writer refers to the "technically competent barbarian."[6]

The Amish way of life highlights the important connection between family values and technology. They claim that "by holding technology at a distance, by exercising restraint and moderation, and by accepting limitations and living within them, the Amish have maintained the integrity of their family and community life" (Hostetler 1980, 371). On the one hand, technology threatens the family values. On the other hand, in many rural areas "popular, ancestral proverbs still partake of an instrumental grasp of the world as object. A rural statement of fact, such as 'the weather is fine' keeps a real link with the usefulness of fine weather."[7] Just as the simple statement of weather ultimately depends on an instrumental or technological logic, parental authority can appeal to a peremptory "because" when confronted with too many "whys" about the causality of nature. Myth depends on common sense. It answers over and over again, "because it just is, that's why."

In challenging the inevitable progression of using more and more "useful" and "convenient" technologies, the Amish also challenge common sense. They suggest a counter-common sense that invents absurd limits and barriers to naturalizing the mythologies of technological progress, democracy of the majority, the value and necessity of high school education, and the freedom of individual choice. Rather than a quaint pastoral peasantry, the people, "as seen in a movie," look silly and absurd in their costumes and in fulfilling their customs. When taken out of the moral packaging of "simpleness," this silliness resembles the foibles of a country bumpkin living in the modernized world. As an inverted reflection of modernity, they demonstrate against the naturalized myths circulating around the suburbs and tourists that increasingly surround them.

The mythology of the simple peasantlike Amish depends on defining them as premodern. Only then can they exist as something that modern observers idealize in terms of something "we miss" and "suspect we have lost" (Olshan, 235). In supporting this commonsense point of view, Hostetler assumes that one can define modernization as the "acceptance of technology and material culture" (Hostetler, 364). Kraybill and Olshan offer alternative counterintuitive definitions. Kraybill gives a number of factors involved in modernity, especially decontextualization. Modernity decontextualizes and abstracts information.[8] Although Kraybill argues that the Amish do not decontextualize the knowledge they learn, and resist abstract thought, one could argue that their belief system depends on abstract rules and regulations. The rules' arbitrary basis only adds to the obviousness of these rules' abstractness. The rules do not depend on a particular context or a natural expedient necessity. They depend on making obvious the abstractness of the rule. Olshan argues that modernity depends on a belief system premised on free choice rather than fate.[9] By actively selecting and choosing which technologies to use, the Amish appear equally as modern as their non-Amish neighbors. Their contrived and artificial lifestyle challenges the mythic image of the natural and simple Amish folk.

Family Values as Method

In contemporary discourse, the advocates of family values conjure up the evils of television and the importance of transcending worldliness's whims of fashion in favor of community authority. In fact, the worldliness of media technology and the simple, religion-centered family life are imbricated one upon the other. The latter depends on media's power to allow outsiders to witness the simple life even as that life mocks the outsider's beliefs in progress, instrumental logic, and social customs. The phrase family values has recently taken on an ominous insinuation of radical changes in the separation of church and state, the role of education, and the challenging of individual negligence in favor of local community's authority. Because it intervenes in changing the educational curriculum from a rational national agenda to a local, often religion-centered discipline, the phrase highlights the confrontations in discussions about the future of education in America. Although this debate currently focuses on high school and elementary school, it has already had an impact through its association with the conservative criticisms of decadent higher education curricula.

Scholars have usually studied the family unit in sociological or psychological terms. Only recently have cultural studies of the historical development of the contemporary family appeared. While Queer theory has challenged scholars to examine methodologies as well as the scope of their work, no one has yet suggested a method of research premised on the essence of the family. That is, the methods should reflect the change in focus. Some might argue that the dominance of the family has already shaped scholarship. Yet, the essence of family values challenges the centralized authority of efficient rationality and instrumental logic. All the attention to the phrase has persuaded the public and educators that the problem of either too much family values or not enough is both real and severe. Academic research calls for new methodologies even as it continues to merely describe, for example, the Amish family structure. This chapter suggests a *family values methodology* rather than merely a description of the Amish alternative or marginalized cultural practice. To understand the implications of family values for scholarship demands a philosophical analysis of those values. In this chapter I examine a specific occurrence of family values in a supposedly unsophisticated or spoiled environment in order to speculate about those values' relationship to particular forms of power and knowledge. Although theorists since Freud have discussed the identity formation found in family groups, the particularly fervent stress on rural family values found in the Amish will have other consequences for identity formation. More importantly, the political and social customs of this simple family life suggest an alternative to representation in general. Using family values challenges naturalization and foregrounds the process of representation usually effaced in efforts to describe or explain social and cultural practices.

In his report from Rome and in a December meeting of his Seminar IV in 1956, Lacan discusses the practice of "bundling."[10] Bundling, sometimes called bed-courtship, practiced widely among working-class Europeans during the nineteenth century, became in the twentieth century an unusual ritual practiced only by the Old Order Amish in the United States. The Swiss-German Brethren sect of the Anabaptists, who are directly linked to the Amish, abandoned the practice during the nineteenth century. The Amish continued to practice bundling until newer splinter groups, especially the more progressive New Order, began objecting to the practice in the late 1960s. Although the Europeans had discontinued the practice, and even strongly objected to the Amish continuing to bundle, the Old Orders saw the ritual as part of a link with tradition.[11] The practice involved a man and a woman spending the night together in the same bed, fully clothed with a bundling board between them. As part of a courting ritual, it allowed for intimacy without premarital sex and for talking. The play between the obviously intense attraction of the couple and the artificial limits allowed for and encouraged reserve and a parrying between approach and retreat.

In his discussion, Lacan uses this practice not as an object of study — he does not apply psychoanalysis to bundling — but as a particularly apt model of the analytic situation. He argues that his appreciation of the practice is not merely the occasion for a pleasant fantasy about peculiar social mores. Instead, the practice teaches us about how analysis allows for talking by limiting a kind of humanistic immediacy. The analysand feels free to talk without aim. Bundling also allows for a witnessing. From the distance between them, the analyst can begin to hear what otherwise would never rise above intended meanings and self-conscious statements. Eventually, the witnessing provoked by bundling also encouraged outsiders to look on it as a perverse and kinky practice. When the Amish began learning of how others witnessed their custom from afar, they began phasing out the practice. For outsiders, Lacanian analysis often has a similarly negative reputation because of the distance between participants, instead of the encouraging smiles and even hugs found in therapeutic approaches.

A number of important Lacanian media and cultural critics also use Lacan's unique style of employing examples. For example, much of the work of Slavoj Žižek uses this approach to cultural artifacts — Žižek uses popular films — to explain analysis rather than using some abstract notion of analysis to explain popular films. In the allusions to bundling, Lacan teaches us how to read these cultural examples as something other than objects of study. The practice is *not* used to help explain structures of the Amish, *nor* does it serve as a symptom of deep conflicts and contradictions among this group. Again, what bundling explains is the relations between analysand and analyst.

Lacan uses bundling to explain how the analytic situation suspends approval because the analyst does not know what the analysand's speech means — and it certainly does not mean what the analysand intends it to mean. The understanding is in reserve. The analyst does not try to elicit a positive response — does not try to *unbundle* the analysand. The goal is simply to incite the subject to speak. She or he says to the analysand, in some way, "give oneself freely to free association. Say anything, don't choose, don't respond to my smiles. Say stupid trivial things. You go to the analyst not to jump and sing and hug or learn to fuck, but to talk about what you don't know." This unusual relationship with the subject is why Lacan eventually indicates the subject with an X rather than a capital S. The X indicates the bundling as an always in reserve.

Bundling is not merely a pleasant fantasy for the witnesses of peculiar social mores—whether that fantasy is about a preindustrial utopian community, an example of group cohesion and kinship rituals, or simply a kinky game of denial and excitement. Instead, it unsettles the habituated social-scientific approaches to culture as well as the smiling sympathetic approaches to sociopolitical issues that naturalize self-conceptions and opposition like technology versus the natural.

The Amish family does not so much transcend or resist technologies, especially the supposedly pernicious media like television, but instead depends on arbitrary moral selection of technologies. The limiting of what children watch or listen to only becomes an issue within the logic of accepting particular media technologies. The family allows the television a place in the home only if it can then code it with arbitrary morality. The Amish allow for technology in every aspect of their lives. They simply morally code those unacceptable technologies as merely for instrumentality. The strange logic of this code suggests the following syllogisms: telephones but not in the house, engines but not on the road, tractors but not in the fields, television but not to be watched. It seems absurd in theory only. The Amish represent in practice the struggle between earth and world that Heidegger philosophizes about.

As Seen

The image of the Amish appears in a number of Hollywood films including *Violent Saturday* (1955), featuring Ernest Borgnine as an Amish farmer who has his barn taken over by fleeing bank robbers; *The Night They Raided Minsky's* (1968), written by Norman Lear and featuring Britt Ekland as a young Amish girl who goes to the city to dance; and sentimental films like *Birch Interval* (1977) and *A Stoning in Fulham County* (1988), which focus on the struggles of Amish life. The most famous portrayal is Peter Weir's *Witness* (1985), which grossed more than $100 million. In the movie *Witness*, Harrison Ford plays a detective who lives on an Amish farm to protect a small boy who has witnessed a brutal killing. "The filming of the movie *Witness* in Lancaster County Pennsylvania created apprehension and displeasure among the Amish people."[12] They did not protest against the content of the film because they do not attend movies of any kind. They objected to the Amish functioning as a tourist lure and the movie creating an atmosphere where the Amish attracted even more attention. They especially objected to the slogan used by the Pennsylvania Dutch visitors' bureau: "As Seen in the Movie *Witness.*" The Amish, in their efforts to avoid using technology, especially cinematic and electronic media, have become movie characters for the rest of us.

Their lives now represent an important tourist site and crucial component to a thriving economy in Pennsylvania. Marc Olshan's essay "What Good Are the Amish?" argues that the Amish do not fit the Disneyfied image of goodness usually associated with this group. The association is so strong that the name becomes associated with products, like Amish Software, rejected by the Amish. Olshan notes that the Mennonites do not function as a symbol of goodness, simplicity, or family values even though they share the same moral values and many of the same practices. They do not have the "full panoply of archaic dress" associated with the Amish (Olshan, 235). Further, Olshan explains that parts of the Amish sensibility would not appear as good or compassionate to outsiders. For example, one boy described to Olshan how a cat can be used to check for the buildup of gas in a silo. The boy used a cat because "it doesn't matter" if the cat dies. In fact, Amish have been arrested for animal abuse, something other Americans might find counter to an idealized image of compassion. The mythic association depends not on an internal *moral* code but rather on the image of an artificial and contrived archaic *dress* code.

The charm of their supposedly simple life has brought suburbanites out to share the pastoral setting and to watch the Amish as if seen in a movie. The Amish are not just other, they are simulated, literally in the roadside attraction that uses pneumatic figurines to represent the Amish "scholars" or students and figuratively in their status as seen in a major motion picture. Although Jean Baudrillard, who describes how simulations escape any original reference, would love this unfortunate situation, the purpose of this chapter is *not* to revel in the appreciation of these people becoming characters in someone else's movie. The crucial issue is how technology interacts with the simple life—the cinema highlights the importance of representation in conjuring this life as a complete and coherent separate entity. The Amish were characters in a movie long before the birth of the cinematic apparatus. They had to make themselves into a spectacle and imagine themselves as a group that represented simple, plain living, which nevertheless resisted instrumentality.

The Amish as seen in a movie allow for precisely the vacillation described earlier in chapter 1 of this book in terms of artificial mythology. The sense of witnessing as if in a movie neither transcends the view to direct access nor eliminates the reality of the Amish looking and talking back. It simply changes the outsider's focus *as in a movie*. As chapter 1 explains, the moments punctuated by that "like-a-movie" sense destabilize naturalized myths or realities. The Amish just do not seem real or natural. In that sense, they challenge the witnesses' own naturalized myths of costume, social customs, and even language. The artificiality and distance that occur when one sees an event unfolding as a movie also create the vacillation between what one sees and how one sees it. The cinematic image allows the witness to notice things usually left unseen. For example, haystacks look different in an Amish field. This difference makes all haystacks allude to labor practices, mechanized farming, and social customs. Just as psychoanalysis makes conscious unconscious thoughts, the as if seen in a movie sensibility makes the previously unconscious available for witnessing. This cinematicity, with all the special effects of horse-drawn plows jumping into the foreground of attention or the crosscutting between buggies and RVs along a rural road, allows the audience to see reality as something unfamiliar and differently than from a naturalized conscious position. Witnessing the Amish "as seen in a movie" implicates the viewer as well as the people looked at. The witnessing fractures the "economy" of identification (i.e., disrupts our appreciation of a work's beauty, unity, creative use of conventions, etc.), and it creates a "screen" for the release of utopian possibilities. The aura of the Amish contains the locus of community. In some sense, the figurative and literal movie of the Amish destroys that aura. Walter Benjamin notices that "aura" also suggests the "reciprocal gaze" of inanimate objects. In the modern world neither art nor nature returns the gaze, but in primitive societies charged objects gaze back at the spectator. Benjamin argues that certain works combine both the experience of the loss of aura (i.e., the present as ruin or crisis and art as an exchangeable commodity) and suggestions of alternative possibilities. The Amish as seen in a movie return the witnesses' look, implicating modernity and witnessing even as all the attention seriously threatens their communities.

As seen in a movie, the characters make up strange and arbitrary rules, flout the social and legal customs of their country, and look like and sound like foreigners rather than indigenous people. They do not have a consistent logic or rationality. In their living in proximity to more mainstream Americans, they constantly remind themselves and others that the naturalized rules and mythologies that rule over social customs have less to do with instrumentality than with arbitrary limits and values. The Amish movie examines the representation of the tension between that which exceeds instrumentality and a worldliness that constantly seeks to reduce everything to function, convenience, and rationality. The movie is about witnessing, and the implications of witnessing for the Amish people and for outsiders. It is naïveté looked at. To simply live a difficult life is not enough. The Amish need the "witness" to elevate their own mythologies to an artificial mythology. Only when someone looks at the Amish or when the Amish consider themselves as an object of the outsiders' witnessing does their noninstrumental essence or family values stand out. The Amish must have a boundary and strict separation between Amish and non-Amish, and between those who they shun and those within the fold. To maintain this inside/outside opposition, they must constantly reinforce themselves as "other" in a larger community. If everyone is Amish, then the Amish articles of separation do not make sense. The Amish exist from the beginning to be witnessed. As a representation, they have a doubled message. On the one hand, they seem to find the strangest arbitrary reasons for doing things the way they do (e.g., the children use scooters instead of bikes). In fact, with their costumes of big black hats or white bonnets, rolled or longish hair, and their purposefully difficult techniques, they look silly and comical. To make this claim might strike some as ethnocentric and as prejudiced against these people. Yet, that "as if seen in a movie" feeling actually denaturalizes these people as just another chapter in a humanities textbook or another stop on a vacation. Once they appear odd and even silly, then the other message appears. Their way of life defamiliarizes the naturalized choices of our different way of life because they so obviously do not naturalize their choices. They very explicitly claim that all their choices derive from a community's decisions. In our culture, the parent answers the over-inquisitive child's demand to know why one more time with the slogan for naturalization: "because that's just the way it is." The Amish refer all questions back to their choices. As neighbors, the Amish quickly fall back into the mythologized natural position. They are different because of a particular set of events. As a naturalized mythology, they appear as "good farmers with high yields" rather than as caught in an absurdly difficult life by choice. As a naturalized mythology, they appear as "plain" folks who live and let live rather than as a constant protest and commentary on the surrounding world's customs and sense of historical, economic, and technological progress. As a movie, as a representation, they appear as something witnessed. They exist from the beginning only as obviously different from the world around them. Their family values function to defamiliarize, denaturalize, and demythologize everyone's family values.

The current emphasis on multiculturalism and "authentic" cultural expression makes the Amish particularly appealing as the pastoral past of American iconoclasm. These efforts at respecting their culture and preserving it without interference actually naturalize the group into a "family of man" model in which the overall similarities in a world of differences are stressed. Look again. As the old saying goes, the Amish prohibitions, similar to all tight-knit family systems of authority, bang down any nails that stick up. There is such strong social control that any differences from either the outside or inside are strictly prohibited and shunned. Although commentators argue that the Amish are not racist, they are the epitome of xenophobic shunning of anyone outside the group. Clearly, they are not controlled like many contemporary cults with guns and intimidation. Many of the Amish salespeople joke with outsiders, the social system protects and respects the elderly, unusual Amish groups like dwarfs have their own newsletter, the families care for the disabled, and a mutual-aid system protects all the members from falling into poverty or dire need. The homogenization, neither demonic nor cruel, has a delightful characteristic for the witnesses. Even the Amish, aware of their differences, enjoy the befuddled looks at their costume and customs. In contrast to the conspiratorial tragedy with big doses of ecstatic devotion found in some contemporary religious cults, the Amish do not attend church or revivals and do not believe in evangelical prayer or proselytization. Their form of smoothing differences has a comical quality even for the Amish. The physical signs of the rules, limits, and prohibitions are not creepy but delightfully humorous. To make fun of the Amish might seem to go against calls for tolerance in American society. The new mythologies of tolerance, a necessary political stance in the face of violent attacks on minorities in a community including the Amish, smooth over the hilariously glaring differences and the implications of those differences. Understanding the community as a representation, as something that exceeds their functioning or failing, allows them to disrupt the naturalized view of their customs.

Although the Amish object to the movie and the attention, their discomfort and unhappiness do not lessen the implications of the tourist bureau using the slogan of the Amish as seen in a movie. They do exist in terms of a more general technological ethos in which commentators discuss their ability to survive for such a long time, to farm so productively, to have unique customs for performing their duties, and so on. Beyond this technological explanation of their lives, an explanation they explicitly protest against, there is an explanation based on essence or value—family values—that exceeds instrumental and causal explanations in favor of something like Heidegger's explanation of the essence of technology as that artlike quality that exceeds its function. Some argue that many of the Amish prohibitions, including no electricity in the house, stem from an effort to limit any exposure to film and television. The more they resist art and media technology, the more they begin to resemble art and media. Their quilts do not function in a marketplace as merely folksy artifacts; they are thought of as similar to modern art because they use only solid colors without patterns. Their lives look more and more like a performance art piece or as characters' lives in a lyrical movie. In fact, they depend on a constant sense of being witnessed not only by outsiders but primarily by a god. That god does not predetermine their movements or actions. He does not function as a puppeteer or a director of a play on earth. He does not obviously intervene in personal choices. In fact, the adult must choose to enter into this arrangement with their god.

In that sense, the particular relationship between the Amish and the witness is one of movie to audience. Although Harrison Ford represents the legal government, and he supposedly lives among the Amish to protect the young witness, the Hollywood film also suggests that he is a witness of a different lifestyle. Hollywood fetishizes action, making the police agent, played by Ford, the necessary antidote to this too passive and pacifist lifestyle. The movie includes the requisite scene where the Amish are taunted by rednecks only to have Ford, in disguise as an Amish man, punch them out. To this the patriarch says, "He is our cousin from Ohio," alluding to the differences of custom among the different groups. The film makes fun of pacifism by assuming that the only protest that has any success requires force and guns. Finally, at the climax of the film, the young Amish boy helps Ford, and this symbolic moment shows that the Amish can take active steps to defend themselves. Of course, the type of protest that the Amish do exact on the surrounding community is lost in the film because it can only appear as Puritanism—even though the characters are sympathetic. Instead of using a review of the film as a pretext to examine the group, an artificial mythology uses the slogan of the tourist bureau as a starting point to understand the peculiar implications and position of the Amish values, family values.

To end a book on cultural invention with an entire chapter devoted to the Old Order Amish will certainly strike some readers as absurdly inappropriate. For politicians and tourists alike, the image of the Amish family has come to represent the epitome of unchanging tradition, a now lost simplicity, and resistance to technological change. That image takes on a different meaning when one looks more closely. When this image is studied, the Amish family represents a counterintuitive image of cultural change, innovation, and protest. They do not resist technology but use it in ever changing configurations to demonstrate technology's potential rather than merely its instrumental value. Once students of culture and media appreciate this allegorical potential, then guides for cultural invention might exist in the most unlikely places. These guides appear in decay, accidents, and jokes. They appear in plain view in mass media and public controversies. One finds these guides in a leaky roof, a doctored photograph, an old film of a train ride, the image of the academic as a whipping boy, and even in a faceless doll, a bundling ritual, and a tourist bureau's slogan. Cultural invention is not born from a bolt out of the blue but found in smudged, effaced, clichéd, and corny images. Look right there in old worn-out myths.

7 | Wonder

Students often complain about demystifications of culture and media because these analyses supposedly take the fun and wonder out of spectatorship. Even as they make these claims against demythologies, students and teachers suppose that ironic detachment has won the day from fascination. The more heroic connotations of wonder—awe, amazement, and marveling at the mysterious—seem anachronistic in the current cultural climate infused with suspicions, ironies, exposés, and rapidly shifting distractions. Beyond this resignation, cultural historians also point to fascist propaganda as an exemplary warning about fascination's dangers. In these contexts, advocating the capacity to wonder will strike some as naive at best.

Just as "natural" or "all natural" markets products, the adjective *wonder* has sold everything from bread to bras. "The wonderful world" becomes an allusion to Disney rather than a utopian possibility. This cheap vulgarized version may seem like an unlikely place to look for methods of cultural analysis and social action. While the earlier and grander connotations seem untenable, these commercialized versions of wonder seem unworthy of anything but transient interest. There is an old barb about Wonder Bread in which a shopper responds to the ingredients and the bread's name by asking, "I *wonder* what's in it?" This question emblematizes the *artificial* version of popular culture's wonder. Artificial mythologies mix that shopper's doubt, curiosity, and levity with wonder's other connotations. They combine the amazement and surprise found in Alice's Wonderland with the attitude of that bemused shopper. Using the ready-made artificiality of mass culture's images and myths, this method seeks to reinvigorate the capacity to wonder at media and culture.

Maybe one can explain the methodology in the context of a generation of critics, artists, journalists, and scholars beginning to have a profound impact on contemporary culture: a generation that grew up during the "wonder years," watched the Wonderful World of Disney on television, and ate Wonder Bread with abandon. Maybe artificial mythology makes sense only as a symptom of a particular generation's sensibility. From this sensibility, mixing doubt and curiosity with the fantastic and marvelous, this book offers a contemporary version of Baldassare Castiglione's advice about acting in and understanding the world: the combination of *sprezzatura* and *mediocrita*. This new artificial subjectivity will no doubt meet with criticism from both those enamored with the heroic connotation of the capacity to wonder and those suspicious of all fascinations. Artificial mythology offers an alternative to the hermeneutics of suspicion as well as to myth's effaced contradictions.

The new wonders of the world, the twentieth century's legacy, are not pyramids or gargantuan statues. Now we wonder at decaying inner cities, contentious public controversies, oddball religious cults, and media spectacles. Given these peculiar and troubling wonders of the world, artificial mythology finds a collection of details that may not fit within prevailing analyses of culture and media. In that sense, this book is a collection of details, a *Wunderkammer* or cabinet of wonders, consisting of many objects and situations including a leaky roof, a doctored photograph, an old film of a train ride, the image of the academic as a whipping boy, and a faceless doll. This cabinet of wonders satirizes academic studies of culture and media even as it also contains unforeseen connections with an emergent alternative methodology. It mixes the wonder of the world with a "wonder what's in Wonder Bread" attitude. With this attitude, artificial mythology intervenes in the reception and conceptualization of photography, cinema, television, architecture, and public relations. It does not merely seek to challenge representations in media and culture. It considers the wondrous problems of the world not as representations of underlying conditions but as situations, actions, and events waiting for the actors reading this book to perform. Its value exists in how it vibrates the reflexes of the future.

Artificial mythology examines details that do not fit into the prevailing grand narratives whether those narratives advocate an anti-humanist postmodernism or a program for social engagement. The details have great promise only for those willing to suspend their allegiance to the power of the particular narratives anchoring the usual problem-solving strategies. Other similar analyses might attempt to argue against a particular grand narrative. Making an artificial mythology from the cornerstones of cultural invention (willful subjectivity, creative intention, and social action), in spite of the many demythologies of these terms, produces an alternative to the tradition of unmasking illusion. It does *not* settle for merely seeing through the trick of naturalization. It sides with the conjurer's charm in the context of discovery rather than the analyst's soberness in the context of justification. It avoids any mean-spirited attacks in favor of making a clearing to allow students of culture to appreciate that which might resist grand narratives. It does not advocate any particular post-this or post-that. It rescues scholars like Barthes for a different project entirely: infusing the study of media and culture with a taste of wonder.

The specific strategy for changing scholarly tastes involves a method of practicing and preparing for a spontaneous improvisational use of knowledge the way a rap poet practices the immediacy necessary for poetry slams and hip-hop jams. Just as a particular rap may leave you cold, the methods in this book may sometimes lead to a dead end. From this practiced improvisation with details, things, and scholars, one can avoid contextualizing information in terms of a prevailing grand narrative. Some may want to hold on to these schemas; some may want to try something else as an artificial experiment.

This experiment suggests a fluid, heterogeneous self-construction: favoring becoming rather than Being. This self uses productively something like a thrift-shop fashion sense. It does not simply reject the taste for the artificial as a ruse. Perhaps those details that appear to escape a self's narratives have a more significant sway than more general notions of true character, inner self, and so on. It is not a coincidence that alternative notions of subjectivity arose when feminists entered influential positions in universities, because the alternatives depend on feminist analyses of subjectivity. Artificial ideas, apparently irrelevant details, or found objects are not merely an indication of ornamentation or illusory seductive wiles as in a patriarchal fantasy. The feminists taught how to make "faking it" into a methodology, as in Cindy Sherman's photographs. One wonders about fake thinking, criticism, and mythmaking.

In the prevailing logic and scholarly tastes, this project may strike some as fake scholarship, in the style of Marcel Duchamp's ready-mades, because it enlarges details to often absurd proportions; it mixes the cornerstones of humanism, creativity, and individual performance with theories usually associated with a criticism of humanism; it parades its use of the apparently irrelevant, and it rescues relatively passé thinkers, unpopular ideas, and kitsch. It would be easy to write a post-structuralist dismissal of invention, and just as easy to write a humanist defense of creative intention and socially engaged subjectivity. The challenging endeavor is to put the two discourses into conjunction with each other. That conjunction will put ideas together in ways that might challenge both discourses, both contexts, both grand narratives. Combining the hero of humanism, Castiglione, with the theorist of "the death of the author," Barthes, unsettles the debate. It shifts the ground and terms of the supposed conflict to rescue both for other ends besides those most commonly associated with these thinkers. This strategy risks making a spoof of Barthes's work as an American-ized and vulgarized version: Barthes as Oprah. It does not dismiss his work. It uses that work in a different (artificial) context. Some readers will recognize this joke grenade as something more than a conservative corrective, as most jokes depend on group cohesion and consensus. The joke in this case allows incongruity to shake received ideas about theory and culture.

Advocating a mixed-up identity politics affects how to study media (photography, film, and television). Just as multiculturalism as a research methodology wants to challenge the self-complacency of a culture that admits no mixing, the early cinema may have encouraged the thrill of hybridity with its promise of "becoming other" as a multicultural, out-of-self, virtual-reality ride. Of course, this unusual project in identity politics has far reaching implications for social policy. In examining the aesthetics of social policy, this project entertains a Situationist solution to urban decay that might appreciate the pleasures of decay. While the threat of death, rape, harm, armed robbery, and vandalism do not warm us to the marrow, urban areas do have an element of unpredictability and excitement that exceeds the needs of a rational corporate market, and those excesses do not necessarily involve death and destruction. Decay does not always end in apocalyptic downfalls. The urban dump has many twinkling fragments and shards. The modest proposal suggested in this project uses Ilya Kabakov's transformation of a leaky roof into water music as a guide to appreciating decay.

When conservative critics focused on what they saw as academics' grand narratives rather than on the specific readings of aesthetic forms and textual practices, they missed the trees for the forest. When a specific feminist reading practice is examined in conjunction with the conservatives' attacks, the scene no longer appears only as a conflict. Understanding the importance of aesthetic decisions, and reading the conservatives' aesthetics in terms of a particular feminist aesthetic, shifts the understanding of the changes confronting higher education from a cultural war to a scene of artificial mourning and masochism. The artificial is *not* merely the demythologizing of the natural. Instead, it recognizes that the worldly and the natural are always imbricated one upon the other. The natural has not shriveled and disappeared, nor should it. Centered attention should not give way to aberrant attention. The advocacy for appreciating the richness of detail and particularities does not simply imply that more and more examples prove a point or exemplify a theory. It does not advocate that readers let any detail influence them without any thought. The strategy explains how to transform the otherwise ignored and irrelevant into something significant and useful. The authors of mass culture may not intend to leave these fascinating details behind. The readers and spectators intend to find them anyway.

I have examined grand narratives common in studies of culture and media: social policies on urban problems, multiculturalism and media, and so on. Rather than entering into a debate with these narratives, this project finds promising details that may lead to unimagined possibilities. The experiment may only produce fascination, amazement, doubt, or levity in wondering about a leaky roof, a faceless doll, a news photo, or even an artificial mythologist. I hope readers will not stop at criticisms and will not settle for facile demythologies. The artificial is neither an antonym of the natural nor a synonym for irony. The demonstrations and theories presented here suggest ways to move to something besides unmasking. Some readers might miss this use of the artificial in their delight in demythologizing this book's arbitrary and artificial constraints. For those readers this conclusion simply adds that the ironic detachment of the critic is only a very small part of the project. Those readers will have forgotten the other side of wonder. How does one answer the critics? How does one change tastes? I wonder.

Notes

Foreword

1. Roland Barthes, *Mythologies* (New York: Hill and Wang, 1972), 12.
2. See Paul Smith, *Discerning the Subject* (Minneapolis: University of Minnesota Press, 1988), 42.
3. Quintin Hoare and Geoffrey Nowell Smith, preface to *Selections from the Prison Notebooks of Antonio Gramsci* (New York: International Publishers, 1971), xi.
4. Smith, *Discerning the Subject*, 109.
5. Baldassare Castiglione, *The Book of the Courtier*, trans. Charles S. Singleton (New York: Anchor, 1959), 43–44. Thanks to Jim Chandler for the reference.
6. Norbert Elias, *The History of Manners* (New York: Urizon, 1978), 79–80.
7. Robert Hughes, *Culture of Complaint: The Fraying of America* (New York: Warner, 1993).
8. Nelson Fu, "Woo's on First! Motion Picture Director John Woo," *Transpacific* 9, 5 (August 1994): 44.
9. Barthes, *Mythologies*, 12.

Chapter 1. Artificial Mythologies and Invention

1. Karl Marx, *The Eighteenth Brumaire of Louis Bonaparte* (New York: International Publishers, 1963), 149–59.
2. Peter Stallybrass and Allon White, *The Politics and Poetics of Transgression* (New York: Cornell University Press, 1986), 14. See also John Fiske, *Understanding Popular Culture* (Boston: Unwin Hyman, 1989), 100–1.
3. Stallybrass and White, *The Politics and Poetics of Transgression*, 14.
4. Roland Barthes, *Mythologies*, trans. Annette Lavers (New York: Hill and Wang, 1972). Hereafter cited in the text as *M*.

5. Cf. Timothy Murray, *Like a Movie: Ideological Fantasy on Screen, Camera, and Canvas* (London: Routledge, 1993).

6. Jerome Singerman, who also attended the fair, testifies that he particularly enjoyed "driving" the Thunderbirds. My memory is of the Mustangs only. Cf. Daniel J. Boorstin, *The Image: A Guide to Pseudo-Events in America*, (New York: Bantam, 1963).

7. Roland Barthes, *Empire of Signs*, trans. Richard Howard (London: Cape, 1983), 28. Hereafter cited in the text as *ES*.

8. For an explanation of bathmology see Réda Bensmaïa, *The Barthes Effect: The Essay as Reflective Text*, trans. Pat Fedkiew (Minneapolis: University of Minnesota Press, 1987), 59–62. Bathmology is crucial for the "Barthes effect."

9. Kevin Lynch, *The Image of the City* (Cambridge, Mass.: MIT Press, 1960), 4.

10. Fredric Jameson, "Cognitive Mapping," in *Marxism and Interpretation of Culture*, ed. Cary Nelson and Lawrence Grossberg (Urbana: University of Illinois Press, 1988), 353.

11. Jacques Derrida, *Disseminations*, trans. Barbara Johnson (Chicago: University of Chicago Press, 1981), 103.

12. Roland Barthes, "Schumann's Lieder Cycles," in *Responsibility of Forms*, trans. Richard Howard (New York: Hill and Wang, 1983), 90. Hereafter cited in the text as *RF*.

13. Roland Barthes, *Roland Barthes*, trans. Richard Howard (New York: Hill and Wang, 1977), 145. Hereafter cited in the text as *RB*.

14. Roland Barthes, *Camera Lucida: Reflections on Photography*, trans. Richard Howard (New York: Hill and Wang, 1981). Hereafter cited in the text as *CL*. Cf. Jane Gallop, "Carnal Knowledge," in *Thinking through the Body* (New York: Columbia University Press, 1988), 135–59; and Dana Polan, "Roland Barthes and the Moving Image," *October* 19 (1985): 41–46. For an excellent discussion on the connection between "fading" of the subject, voice, or presence and the "punctum," see Ned Lukacher, "Prosopopoeia," in *Primal Scenes: Literature, Philosophy, Psychoanalysis* (Ithaca, N.Y.: Cornell University Press, 1986), 68–96. Lukacher argues, among other things, that Barthes teaches us how to locate instances of "tonal instability" or "fading." These interpretations of the fading voice signal "the ending of the Platonic notion of voice as presence. Anamnesis enables memory to make voice present to the self in the absence of the voice" (72–73). Lukacher also connects Barthes's project to Derrida's and Lacan's theories. Although it exceeds the scope of this chapter, I would argue that the punctum is similar to Lacan's *objet a*. For a reading of the *objet a* as similar to the punctum, see Craig Saper, "A Nervous Theory: The Troubling Gaze of Psychoanalysis in Media Studies," *diacritics*, winter 1991: 33–52.

15. Nancy M. Shawcross, *Roland Barthes on Photography: The Critical Tradition in Perspective* (Gainesville: University of Florida Press, forthcoming), ch. 4. Shawcross goes to great pains to point out the differences between involuntary memories and the punctum. She also explains the significance of those differences.

16. Stephen C. Ferruolo, "*Parisius-Paradisus*: The City, Its Schools, and the Origins of the University of Paris," in *The University and the City: From Medieval Origins to the Present*, ed. Thomas Bender (New York: Oxford University Press, 1988), 24–25.

17. Robert Sternberg with Lynn Okagaki, "Teaching Thinking Skills: We're Getting the Context Wrong" (unpublished manuscript, 1989), 1.

18. Susan Stewart, *Nonsense* (Baltimore: Johns Hopkins University Press, 1986), 204.

19. Sternberg with Okagaki, "Teaching Thinking Skills," 9.

20. Ibid.

21. Susan Horton, *Thinking through Writing* (Baltimore: Johns Hopkins University Press, 1982), 7.

22. In the missing photograph of *Camera Lucida*, "the mask vanished" and the air was "consubstantial with her face," but instead of the past made present ("it is happening"), the past *arrests* the present (109). This puncture or arrest in reading functions as an index of a past reality, an identification of "that has been." It cynically proves that reality is missing and dead. In regard to this death, Barthes's choice of the word "consubstantial" alludes to André Bazin's theory of cinema. Bazin makes an analogy between the photographic image and the shroud of Turin, but Barthes has perverted this religious metaphor by casting his mother in the role of Christ; he personalizes the truth. The religious idea that Christ's flesh and blood coexist with the wine and bread given during the Eucharist closely resembles Bazin's notion that the dead past coexists in the present. Barthes perverts the analogy by suggesting we feel pity, instead of guilt or exaltation, for the past, and he raises this pity to such a mad intensity that it suggests a death without heaven, without return.

23. Roland Barthes, *A Lover's Discourse: Fragments*, trans. Richard Howard (New York: Hill and Wang, 1978), 60. Hereafter cited in the text as *LD*.

24. Roger Cardinal, "Pausing over Peripheral Detail," *Framework* 30/31 (1986): 113.

25. Ibid., 114.

26. Jacques Lacan, *The Four Fundamental Concepts of Psychoanalysis, Seminar XI*, trans. Alan Sheridan (New York: Norton, 1978), 73.

27. Gallop, "Carnal Knowledge," 153.

28. Ibid., 158.

29. Philip Thody, *Roland Barthes: A Conservative Estimate* (Atlantic Highlands, N.J.: Humanities Press, 1977), 122.

30. Roland Barthes, *The Pleasure of the Text* (New York: Hill and Wang, 1977), 22.

31. Gilles Deleuze and Félix Guattari, *Kafka: Toward a Minor Literature*, trans. Dana Polan (Minneapolis: University of Minnesota Press, 1986), 17. Cf. Roland Barthes, "Kafka's Answer," in *Franz Kafka*, ed. Leo Hamalian (New York: New Directions Press, 1974), 140–43; Alan Udoff, "Introduction: Kafka's Question," in *Kafka and the Contemporary Critical Performance*, ed. Alan Udoff (Bloomington: Indiana University Press, 1987), 4–10. Barthes explains that "Kafka's narrative is not woven of symbols, as we have been told so often, but it is the first of an entirely different technique, the technique of allusion" (142). Udoff objects to Barthes's privileging of "a particular form of multivalency" that valorizes only an interpretation of Kafka. Udoff ends his essay by explaining that "at the root of the *quest* ions that proliferate through Kafka's writings, then, there lies an expeditionary striving . . ." (13). One argument of this book is that Barthes's Kafkaesque expedition through Tokyo *quest* ions *inventio*. *Empire of Signs* offers an alternative to Udoff's opinion that "to read Kafka is to attempt to 'find one's way' . . ." (12). Barthes demonstrates the importance of *losing* one's way.

32. Craig Saper, "Instant Theory: Making Thinking Popular," *Visible Language* 22, 4 (1988): 375.

33. Joan Copjec, "Cutting-up," in *Between Psychoanalysis and Feminism*, ed. Theresa Berman (New York: Routledge, 1989), 238–39.

34. Ibid., 241.

35. Marshall McLuhan, *The Gutenberg Galaxy* (Toronto: University of Toronto Press, 1962), 11.

36. Ibid., 14.

37. Ibid., 11.

38. Julian Jaynes, *The Origin of Consciousness in the Breakdown of the Bicameral Mind* (Boston: Houghton Mifflin, 1976), 276.

39. See for example, Roger Sperry, "Some Effects of Disconnecting the Cerebral Hemispheres," *Science* 217 (24 September 1982): 1223–26.

40. Gilles Deleuze and Félix Guattari, *A Thousand Plateaus: Capitalism and Schizophrenia*, trans. Brian Massumi (Minneapolis: University of Minnesota Press, 1987), 355. Originally published as *Mille Plateaux*, vol. 2 of *Capitalisme et Schizophrenia* (Paris: Les Editions de Minuit, 1980).

41. David Carroll, *Paraesthetics: Foucault, Derrida, Lyotard* (New York: Metheun, 1987), 208.

42. Jacques Derrida, "Passe-Partout," in *Truth in Painting*, trans. Geoff Bennington and Ian McLeod (Chicago: University of Chicago Press, 1987), 12.

43. Carroll, *Paraesthetics*, 144.

44. Deleuze and Guattari, *A Thousand Plateaus*, 110.

45. Jean-François Lyotard, *The Postmodern Condition: A Report on Knowledge*, trans. Geoff Bennington and Brian Massumi, Theory and History of Literature, vol. 10 (Minneapolis: University of Minnesota Press, 1984), 15.

46. Ludwig Wittgenstein, *Philosophical Investigations*, trans. G. E. M. Anscombe (London: Oxford University Press, 1968), 18. Cf. Robert Ackermann, *Wittgenstein's City* (Amherst: University of Massachusetts Press, 1988). Ackermann's reading of Wittgenstein divides the city into neighborhoods containing "clear linguistic assertions."

47. Michel de Certeau, *The Practice of Everyday Life*, trans. Steven Rendall (Berkeley: University of California Press, 1984), 101. Hereafter cited in the text as *Life*.

48. See also John King and Andy Gill, "At Home He's a Tourist," song lyrics, song recorded by The Gang of Four on the LP recording *Entertainment* (1982).

49. Eric Charles White, *Kaironomia: On the Will-to-Invent* (Ithaca: Cornell University Press, 1987).

50. Cicero, *De Oratore*, I, xxxi, trans. E. W. Sutton (Cambridge, Mass.: Harvard University Press, 1959–60), 142–43.

51. Roland Barthes, *The Fashion System*, trans. Matthew Ward and Richard Howard (New York: Hill and Wang, 1983), 293.

52. Roland Barthes, *S/Z: An Essay*, trans. Richard Miller (New York: Hill and Wang, 1974).

53. Gregory Ulmer, "Fetishism in Roland Barthes's Nietzschean Phase," *Papers on Language and Literature* 14, 3 (1983): 340.

54. Robert Ray, "The Bordwell Regime and the Stakes of Knowledge," *Strategies* 1, 1 (fall 1988): 162.

55. Ibid., 163.

56. Ibid., 163–64.

57. Armand Mattelart and Yves Stourdze, *Technology, Culture, and Communication: A Report to the French Minister of Research and Industry* (New York: North-Holland, 1985), 122–23.

58. James Clifford, *The Predicament of Culture: Twentieth-Century Ethnography, Literature, and Art* (Cambridge: Harvard University Press, 1988), 226. See also Fredric Jameson, *The Political Unconscious: Narratives as a Socially Symbolic Act* (Ithaca: Cornell University Press, 1981), 47.

59. Clifford, *The Predicament of Culture*, 226.

60. Michel de Certeau, *Heterologies: Discourse on the Other*, trans. Brian Massumi (University of Minnesota Press, 1986), 194. Hereafter cited in the text as *Heterologies*.

61. Gregory Ulmer, "Barthes's Body of Knowledge," *Studies in Twentieth Century Literature* 5, 2 (spring 1981): 223–24.

62. Paul Feyerabend, *Against Method* (London: Verso, 1975), 26–27.

63. Deleuze and Guattari, *A Thousand Plateaus,* 244–46.

64. Deleuze and Guattari, *Kafka,* 19.

65. Roland Barthes, "Event, Poem, Novel," afterword to *Event,* by Phillipe Sollers, trans. Bruce Benderson and Ursula Molinaro (New York: Red Dust, 1986), 104.

66. These three sentences directly allude to Barthes's discussion of mythology. At the beginning of his essay "Myth Today" in *Mythologies,* he writes, "What is myth, today? I shall give at the outset a first, very simple answer, which is perfectly consistent with etymology: *myth is a type of speech"* (109).

Chapter 2. Mapping Television

1. Walter Goodman, "TV Critic's Notebook: On Television, the Theater of War," *New York Times,* Jan. 17, 1991, International section, A19.

2. Ibid., A19.

3. Howard Kurtz, "On Television, Gunfire Is Heard, but Not Seen," *Washington Post,* Jan. 17, 1991, A28.

4. Tom Shales "The Bombing of Baghdad: Television on the Front Line," *Washington Post,* Jan. 17, 1991, Style section, C1.

5. Editorial, "Exit from Hell?" *Village Voice,* Feb. 5, 1991, 25.

6. Goodman, "TV Critic's Notebook," A19.

7. Mitchell Cohen, "War in the Gulf," *Dissent* (winter 1991): 7.

8. Walter Benjamin, "The Work of Art in the Age of Mechanical Reproduction," in *Illuminations,* trans. Harry Zohn, ed. Hannah Arendt (New York: Harcourt, Brace and World, 1968.) This version contains the footnotes. A reprint of Benjamin's article without the footnotes appears in Gerald Mast, Marshall Cohen, and Leo Braudy, eds., *Film Theory and Criticism* (New York: Oxford University Press, 1992), 665–81.

9. Noël Burch, "Narrative/Diegesis—Thresholds, Limits," *Screen* 2 (1982): 31. Hereafter cited in the text as Burch.

10. Jean Baudrillard, "The Structural Law of Value and the Order of Simulation," in *The Structural Allegory: Reconstructive Encounters with the New French Thought,* ed. John Fekete (Minneapolis: University of Minnesota Press, 1984), 71. See also Jean Baudrillard, *America,* trans. C. Turner (New York: Hill and Wang, 1982).

11. Benjamin, "The Work of Art in the Age of Mechanical Reproduction," 234.

12. Ibid., 237.

13. Ibid., 232.

14. Benjamin, "The Work of Art in the Age of Mechanical Reproduction."

15. John Berger, *Ways of Seeing* (London: BBC and Pelican Books, 1980), 13. The first chapter applies many of the ideas in Benjamin's "The Work of Art." See also John Berger, "Uses of Photography: For Susan Sontag," in *About Looking* (New York: Pantheon Books, 1980).

16. Theodor Adorno, "On the Fetish-Character in Music and the Regression of Listening," (1938) in *The Essential Frankfurt School Reader,* ed. Andrew Arato and Eike Gebhardt (New York: Urizen Books, 1978), 270–99.

17. Bill Nichols, *Ideology and the Image: Social Representation in the Cinema and Other Media* (Bloomington: Indiana University Press, 1981), 174–78. Hereafter cited in the text as *Image.*

18. Christian Metz, *Film Language: A Semiotics of the Cinema*, trans. Michael Taylor (New York: Oxford University Press, 1974).

19. For an explanation of the current trend in psychoanalytic cultural studies away from the Althusserian mode, see James Donald, ed., "On the Threshold: Psychoanalysis and Cultural Studies," in *Psychoanalysis and Cultural Theory: Thresholds* (London: Macmillan with the ICA, 1991), 1–10. For explanations of where psychoanalytic theories went wrong, and where they might now go, see Joan Copjec, "The Orthopsychic Subject: Film Theory and the Reception of Lacan," *October* 49 (spring 1989): 1–28; Slavoj Žižek, "Looking Awry," *October* 50 (fall 1989): 31–56; Slavoj Žižek, *Looking Awry: An Introduction to Jacques Lacan through Popular Culture* (Cambridge: MIT Press, 1991); Craig Saper, "A Nervous Theory: The Troubling Gaze of Psychoanalysis in Media Studies," *diacritics* (winter 1991): 33–52.

20. John Fiske, "British Cultural Studies," in Robert C. Allen, ed., *Channels of Discourse: Television and Contemporary Criticism* (Chapel Hill: University of North Carolina Press, 1987), 254–89. See also John Fiske, *Understanding Popular Culture* (Boston: Unwin Hyman, 1989).

21. Hamid Naficy, *The Making of Exile Cultures: Iranian Television in Los Angeles* (Minneapolis: University of Minnesota Press, 1993).

22. Judith Williamson, "The Problems of Being Popular," *New Socialist* (Sept. 1986): 14–15; as quoted in Meaghan Morris, "The Banality in Cultural Studies," in *Logics of Television: Essays in Cultural Criticism*, ed. Patricia Mellencamp (Bloomington: Indiana University Press, 1990), 14–43.

23. Morris, "The Banality in Cultural Studies," 14.

24. When reading current left-wing discussions of the Gulf War, one might even imagine a game show, "Body Count," in which contestants would name how many corpses the United States has produced in the five wars during the Reagan-Bush years, and the "them" versus "us" kill ratio; during a bonus round called "in harm's way," contestants would list special situations where the enemies "we" bombed actually caused the deaths (e.g., Muammar al-Qaddafi's 15-month-old daughter, the 1988 shooting down of an Iranian jetliner, which killed 290 people, the people in the Iraqi bomb shelter, etc.). After each correct answer, the announcer would ask rhetorically, "Any news photos of the dead?" Of course, it is the irony, not the facts, that saves this perverse example from the quiz-show logic.

25. Fred Smoler, "The Arming of Saddam Hussein," *Dissent* (summer 1991): 245–48.

26. William Boddy, "The Seven Dwarfs and the Money Grubbers: The Public Relations Crisis of US Television in the Late 1950s," in Mellencamp, ed., *Logics of Television*, 107.

27. Ibid.

28. Todd Gitlin, "On Thrills and Kills: Sadomasochism in the Movies," *Dissent* (spring 1991): 245–48. Subsequent page references will be given in the text.

29. Homi Bhabha, "A Question of Survival: Nations and Psychic States," in Donald, ed., *Psychoanalysis and Cultural Theory*, 101. Subsequent page references will be given in the text.

30. Sigmund Freud, *The Problem of Anxiety* (New York: Psychoanalytic Quarterly Press and W. W. Norton, 1936), 111.

31. Ibid., 106.

32. Shoshana Felman, "Psychoanalysis and Education: Teaching Terminable and Interminable," in *Jacques Lacan and the Adventure of Insight: Psychoanalysis in Contemporary Culture* (Cambridge: Harvard University Press, 1987), 80.

33. Leslie Good, "Power, Hegemony, and Communication Theory," in *Cultural Politics in Contemporary America*, ed. Ian Angus and Sut Jhally (New York: Routledge, 1989), 61.

34. Jacques Lacan, "On Logical Time," *Newsletter of the Freudian Field* 2, 2 (fall 1988): 9–10.

35. Jacques-Alain Miller, "To Interpret the Cause: From Freud to Lacan," *Newsletter of the Freudian Field* 3, 1 and 2 (spring/fall 1989): 33–34.

36. Ibid., 35.

37. Roland Barthes, *Camera Lucida* (New York: Hill and Wang, 1980).

38. Leo Bersani, "Is the Rectum a Grave?" *October* 43, special issue on "AIDS: Cultural Analysis, Cultural Activism" (winter 1987): 212.

39. Slavoj Žižek, "Why Lacan Isn't a Poststructuralist," *Newsletter of the Freudian Field* 1, 2 (1988): 35.

40. Peter Brunette and David Wills, *Screen/Play: Derrida and Film Theory* (Princeton: Princeton University Press, 1989), 117. See also Jacques Derrida, "The Deaths of Roland Barthes," trans. Pascale-Anne Brault and Michael Naas, in *Philosophy and Non-Philosophy since Merleau-Ponty*, ed. Hugh J. Silverman, Continental Philosophy, vol. 1 (London: Routledge, 1988), 259–96.

Chapter 3. Multiculturalism and Identity Politics in Photography and Film

1. Roland Barthes, *S/Z: An Essay*, trans. Richard Miller (New York: Hill and Wang, 1974). Barthes writes in *S/Z*: "Realism (badly named, at any rate badly interpreted) consists not in copying the real but in copying a (depicted) copy of the real: this famous *reality*, as though suffering from a fearfulness which keeps it from being touched directly, is *set further away*, postponed, or at least captured through the pictorial matrix upon which it has been steeped before being put into words" (55).

2. D. A. Miller, *Bringing Out Roland Barthes* (Berkeley: University of California Press, 1992). Hereafter cited in the text as Miller.

3. James Clifford, "Introduction: Partial Truths," in *Writing Culture: The Poetics and Politics of Ethnography*, ed. James Clifford and George Marcus (Berkeley: University of California Press, 1986), 12.

4. Edward Said, *Orientalism* (New York: Random House, 1979), 2.

5. Clifford, *Writing Culture*, 12.

6. Jonathan Culler, *Framing the Sign: Criticism and Its Institutions* (Norman: University of Oklahoma Press, 1988), 167.

7. Kristin Ross, *The Emergence of Social Space: Rimbaud and the Paris Commune* (Minneapolis: University of Minnesota Press, 1988), 95.

8. Dean MacCannell, *The Tourist: A New Theory of the Leisure Class* (New York: Schocken Books, 1989), 103.

9. Marianna Torgovnick, *Gone Primitive: Savage Intellects, Modern Lives* (Chicago: University of Chicago Press, 1990), 187.

10. Said, *Orientalism*, 113.

11. James Michael Buzard, "Forester's Trespasses: Tourism and Cultural Politics," *Twentieth Century Literature* 34, 2 (summer 1988): 155.

12. MacCannell, *The Tourist*, 200.

13. Roland Barthes, *Empire of Signs*, trans. Richard Howard (London: Cape, 1983), 3. See also Craig Saper, "Learning from Being Lost," *Journal of Urban and Cultural*

Studies 1, 2 (1990): 67–86. Cf. Jay Caplan, "Nothing But Language: On Barthes' *Empire of Signs,*" *Visible Language* 6, 4 (1977): 341–54; Scott Malcomson, "The Pure Land beyond the Sea: Barthes, Burch, and the Uses of Japan," *Screen* 26, 3/4 (May/ August 1985): 23–33.; Zhang Longxi, "The Myth of the Other: China in the Eyes of the West," *Critical Inquiry* 15, 1 (1988): 108–31; Maureen Turim, "Signs of Sexuality in Oshima's Tales of Passion," *Wide Angle* 9, 2 (1987): 32–46; Miller, *Bringing Out Roland Barthes.*

14. For an explanation of Burson's technique, see "The Age Machine," an interview with Nancy Burson and David Kramlich by Senior Curator France Morin, pamphlet for the exhibit, New Museum of Contemporary Art, New York, 1992.

15. Nancy Burson and David Kramlich, *The Age Machine,* interactive computer station, New Museum of Contemporary Art, New York, Jan.–Apr., 1992.

16. T. S. Eliot, "Commentary," *The Criterion* 13 (Oct. 1933–July 1934): 115; as quoted in Russell Kirk's "Introduction to Irving Babbitt," in *Literature and the American College* (Washington: National Humanities Institute, 1986), 2.

17. Randolf Bourne, "Trans-National America," in *History of a Literary Radical and Other Essays,* ed. Van Wyck Brooks (New York: B. W. Huebsch, 1920), 274. Subsequent page references will be given in the text.

18. Daniel J. Boorstin, as quoted in Tad Szulc, "The Greatest Danger We Face," *Miami Herald, Parade Magazine,* July 25, 1993, 4.

19. Ibid., 5.

20. Cornel West, "Diverse New World," in *Debating P.C.: The Controversy over Political Correctness on College Campuses,* ed. Paul Berman (New York: Dell, 1992), 331.

21. Simon Frith, "Britbeat: I Am What I Am," *Village Voice,* Aug. 3, 1993, 82.

22. Ibid.

23. Roland Barthes, *Responsibility of Forms,* trans. Richard Howard (New York: Hill and Wang, 1983), 239.

24. Michel de Certeau, *The Practice of Everyday Life,* trans. Steven Rendall (Berkeley: University of California Press, 1984), xiii.

25. Jacques Derrida, *Of Grammatology,* trans. Gayatri Spivak (Baltimore: Johns Hopkins University Press, 1976); and Torgovnick, *Gone Primitive.*

26. Nelson Graburn, introduction to *Ethnic and Tourist Arts: Cultural Expressions from the Fourth World,* ed. Nelson Graburn (Berkeley: University of California Press, 1976), 2. Subsequent page references will be given in the text.

27. Jill Sweet, "Burlesquing the 'Other' in Pueblo Performance," *Annals of Tourism Research* 16, 1 (1989): 71. Cf. Dick Hebdige, *Subculture: The Meaning of Style* (London: Methuen, 1979).

28. Constance Perin, *Belonging in America: Reading between the Lines* (Madison: University of Wisconsin Press, 1988), 146.

29. Ibid., 23.

30. Louis Hieb, "Masks and Meaning: A Contextual Approach to the Hopi *Tüvi' Kü,*" in *Ritual Symbolism and Ceremonies in the Americas,* ed. N. R. Crumrine, Studies in Symbolic Anthropology (Greeley, Colo.: Museum of Anthropology, University of Northern Colorado, 1979), 62–79.

31. Alexander Stephen, "Hopi Indians of Arizona," *The Masterkey* 14: 103, as quoted in Louis Hieb, "Masks and Meaning."

32. Sergei Eisenstein, *Immoral Memories: An Autobiography,* trans. Herbert Marshall (Boston: Houghton Mifflin, 1983), 209.

33. Sergei Eisenstein, *Film Sense,* ed. and trans. Jay Leyda (New York: Harcourt, Brace and World, 1960), 32.

34. Paul Virilio, *War and Cinema: The Logistics of Perception*, trans. Patrick Camiller (New York: Verso, 1989), 83.

35. Ibid., 40.

36. Walter Benjamin, "The Work of Art in the Age of Mechanical Reproduction," in *Illuminations*, ed. Hannah Arendt, trans. Harry Zohn (New York: Harcourt, Brace and World, 1968), 238.

37. Tom Gunning, "An Unseen Energy Swallows Space: The Space in Early Film and Its Relation to American Avant-Garde Film," in *Film before Griffith*, ed. John L. Fell (Berkeley: University of California Press, 1983), 361. See also Raymond Fielding, "Hale's Tours: Ultrarealism in the Pre-1910 Motion Picture," in Fell, *Film before Griffith*, 116–30. To understand how Gunning distinguishes this fascination with movement from narrative cinema, see his "The Cinema of Attractions: Early Film, Its Spectator and the Avant-Garde," *Wide Angle* 8, 3/4 (1986): 63–70.

38. Gunning, "An Unseen Energy Swallows Space," 362.

39. In respect to what the film of this type might show, Gunning writes: "Interestingly the idea of providing an onlooker as a sort of stand-in for the audience appears in some early films and then seems to be dropped. One of the earliest surviving panorama films, Edison's *Mt. Tamalpais RR No 2* from 1898, angles the camera so that a woman tourist is seen in the foreground watching the landscape unwind around her. But the vast majority of these panoramas present the landscape unmediated. Our only connection with it is the unseen, but experienced camera" (Gunning, "An Unseen Energy Swallows Space," 363). Cf. Roland Barthes's discussion of cinema in *Camera Lucida* and my discussion in this book of the possibility of finding what Barthes calls a punctum in films.

40. Gunning, "An Unseen Energy Swallows Space," 363.

41. Michel de Certeau, *Heterologies*, trans. Brian Massumi (Minneapolis: University of Minnesota, 1986).

42. Roland Barthes, *Mythologies*, trans. Richard Howard (New York: Hill and Wang, 1972), 128–29.

43. Culler, *Framing the Sign*, 155.

44. Certeau, *Heterologies*, 220.

Chapter 4. Urban Decay and the Aesthetics of Social Policy

1. Debra Prothrow-Smith, *Deadly Consequences*, with Michael Weissman (New York: Harper Collins, 1991).

2. Bernard Tschumi, "Fireworks," *A Space: A Thousand Words*, exhibition catalogue, Royal College of Art Gallery (Feb. 1975), unnumbered pages; as quoted in Bernard Tschumi, *Questions of Space: Lectures on Architecture* (London: Architectural Association, 1990), 26 n. 9. Also published as "Questions of Space: The Pyramid and the Labyrinth (or the Architectural Paradox)," *Studio International* 190, 977 (Sept.–Oct. 1975): 136–42. In *Questions of Space*, Tschumi writes that "making architecture is not unlike burning matches without a purpose" (52).

3. Meaghan Morris, "The Banality in Cultural Studies," in *Logics of Television: Essays in Cultural Criticism*, ed. Patricia Mellencamp (Bloomington: Indiana University Press, 1990), 29.

4. Ibid.

5. Marshall Blonsky, *American Mythologies* (New York: Oxford University Press, 1992), 331.

6. Beatriz Colomina, *Architectureproduction* (Princeton, N.J.: Princeton University Press, 1988), 7. For a brief discussion of an architect's use of *Empire of Signs,* see Kisho Kurokawa, "Le Poetique in Architecture," *Japan Architect* 60 (Feb. 1985): 25–30.

7. Colomina, *Architectureproduction,* 9–10.

8. Edward W. Soja, *Postmodern Geographies: The Reassertion of Space in Critical Theory* (New York: Verso, 1989), 78–79.

9. Greil Marcus, *Lipstick Traces: A Secret History of the Twentieth Century* (Boston: Harvard University Press, 1990), 173.

10. Christine Wick Sizemore, *A Female Vision of the City: London in the Novels of Five British Women* (Knoxville: University of Tennessee Press, 1989), 154.

11. Ibid., 155.

12. Paul Rabinow, *French Modern: Norms and Forms of the Social Environment* (Cambridge, Mass.: MIT Press, 1989), 6. See also Michel Foucault, *Discipline and Punish: The Birth of the Prison,* trans. Alan Sheridan (New York: Vintage Books, 1979). Subsequent page references will be given in the text.

13. Maurice Roncayolo, *Histoire de la France urbaine* (Paris: Seuil, 1985), 5; as quoted in Rabinow, *French Modern,* 370.

14. Walter Benjamin, "Karl Kraus," in *Reflections,* ed. Peter Demetz (New York: Schocken Books, 1986), 247.

15. Avital Ronell, "Street Talk," *Studies in Twentieth Century Literature* 11, 1 (1986): 128.

16. Ibid., 129.

17. Roland Barthes, *Empire of Signs,* trans. Richard Howard (London: Cape, 1983), 33. Subsequent page references will be given in the text.

18. Marc Eli Blanchard, *In Search of the City: Engels, Baudelaire, and Rimbaud,* Stanford French and Italian Studies, 37 (Saratoga, Calif.: Anma Libri, 1985). Blanchard focuses on the three thinkers as respectively investigator, *flâneur,* and spectator. Cf. Burton Pike, *The Image of the City in Modern Literature* (Princeton: Princeton University Press, 1981). Pike examines the relationship between an individual and the mass, and utopian visions of cities. Cf. Raymond Williams, *The Country and the City* (New York: Oxford University Press, 1973); Lewis Mumford, *The City in History* (New York: Harcourt Brace, 1961); and David R. Weimar, *The City as Metaphor* (New York: Random House, 1966).

19. Jacques Barzun, introduction to *Les Nuits de Paris* by Restif de la Bretonne (1788), trans. Linda Asher and Ellen Fertig (New York: Random House, 1964), xiv.

20. Gerard Nerval, *Journey to the Orient,* trans. Norman Glass (London: Peter Owen, 1972), 23.

21. Charles Baudelaire, *Le Spleen de Paris,* trans. Edward Kaplan (Athens: University of Georgia Press, 1989), 1.

22. André Breton, *L'Amour fou* (1937), trans. Mary Ann Caws (Lincoln: University of Nebraska Press, 1987), 25, 87. Cf. Breton, *Nadja* (Paris: Gallimard, 1928).

23. Richard Dawkins, *The Selfish Gene* (New York: Oxford University Press, 1976), 203–16.

24. Slavoj Žižek, *The Sublime Object of Ideology* (New York: Verso, 1989), 96.

25. Ibid., 101.

26. Dean MacCannell, *The Tourist: A New Theory of the Leisure Class* (New York: Schocken Books, 1976).

27. Oswald Spengler, *The Decline of the West* (New York: A. A. Knopf, 1932).

28. Slavoj Žižek, *Enjoy Your Symptom* (New York: Routledge, 1992), 151.

29. Walter Benjamin, "Paris, Capital of the Nineteenth Century," in *Reflections,* trans. Edmund Jephcott (New York: Schocken Books, 1978), 156.

30. Alexander Gelley, "City Texts: Representation, Semiology, Urbanism," in *Politics, Theory, and Contemporary Culture,* ed. Mark Poster (New York: Columbia University Press, forthcoming). See my article on Tschumi, "The Music of Visual Poetry and Architecture," *Yearbook of Interdisciplinary Studies* 1, 2: 155–70. Cf. Soja, *Postmodern Geographies*; cf. Celeste Olalquiaga, *Megalopolis* (Minneapolis: University of Minnesota Press, 1992).

31. Tschumi, *Questions of Space,* 98.

32. See J. A. Place and L. S. Peterson, "Some Visual Motifs in Film Noir," *Film Comment,* January 1974: 30–35.

33. Mike Davis, *City of Quartz: Excavating the Future in Los Angeles* (New York: Random House, 1972), 38. Subsequent page references will be given in the text.

34. Carolee Schneemann, "Parts of a Body House," in *Fantastic Architecture,* ed. Wolf Vostell and Dick Higgins (New York: Something Else Press, 1969). Apparently George Maciunas agreed with Vostell when he included Uology (a typographical variation of Urology) in his "Learning Machine," a grid that organized all knowledge. For a more complete discussion of the "Learning Machine," see Craig Saper, "Fluxacademy," *Visible Language* 26, 1/2 (winter/spring 1992): 79–96. I argue that Uology is the intended spelling, but in the context of this quote from Schneemann, it appears as a typographic error for Urology.

35. Ilya Kabakov, "What Is a Communal Apartment," in *Ten Characters,* exhibit catalog (New York: ICA with Ronald Feldman Fine Arts, 1989), 50. Subsequent page references will be given in the text.

36. Ilya Kabakov, "Incident at the Museum or Water Music," at Ronald Feldman Fine Arts Gallery, Sept. 12–Oct. 17, 1992.

Chapter 5. The Role of the Public Intellectual

1. Roland Barthes, *Leçon* (Paris: Seuil, 1978), 4. Translated as "Inaugural lecture, Collège de France," in *A Barthes Reader,* ed. Susan Sontag (New York: Hill and Wang, 1982).

2. Alexander Astin, *What Matters in College?* (San Francisco: Jossey-Bass Publishers, 1993), 397.

3. Ibid., 398.

4. See also Richard Grenier, "The New Treason of the Clerks," *National Review* 42 (July 23, 1990): 42–45; Jefferson Morley, "The Washington Intellectual," *New Republic* 195 (Aug. 11–18, 1986): 10–12; Jeffrey Peter Hart, "What Must Be Done," *National Review* 40 (July 22, 1988): 28; Jon Wiener, "Why the Right Is Losing in Academe," *The Nation* 242 (May 24, 1986): 724–26; Michael Novak, "The Left Still Owns American Culture," *Forbes* 145 (March 5, 1990): 118; Michael Stanford, "The Stanford Library (Revised Western Civilization Course)," *New Republic* 201 (Oct. 2, 1989): 18; Otto Friedrich, "Minding Our Manners Again," *Time* 124 (Nov. 5, 1984): 62–63; Peter L. Berger and Brigitte Berger, "Our Conservatism and Theirs," *Commentary* 82 (Oct. 1986): 62–67; Rick Henderson, "Oh, Grow Up (Young Conservatives Employed by Washington Think Tanks)," *Reason* 24 (Feb. 1993): 38–39; Russell Jacoby, "The Lost Intellectual: Relativism and the American Mind," *New Perspectives Quarterly* 4 (winter 1988): 30–35; Stephen J. Tonsor, "Why I Too Am Not a Neoconservative," *National Review* 38 (June 20, 1986): 54–56.

5. Paul Berman, "Introduction: The Debate and Its Origins," in *Debating P.C.: The Controversy over Political Correctness on College Campuses*, ed. Paul Berman (New York: Dell, 1992), 2. Cf. Marjorie Perloff, "Ca(n)non to the Right of Us, Ca(n)non to the Left of Us: A Plea for Difference," *New Literary History* 18, 3 (spring 1987): 633–56.

6. For a discussion of the distinction between American and British cultural studies, and the apparently more pessimistic attitude of the American critics, see John Caughie, "Popular Culture: Notes and Revisions," in *High Theory/Low Culture: Analyzing Popular Television and Film* (New York: St. Martin's Press, 1986), 158–59.

7. Laura Mulvey, *Visual and Other Pleasures* (Bloomington: Indiana University Press, 1989), 163–64.

8. Annette Kuhn, "Deconstruction," in *Women's Pictures: Feminism and Cinema* (New York: Routledge, 1986), 160–67.

9. Nöel Burch, "Film's Institutional Mode of Representation and the Soviet Response," *October* 11 (winter 1979): 77–96; see also Nöel Burch with Jorgé Dana "Propositions," *Afterimage* 5 (spring 1974): 40–66.

10. See, for example, the first three issues of *m/f*.

11. Cf. Jane Gallop, *The Daughter's Seduction* (London: Macmillan, 1982).

12. Gaylyn Studlar, *In the Realm of Pleasure: Von Sternberg, Dietrich, and the Masochistic Aesthetic* (Urbana: University of Illinois Press, 1988). Subsequent page references will be given in the text.

13. Robert Hughes, *Culture of Complaint: The Fraying of America* (New York: Oxford University Press, 1993), 72. Subsequent page references will be given in the text.

14. Henry Louis Gates Jr., "The Weaning of America," *New Yorker*, April 19, 1993: 113. Hereafter cited in the text as Gates.

15. Camille Paglia, *Sexual Personae: Art and Decadence from Nefertiti to Emily Dickinson* (New York: Random House, 1991), 34. Subsequent page references will be given in the text. See also Camille Paglia, *Sex, Art, and American Culture: Essays* (New York: Random House, 1992).

16. Robert Richards, *Darwin and the Emergence of Evolutionary Theories of Mind and Behavior* (Chicago: University of Chicago Press, 1987). See also James Baldwin, *Individual and Society or Psychology and Sociology* (Boston: Badger, 1911).

17. For an indication of the relatively recent reemergence of Baldwin's importance for studies of social-symbolic interactions, see Sheldon Stryker, *Symbolic Interactionism: A Social Structural Version* (Menlo Park, Calif.: Benjamin/Cummings Publishing Co., 1980), 23–24.

18. The merger of "identity politics" and "a New World spin on Parisian ideas" produced endless analyses of "race, class, and gender." Although many within media and cultural studies agreed with that assessment of the situation, the conservative critics claimed that these theories also produced a widespread conspiracy among self-righteous academics. For the scholars, agreements, let alone conspiracies, were few and far between. Only in hindsight have theorists begun to recognize patterns. The development of these patterns included fractious struggles and widely divergent variations.

19. Stanley Fish, "There's No Such Thing as Free Speech and It's a Good Thing, Too," in *Are You Politically Correct? Debating America's Cultural Standards*, ed. Francis Beckwith and Michael Bauman (Buffalo: Prometheus Books, 1993), 49.

20. Roland Barthes, *Camera Lucida: Reflections on Photography*, trans. Richard Howard (New York: Hill and Wang, 1980), 73.

21. Barthes, *Leçon*, 4.

22. Ibid.

23. Roland Barthes, *A Lover's Discourse: Fragments,* trans. Richard Howard (New York: Hill and Wang, 1978), 15.

24. Ibid., 37.

25. Steven Ungar, *The Professor of Desire* (Lincoln: University of Nebraska Press, 1983), 97.

Chapter 6. Family Values and Media Technology

1. Marc. A. Olshan, "Conclusion: What Good Are the Amish?" in *The Amish Struggle with Modernity,* ed. Donald B. Kraybill and Marc A. Olshan (Hanover: University Press of New England, 1994), 234. Hereafter cited in the text as Olshan.

2. John A. Hostetler, *Amish Society,* 3d ed. (Baltimore: Johns Hopkins University Press, 1980), 3. Hereafter cited in the text as Hostetler 1980.

3. Martin Heidegger, *Poetry, Language, Thought,* trans. Albert Hofstader (New York: Harper and Row, 1975), 33. Subsequent page references will be given in the text.

4. Jacques Derrida, "Restitutions: Truth to Size," in *Truth in Painting* (Chicago: University of Chicago Press, 1987). Hereafter cited in the text as Derrida. See also Herman Rapaport, *Heidegger and Derrida: Reflections on Time and Language* (Lincoln: Nebraska University Press, 1989). Rapaport writes that this is "one of Derrida's finest and wittiest essays" (154). See also Meyer Schapiro, *Modern Art: 19th and 20th Centuries* (New York: Braziller, 1978).

5. Martin Heidegger, *The Question concerning Technology and Other Essays,* trans. William Lovitt (New York: Harper & Row, 1977); hereafter cited in the text as *QCT.*

6. Franklin H. Littell, "Holding the New Barbarians in Check," in *Amish Roots: A Treasury of History, Wisdom, and Love,* ed. John A. Hostetler (Baltimore: Johns Hopkins University Press, 1989), 290.

7. Roland Barthes, *Mythologies* (New York: Hill and Wang, 1983), 154.

8. Donald Kraybill, "The Amish Encounter with Modernity," in Kraybill and Olshan, *The Amish Struggle with Modernity,* 30.

9. Marc Olshan, "Modernity, the Folk Society, and the Old Order Amish," in Kraybill and Olshan, *The Amish Struggle with Modernity,* 189.

10. Jacques Lacan, "De l'analyse comme *bundling,"* *Le Séminaire de Jacques Lacan, Livre IV, La Relation d'object,* text established by Jacques-Alain Miller (Paris: Editions du Seuil, 1975), 87.

11. Paton Yoder, *Tradition and Transition: Amish Mennonites and Old Order Amish, 1800–1900* (Scottsdale, Pa.: Herald Press, 1991), 32–33.

12. Name withheld, "A Letter to Governor Thornburgh," in Hostetler, ed., *Amish Roots,* 275.

Index

Craig J. Saper is an assistant professor of English at the University of Pennsylvania.